THE RED BOOK OF CHINESE MARTYRS

THE RED BOOK
OF
CHINESE MARTYRS

Testimonies and Autobiographical Accounts

EDITED BY GEROLAMO FAZZINI

Translated by
Michael Miller

With a Preface by Joseph Cardinal Zen
Bishop of Hong Kong

IGNATIUS PRESS   SAN FRANCISCO

Original Italian edition:
Il Libro Rosso Dei Martiri Cinesi
© 2006 by Edizoni San Paolo, Milan

Cover art:
Narrative account by Gertrude Li Minwen
smuggled out of prison in a shoe
and photograph of
Red Guard soldiers and an unidentified victim
Pontifical Institute for Foreign Missions (PIME)

Cover design by John Herreid

ISBN-978-1-58617-244-2
Library of Congress Control Number 2008936285
Printed in the United States of America ∞

CONTENTS

PREFACE

I am not only happy but also honored to be able to present to Italian readers *Il libro rosso dei martiri cinesi* [The Red Book of Chinese Martyrs]. I hope that my words are not taken as a rhetorical gesture. It is truly an honor and a privilege to be able to give voice to the many brothers and sisters of my people who have suffered, often to the point of martyrdom, under a very severe and sometimes ruthless persecution. As I write I experience the same sentiments as I did several months ago when the Holy Father Benedict XVI elevated me to the rank of cardinal in February of 2006. While I was in Rome, I celebrated a Mass (broadcast by Vatican Radio) for the Catholics of my nation, China, in which I recalled: "The color red that I wear expresses the willingness of a cardinal to shed his own blood. But it is not my blood that has been shed: it is the blood and tears of the many unnamed heroes of both the official and the underground Church who have suffered for being faithful to the Church."

Of the numerous Catholics who have been imprisoned for thirty years or more in China, quite a few have left us their memoirs. Many of these have been kept in a drawer for a long period of time. There were valid reasons for doing so: no one wanted to run afoul of the political authorities and to put even more of our Catholic brethren in danger. Yet I must admit that there was also a sort of reluctance, even on the part of Church members, to denounce openly the persecutions experienced during the Mao regime. For many years Maoism has been extolled beyond any reasonable bounds. Even those who did not agree with it did not have the courage, or the interior freedom, to speak outside of the ideological choir, perhaps because they feared being numbered among the reactionaries.

To continue today on the path of silence would be an incomprehensible and unpardonable error. As John Paul II often reminded us, we have the duty to remember without further reticence all the martyrs under any regime whatsoever, particularly the martyrs of the twentieth century.

The confessors and martyrs of the Church of China belong to Christianity as a whole, and it is our duty, as well as our right, to present their testimonies so that they might nourish the faith of Christians throughout the world.

Aside from all these considerations, the victims—or better, the protagonists—of that phase of persecution are now vanishing. There is no longer any real reason to remain silent. And so I hope that the young Chinese priests and lay faithful will gather from the lips of their elders the stories of suffering and martyrdom that have not yet been recorded; otherwise the memory of them may be lost forever. This "harvest of memory", I believe, is one of the services that young Chinese

Catholics can render to our church, to our nation and to the universal Church.

I realize that this book, among the first of its kind, compiles only a fraction of the available testimonies. Be that as it may, the collection presented here is of great human and spiritual value, and I offer my heart-felt congratulations to those who planned and executed this editorial initiative.

As Bishop of Hong Kong, I feel particularly obliged to point out the connections between some of the pro-tagonists of this book and the Church of Hong Kong.

Father Francis Tan Tiande, a student at Aberdeen regional seminary in Hong Kong, spent thirty years doing extremely hard labor in the midst of cold (as low as $-40°$ F), hunger and depression. He is well-known and revered by the Catholics of Hong Kong, who visit him in nearby Canton in great numbers. Our lay faithful continue to be edified by his fortitude and serenity, which are also so evident in his diary, pub-lished in this volume.

> Today, thirty years later, every time that I remember those meetings in which I was criticized and denounced, my knees begin to tremble involuntarily to the point that I can hardly remain standing.... How could I have had that courage then? Where did it come from? Every time that I was denounced, the words of Jesus suddenly came to mind: "They will lay their hands on you and persecute you ... for my name's sake. This will be a time for you to bear testimony." Those words are absolutely true, aren't they? The followers of Jesus cannot avoid persecutions. Therefore I accepted my sufferings joyfully, knowing that they were not in vain!

Father John Huang Yongmu was a priest of the Diocese of Hong Kong and studied in our Aberdeen seminary. He had been assigned to the district of Haifeng, the area of the diocese located within China, which was cut off after the Communists took power in 1949. He spent the final years of his life with us in Hong Kong, residing near Saint Margaret Church and offering his testimony and his service. He, a southerner, lived through twenty-five terrible years in a labor camp in northern China with arctic temperatures. Besides being a priest, his great crime was being the son of a small landowner. During the Cultural Revolution the factory where he was forced to work became an inferno: more than a thousand detainees despaired and committed suicide.

It is no surprise that the same Father Huang experienced "the dark night" of faith:

> During those periods of the dark night of my soul, caused by the mental and physical stresses of the Communist persecution, I suffered so much that I thought there could not be anything worse. During those spiritual crises, only prayer gave me relief and the strength to persevere. If only I had been able to say Mass at least once! In all three of the prisons in which I was confined, many times I secretly made the Stations of the Cross, meditating on Jesus who suffered even unto death. I felt profound regret that I had not offered all my sufferings for the Church and for the souls in purgatory, as I ought to have done. Sometimes I thought of my seminary days, of the statue of the Blessed Virgin, imagining myself under the arbor that covered the shrine praying to Our Lady of Peace in the freedom and safety of the seminary, calmly reciting

the *Salve Regina*. And then the old demon came over
me again to torment me: never again would I be able
to see my relatives, my family, my father, my dearest
friends ...

In that environment of hatred and terror there was
nothing but enmity and cruel hostility. Oh, that oppressive and fatal Communist prison! But despite everything
I was able to say: "*Salve Regina*, Hail, Holy Queen, Mother
of mercy, our life, our sweetness and our hope!"

The protagonists of the "Death March", a very sorrowful Way of the Cross, were the Trappist monks of
Our Lady of Consolation, located in Yangjiaping
(Hebei), about a hundred kilometers northwest of Beijing. In Hong Kong, on the island of Lantau, we are
gifted with the presence of monks who come from
the Trappist monastery of Our Lady of Joy, also in the
province of Hebei, which in its turn was struck by the
fury of the persecution. The testimony of the Trappists, which is highly esteemed by our lay faithful, keeps
us from forgetting one of the most atrocious acts of
cruelty committed by the Communists against the Catholic community.

Also very important are the other testimonies included in this collection: the one by Father Joseph Li
Chang, who also studied in the seminary of Hong Kong,
although he was originally from the neighboring province of Guangdong, and of Gertrude Li Minwen, whose
testimony came to us via "the soles of the shoes strat-
agem", as you will read.

The editor has also asked me to include a note of
personal testimony in this introduction. I was born in

Shanghai but left my native city in 1948, before the Communist Party came to power, because as the Salesian novitiate was in Hong Kong. Therefore, thank God, I was not personally a victim of the regime. But I know well the sufferings inflicted on the Church in my city, which was truly martyred, and on the Salesian Congregation, which had many members in Shanghai.

The most striking incident occurred on the tragic day of September 8, 1955 when in a massive raid the police arrested hundreds of Catholics, from the bishop to the priests, the catechists and the faithful members of Catholic associations, particularly the Legion of Mary. They were brought to the dog racing stadium where the bishop, the heroic Ignatius Gong [Kung] Pinmei (created a cardinal *in pectore* in 1979 while he was still in prison), instead of denying the faith, shouted amid the commotion of the Catholics crowded there and the indignation of the guards, "Long live Christ the King! Long live the Pope!"

The Church of Shanghai counted dozens and dozens of confessors of the faith: priests, religious and lay people who died in prison because of maltreatment and starvation. Many priests of Shanghai were Jesuits, because of the centuries-old presence of the Society of Jesus in my city. The two present bishops are also Jesuits, Louis Jin and Joseph Fan.

There was a family named Zhu which was particularly well-known to the Catholics in Shanghai; their story has moved people throughout the world. The mother Martina, a widow, had eight sons, four of whom became Jesuit priests. With the exception of Michael, who was stationed in Rome at the General Curia of the Order, they were all imprisoned on September 8. (Moreover the oldest son, Francis Xavier, had already been doing forced labor for two years.) Mama Martina, called "the sorrowful mother" by the Catholics of Shanghai, set out to find each one of her sons in the various prisons in which they were interned. For almost three years she traveled on foot, walking for kilometers in order to save the few cents that allowed her to bring them some little gift. Although she was insulted by the guards, she encouraged each one of her sons to persevere, to accept sufferings willingly and to keep trusting God. Finally the sons were transferred to labor camps in distant provinces. For another twenty years Mama Martina did not see them. They were freed only in the early 1980s, but not Francis Xavier, who died in prison in 1983.

Another remarkable figure was the Jesuit Father Bede Zhang, a very well-known personality in Shanghai, who was among the first to be arrested. The government hoped to convince him to persuade the Catholics to separate from the Church and from the Pope. They subjected him to all sorts of pressure, and when it became clear that he would not allow himself to be persuaded, his jailers turned to violence and torture. The detainees in cells near his often heard him invoke the names of Jesus, Mary and Joseph; then, only his moaning was audible. After ninety-four days of detention Father Bede died: the first martyr of our Church of Shanghai.

How many memories I have of my Salesian confreres! Those from foreign lands were expelled, even

though—I can say this from personal experience—
they were not "enemies of the people" at all, but rather
humble, generous men who were dedicated to their
mission and wished us well. And how many innocent
Chinese confreres were led off, like cattle to the slaugh-
terhouse, for long and tormenting detentions!

How many times journalists have asked me: is the
Church in China still persecuted today? It is not easy
to answer this question in a short sentence because, as
you know, the situation is quite complex. The Communist regime that was responsible for the sufferings
described in this book is still in power; while it has
rejected the radical policies of Maoism, it has never
asked pardon for the outrages inflicted on believers and
on so many other innocent Chinese citizens. From the
political perspective, the ultimate cause of the persecution against the Christians is still very much in effect:
the one-party system, which has governed uninterruptedly for almost sixty years without popular mandate or endorsement, without democracy.

Although the systematic, large-scale persecutions of
the Maoist period are a thing of the past, the suffering
of the Church has not entirely ended. The communities and bishops of the official "Patriotic" Church,
which is recognized by the government, are subjected
to constant surveillance, interference, mistreatment and
harassment. Hence the communities of the official
Church and its leaders are not entirely free, although
it may seem so to the casual observer. The so-called
"clandestine" or "underground" communities, which
refuse (with good reason) to submit to the religious

policy of the government, are continually subjected to abuse and even violence, so it would not be an exaggeration to speak, in these cases, of persecution.

I must declare that there are still, unfortunately, several dozen bishops, priests and laymen detained under house arrest or in prison. There are even a few of our brother bishops from whom there has been no news for several years now. I would like to mention in particular Bishop James Su Zhimin of the Diocese of Baoding (Hebei), who disappeared around ten years ago. Nor has there been any news from his auxiliary, Bishop Francis An Shuxin, for nine years. It seems that he has been released, but as these lines are being written the situation is still unclear. There is no alternative but to denounce in the clearest terms this violation of the human rights of my brothers in the episcopate and in the faith. These persons are not only innocent but almost always elderly and sick. Why are they not released?

I, too, like the protagonists of this book, have wondered about the reason for so much suffering and violence. Our faith in God, even if it does not always seem to give us immediate answers, remains the only way to preserve hope and strength. While writing these pages, I read the splendid catechesis that the Holy Father Benedict XVI presented to the faithful on Wednesday, August 23, 2006. In the course of a commentary on the Book of Revelation, he describes with incomparable depth the drama of persecution against the disciples of Christ. I wish to conclude my preface with the Holy Father's own words.

History remains indecipherable, incomprehensible. No one can read it. Perhaps John's weeping before the mystery of a history so obscure expresses the Asian Churches' dismay at God's silence in the face of the persecutions to which they were exposed at that time. It is a dismay that can clearly mirror our consternation in the face of the serious difficulties, misunderstandings and hostility that the Church also suffers today in various parts of the world.

These are trials that the Church does not of course deserve, just as Jesus himself did not deserve his torture. However, they reveal both the wickedness of man, when he abandons himself to the promptings of evil, and also the superior ordering of events on God's part. . . .

Although John's Book of Revelation is pervaded by continuous references to suffering, tribulation and tears—the dark face of history—it is likewise permeated by frequent songs of praise that symbolize, as it were, the luminous face of history. . . .

Here we face the typical Christian paradox, according to which suffering is never seen as the last word but rather, as a transition towards happiness.

Yes, that is exactly how it is: the pages that you will read are not just pages of suffering and sorrow; they are also, and above all, pages of joy. Along with so many others, I can confirm the words of the Holy Father. The many bishops, priests and lay faithful whom I have met during my long stays in China were happy and serene, despite long and terrible periods of confinement. No one can take from us the joy and the beauty of being disciples of Jesus.

† Joseph Cardinal Zen
Bishop of Hong Kong
August 27, 2006

A NOTE ON THE TEXT

The documents collected in this volume were written at different times and by various authors. An attempt has been made, as much as possible, to standardize the spelling of proper names.

In transliterating Chinese names of well-known persons and places we have employed the *pinyin* system that was officially adopted in the People's Republic of China in 1980, instead of the English method (Wade-Giles). In some cases, however, exceptions have been made for practical reasons; the Wade-Giles method has been used to avoid references that would be incomprehensible to the English-speaking reader: we write Chiang Kai-shek (and not Jiang Jieshi, as the name of the founder of the Republic of China is written today), Kuomintang (and not Guomindang).

Finally, preference has been given to the English version of geographical names that have become common usage (for instance Canton, and not Guanzhou).

ACKNOWLEDGMENTS

This volume is the product of the work of several persons in Italy and China who agreed to translate the texts, revise them and provide them with the necessary explanatory notes.

I would like to mention here especially Father Mario Marazzi, who lovingly and closely followed the editorial project and contributed decisively to the revision of the texts with his expertise. Along with him, other PIME missionaries have offered their skills and time in various ways (particularly in preparing the Appendices): Fathers Angelo Lazzarotto, Giancarlo Politi and Gianni Criveller. I thank them individually, just as I thank Father Massimo Casaro, who supervised the publication of this book.

Matteo Nicolini-Zani, a monk in Bose and a China expert, reviewed parts of this book, in particular the chapter about the Trappists of Yangjiaping; his assistance is greatly appreciated. Thanks also to Dehonian Father Antonio Dall'Osto, editor of the magazine *Testimoni*, for allowing the publication of his article on the Trappists of Yangjiaping.

Many people have collaborated in the translation of some chapters and in the revision of the texts. I mention here, besides those already cited: Laura Badaracchi and Anna Pozzi, editors of *Mondo e Missione*; copyeditor Elena Terragni and Isabella Mastroleo, a contributor to the magazine.

Research for illustrations benefited from the collaboration of Mauro Moret from the photo archives of the PIME Center in Milan; the photographic insert and map were prepared by Bruno Maggi. Valuable bibliographic advice was offered by Rosalba Ravelli and Father Lorenzo Chiesa from the Library of the PIME Center in Milan.

INTRODUCTION

In a historic moment like the present, when the eyes of the West are turned toward gigantic China, viewed both as a formidable economic rival and as a promising future market, what point is there in drawing attention to stories of Christian persecution that, for the most part, took place decades ago during the darkest days of Maoism? Doesn't that run the risk of going against the mainstream and, ultimately, of being anachronistic? This sense of "disorientation" might increase as the reader goes on to encounter a spirituality seemingly light-years away from that of present-day Western believers. Gertrude Li, for example, a young Chinese laywoman whose experience of persecution is narrated in the fourth chapter of this volume, expresses herself in a letter from February 1952 in language that today we might find somewhat bewildering, if not disturbing: "It pleases God to water his harvest with the blood of martyrs. Oh, that I might be found worthy of martyrdom!"

We are nevertheless convinced—for reasons to be set forth shortly—that this book will prove to be invaluable for those who read it, believers and unbelievers alike: provided that they are able to consider the events narrated in these accounts carefully, with open hearts and without prejudices. On the one hand, the testimonies collected here are tragically eloquent documents of remarkable historical value; on the other hand, they are spiritual reading of the highest quality. Without fear of rhetorical exaggeration, we do not hesitate to describe them as authentic jewels.

The Protagonists of the Stories

In the strict sense of the term, none of the events recorded here has been recognized solemnly by the Church as a "martyrdom". Nonetheless—the reader will recognize this immediately—the horrific sufferings experienced by the protagonists of these stories, the evangelical patience with which they were accepted and endured and, above all, the faithful witness to Christ that they represent, guarantee that they all have good reason to be included in *The Red Book of Chinese Martyrs*.

Two of the texts that make up this volume—the autobiography of Father Tan Tiande and that of Father Huang Yongmu—are diaries of the imprisonment and forced labor, which lasted thirty and twenty-five years, respectively, of two priests (the former is still living [as of 2006]).

The third document, *Spring Rain*, is the life story of a priest, Father Li Chang, who died in 1981; the compilation and publication of this account (in Hong Kong in 1990) were made possible by his cousin, Li Daoming. This is followed by the autobiographical narrative of the young Catholic woman mentioned before, Gertrude Li Minwen, who was also the object of Maoist hostility for being a fervent Catholic and a friend to the missionaries. The manuscript made its way out of China in an improbable manner: the author penned her story on extremely thin pieces of paper that had been cut out in the shape of the sole of a shoe. This made it possible for her account to travel to the West, thanks to a PIME[1] missionary priest, Father Giovanni Carbone, who hid the pages in the traditional silk shoes that he put on at the moment of his expulsion from China at the end of 1952.

This collection concludes with a sobering report of what can be described without exaggeration as a missionary epic, namely, the martyrdom of thirty-three Cistercian monks of the Strict Observance (Trappists) from the monastery of Yangjiaping, which took place in 1947 at the end of a genuine *Via Crucis*.

Maoism Seen from the Inside

These extraordinary documents report on a span of time that begins with the war between the Communists and the Nationalists (in the mid-1940s—the same period in which the tragedy of the Yangjiaping monastery unfolds). They are concerned primarily with the first period of Maoist religious persecution (from 1949 to the mid-1950s) and continue as far as 1983, the year of Father Tan Tiande's liberation, and the first phase of the "modernization" promoted by Deng Xiaoping upon coming to power after the death of Mao. In

[1] Pontifical Institute for Foreign Missionaries.

perusing these accounts, the reader reviews four crucial decades of contemporary Chinese history, taking
as travel companions eyewitnesses of the events in question. (The historical timeline provided in the appendix is a useful compass to help orient the reader in the
complex series of events in twentieth-century China.)

In other words, the following pages are the memoirs of persons who have experienced in their own
flesh how far the violence of a power blinded by ideology can go, a power which—after winning its battle against an armed enemy (Chiang Kai-shek's
Nationalists)—had decided to exterminate its "enemies
without guns", as Mao in a famous speech described
intellectuals, believers, and opponents of civil society.

From the historical perspective these are contribu-
tions of great value, especially for anyone who wants
to learn about the injustices and brutality of Maoism.
Only in recent years have non-specialists had access to
autobiographical testimonies concerning the *laogai*,[2] the
Chinese forced labor camps. I am thinking, for example, of Chen Ming's *Nubi nere s'addensano* (Black clouds
thicken), recently published in Italy (by Marsilio Press,
2006) but still banned in China. Several years ago Harry
Wu, one of the most famous Chinese dissidents, documented the number, characteristics, and function of
the labor camps in his book *Laogai: The Chinese Gulag*
(1992). But we have a long way to go before we know
about life in the Chinese labor camps in as much detail

---

[2] *Laogai*: an abbreviation of *laodong gaizao*, a Mandarin expression meaning
"reform through labor"—TRANS.

as we know about the Soviet *gulags*, thanks to Solzhenitsyn. *The Red Book of Chinese Martyrs* partially fills this gap. It is a gap that originated in precise politico-cultural circumstances which explain why a book of this sort has never seen the light of day until now.

The Cloak of Ideology

The reason can be summed up in a few words. For a long time a cloak of ideology has weighed heavily upon the real Chinese history of the last half century (as well as upon the living conditions of those who oppose the Communist regime), and it has prevented a calm rereading of entire chapters of recent history. "Every true story, every personal case, offends us with the audacity of its lived reality. It's as if we just keep repeating, 'We already know it all, we already know it all. . . .', and yet we know nothing at all. We have refused to listen to those who tell their stories, and we continue to do so." Such forthright venting—"or, if you will, self-critique"—was written by Renata Pisu, the well-known correspondent for the newspaper *Repubblica*, in her beautiful preface to a book entitled *L'allodola e il drago* (The skylark and the dragon),[3] which received a warm reception when it appeared in 1993. Written by Wang Xiaoling, a Catholic woman whose real name is Catherine Li Kunyi, recently deceased, the book tells of the more than twenty years she spent in the Chinese

---

[3] Originally published in English as *Many Waters: Experience of a Chinese Woman Prisoner of Conscience* (Hong Kong: Caritas Printing Training Centre, 1988).

gulag before her long-awaited liberation and settlement in the United States. The journalist Pisu was among the rank and file of those who fell in love with Maoism during the sixties; in time, however, once the horrors of the Revolution were disclosed, she abandoned such views. Pisu writes:

> This self-critique applies to me personally, as it does to all of us in the West who for years lied to ourselves and to others about China. Yet perhaps—and this is worse in light of what we understand today—many knew that they were lies, but told them "for the right reasons". These were the people—like us?—who considered themselves "friends of the Chinese people". Some friends! ... I broke with this way of thinking in 1978 when I was editing (and writing a preface for) the Italian translation of Jean Pasqualini's book, *Prisoner of Mao*: raised in China, he was imprisoned for unspecified counterrevolutionary crimes during the same period in which Catherine Li lost her freedom. In 1964, Pasqualini managed to obtain a French passport and took refuge in France, where he wrote about the sentence that he had served in a Chinese labor camp, the first testimony ever given about the universe of the Chinese *gulags*. Well, none of the intellectuals believed him, and the French sinologists joined forces against him, claiming that he was in the pay of the American secret services, a CIA agent.

The ideological mortgage encumbering historiography and journalism on the subject of China has severely limited the opportunities for learning about and publicizing these stories of Christian persecution and martyrdom. Not that there haven't been attempts, of course. In the early 1950s, a series of firsthand accounts from missionaries expelled from China were published (see the bibliography at the end of this volume). In 1956, on the heels of the events that are narrated in these pages, Áncora Press published Alberto Galter's *The Red Book of the Persecuted Church*, which is dedicated to the Communist countries, obviously including China. And more recently, in the early 1990s, the Italian Missionary Press (*Editrice missionaria italiana*, EMI) published several eyewitness accounts of anti-Christian persecution in China. In each case, however, the books have not had a significant impact on public opinion, nor have they succeeded in making a dent in the Maoist myth.

The Red Book of Chinese Martyrs, which was printed in the original Italian edition within a few weeks of the thirtieth anniversary of Mao's death (September 9, 1976), intends to be (also) a denunciation of Maoism and its crimes. Although the aging and nostalgic fans of the "Great Helmsman"[4] (who are willing to allow him a thirty percent margin of error) may still be putting up a pathetic resistance, a critical reappraisal of Mao and of his epoch has been underway for some time now in the West. (This is not yet the case in China: the present leadership has preferred thus far to sideline the unwieldy figure and to avoid coming to terms with history.) After decades of ideologically skewed propaganda, a "demythologization of Mao", of his ideology and of his methods, is finally taking place.

---

[4] "Great Helmsman" and "Red Sun" are two of the titles attributed to Mao by the personality cult of which he was made the object.

A decisive contribution along these lines was made recently by the monumental biography by Jung Chang and Jon Halliday entitled, *Mao: The Unknown Story* (2005). If we consider the simple data contained in this and other works (for example, Jasper Becker's exhaustively documented *Hungry Ghosts: Mao's Secret Famine* [1996]), it is no exaggeration to state that Mao Zedong, the "Red Sun", is directly or indirectly responsible for crimes which—in terms of cruelty, intensity and duration—are equal to or even worse than those of Stalin or of Hitler himself. Does this sound like a joke? Far from it. Chen Yizi, a former Party leader who escaped abroad, declares that he saw an internal Communist Party document that put the death toll from "non-natural causes" at eighty million, most of these deaths occurring during the "Great Leap Forward" (1958–1961).

While *The Red Book of Chinese Martyrs*—and this bears repeating—is in no way inspired by political concerns, one cannot help but notice while reading it what a moral, political, and economic tragedy the long season of Maoism proved to be. For example, Father Joseph Li observes,

> The Cultural Revolution had thrown the country into complete and utter chaos. No one worked any more. Young and old, without distinction, spent all their time either in "mass meetings" or in "warfare sessions". People were dragged by force onto platforms where they endured barrage after barrage of accusations and abuse by the crowd. It didn't matter that the charges were contradictory and baseless: they had to stand up there anyway, motionless, while every detail of their private lives

was put on display and made known to all. Among the many who were unable to endure the violence of this moral lynching, some later developed symptoms of mental imbalance, while others committed suicide. It is not far from the truth to say that in those years the whole country had turned into a colossal insane asylum.... The Cultural Revolution spread such a climate of mistrust and suspicion that it threatened to suffocate completely the modicum of natural goodness inherent in every human being.

The point is that whereas in Europe in the 1960s the Maoist program was touted as the "good face" of Communism, enlisting sympathizers even in Catholic circles, in China the cult of the "Great Helmsman" was imposed ruthlessly, by force, so as to subjugate individual consciences and the masses alike. In his autobiography, Father John Huang recalls:

From the time we woke up each morning until we lay down at night, we were compelled to assemble seven or eight times a day in front of Mao's image and to bow repeatedly as a sign of veneration.... Before this image we were obliged to ask forgiveness for our crimes, shouting, "We are all guilty!" And then, raising our heads up to his image, we had to cry out three times "Long live Mao!" ... Thinking back on it now, it's enough to make you laugh! But not at the time, because this comedy had some serious political consequences.

Indeed. In the present cultural climate, which has changed its attitude toward the past, a volume such as *The Red Book of Chinese Martyrs* has a chance of finding a favorable reception—which is our hope—even among readers and intellectual circles that are not particularly interested in religious discussions but have the dignity of man and a passion for freedom at heart.

Enduring Persecution with Faith

It should be emphasized, however, that the purpose of this book is strictly spiritual. Memoirs about concentration camps, forced labor, *gulags* et cetera, have been quite popular for some time now, so much so that one could speak of a publishing trend, but we are not trying to jump on that bandwagon. Nor does the book attempt to reconstruct the context in which the persecution developed, even though there are plenty of keen political observations interspersed throughout the accounts.

In any case, one of the motives for producing this book has been the desire to help paint a picture of the dramatic and heroic experience of Chinese Catholics during the first decades in the history of the People's Republic of China. In this sense, the accounts collected in these pages form pieces of a vast mosaic that is impossible to reassemble in its entirety. It is useful in this regard to recall what Father Giancarlo Politi, one of the foremost authorities on the recent history of the Catholic Church in China, has written in his book, *Martiri in Cina* (Martyrs in China), which records the beautiful faith testimonies of 1,241 believers who have been slaughtered since the Communists seized power:

> Broadly speaking, we can distinguish three major moments during which the Church and Christians have experienced

extreme difficulty which has also led to martyrdom. . . .
A third moment, perhaps the most dramatic, spans the
twentieth century. During the suffering of the first decades
there were numerous martyrs, but then it was still a
question of sporadic and isolated cases. Beginning in the
1940s, however, the persecution became systematic, part
of a perverse plan to suppress and eliminate religion—
and thus the Church—which assumed extremely violent forms.

The Present Situation

And today? Even though disturbing reports continue
to surface from time to time—arrests of bishops and
priests, severe tensions and restrictions, appointments
of illegitimate bishops, heated disputes over church
properties—the present situation of the Church in China
is not even distantly comparable to the environment
reflected in *The Red Book of Chinese Martyrs*. Since the
early 1980s a decidedly different climate has emerged.
That said, being a Catholic in China, as Cardinal Zen
explains very well in the Preface, still involves a great
deal of effort and quite often suffering, especially in
certain regions. Indeed, despite official declarations on
religious liberty (which is formally guaranteed by the
Constitution), the regime refuses to relinquish its claim
to control public expressions of the faith in whatever
form: from liturgical celebrations to social service
initiatives.

In the preface to the Italian edition of James T.
Myers' *Enemies without Guns* (perhaps one of the most
in-depth studies on the Catholic Church in the People's

Republic of China), Father Angelo Lazzarotto, a PIME missionary and an expert on China, makes the following observation:

> Through the dramatic events ushered in by Communist policies in China, a clear light is shed on the fundamental contradictions that still exist that make it extremely dangerous and precarious for Christian communities to safeguard their faith, especially the Catholic faith. For the reigning ideology, it remains intolerable that the churches should claim to offer a different and autonomous answer to the fundamental questions of life and death, and thus to the meaning of man and society, an answer that contradicts the "scientific" version of truth devised by Marxism-Leninism and the thought of Mao Zedong. Here is the key to understanding the persistent uneasiness and the barely concealed repression that the Church still continues to experience today.

The Testimonies of Believers

If today the Chinese Church has survived in spite of the severe and often ferocious opposition of the Party, it is thanks to the granite-like faith of generations of believers who have paid with their blood. The pages of *The Red Book of Chinese Martyrs*, through the words of the protagonists themselves, give us an idea of the extent of the sufferings endured and accepted with heroism and courage, indeed even joy, by believers for the sake of the gospel. The testimonies collected here provide in a very special way the inside story of the daily life of Catholics during the darkest period of religious persecution in China.

All of these accounts are highly charged with the same spiritual tension: here one breathes the crystal-clear faith of the disciple who embraces the cross without hesitation or complaint, following in the Master's footsteps; here a genuinely evangelical mercy shines forth so powerfully that it keeps these pages from coming across as a mere description of the brutal, criminal acts perpetrated by a violent regime. "People might wonder how I was able to survive in those horrific conditions", writes Father Tan Tiande in his diary. "For someone who does not believe, that is a riddle without a solution. For someone who has faith, it is the will of God."

The subjects of these accounts witnessed to their faith, that "pearl of great price", even though we find true martyrdom, strictly speaking, only in the case of the monks of Yangjiaping. What is striking is the freshness of these stories: they are either autobiographical writings or eyewitness reports of the events that are narrated. Hence the reader will not encounter precise but colorless academic essays on the topic but rather pages that ooze blood, sweat, grit and tears, pages written by ordinary people, in a simple style that never indulges in rhetorical excess, even when describing episodes that easily lend themselves to bombastic storytelling.

Minute descriptions of the methods of control, abuse and persecution emerge at various junctures in the volume, enabling the reader to form a vivid idea of the utterly degrading psychological and physical circumstances and the oftentimes extreme conditions under which religious believers (and the "nonaligned" in general) suffered during the harshest years of persecution. The catalogue of brutalities and absurd punishments inflicted upon the prisoners is shocking and in many cases horrifying. For example, we read in Li Daoming's life of Father Li Chang (*Spring Rain*):

> Reeducation could occur in different places and assume different forms: there were the endless interrogations, the mass meetings and "warfare sessions", the indoctrination courses, the humiliation processions, the public condemnations followed by long written confessions. The most violent forms of reeducation, reserved for repeat offenders, included internment in a labor camp or exile to remote and deserted areas where the condemned person had to live in the most complete isolation.

Besides documenting the abyss of cruelty into which the prison wardens had descended, this book demonstrates and authenticates the degree of genuine heroism that characterizes the subjects of these reports, the steadfastness of their faith and their courageous hope in the One who does not forsake His own. These are not clichés. On several occasions all of the protagonists of these reports were assailed by doubt, and all experienced extreme loneliness and a feeling of total abandonment, even abandonment by God. Father Tan Tiande writes as follows in his diary:

> I lived in such conditions as to experience the brutal actions of my companions and to discover what a brute can accomplish.... I would have liked to run into the fields and to shout in a loud voice, "God, where are you?" I don't know how many times I thought of

putting an end to it all. But right at the crucial moment I would see Jesus on the cross looking at me with merciful eyes ... and I would hear Him say, "O man of little faith, do you perhaps doubt that I love you?"

The courage of the believer who dares to believe in God's love against all evidence to the contrary becomes palpable in these pages, and the reader also encounters that anguish before the mystery of evil that can turn into shouts and screams: the cry of the oppressed man, swooning with physical pain, gripped by fear, without any future, without hopes. Besides, what is there to hope for but God in Whom can you place your trust after years and years spent in the *laogai*?

What radically sets this book apart from others like it is that it chronicles events in the lives of believers. We are not dealing with inspiring yet generic stories of political dissidents or human rights activists (however significant they may be). The authors of these various accounts of persecution are Catholics, persecuted because they could not be "assimilated" by the authorities, but above all because they were considered "enemies of the people" by virtue of their faith. As believers, however, they do not bear grudges against their jailers. Not a word of revenge or hatred issues from these pages; on the contrary, we find examples of the persecuted praying for their enemies with the sincerity the Gospels call for. Furthermore, it would be a mistake to interpret this book as merely an attempt at "cultural revisionism" or as a clever publishing strategy adapted to the changing "spirit of the times".

Testimonies as transparent and unaffected as those narrated here cannot help but attract the attention even of nonbelievers. This is another reason why the present volume is so gripping: it is not a collection of edifying human-interest articles or a rhetorical "treatise" on the glories of martyrdom, but rather consists of real-life stories that are genuine through and through. What stands out from these pages, even before the testimony of believers, is the witness to humanity: portraits of women and men of exceptional spiritual and human stature.

New Men

What takes place here before our eyes is a somewhat paradoxical reversal. *Gulag* and *laogai*, which were supposed to be laboratories for molding the "new man" according to the dictates of ideology, have indeed brought to light "new men", but from the newness of the gospel instead: men who, in the hour of trial, discovered the mysterious presence of God and drew from their faith unexpected resources for withstanding difficulties, insults, suffering and torture. Moreover, in the hell of prison, some found themselves hard-pressed to find answers to life's toughest questions: Why is there evil in the world? Where do believers get the strength to resist it? Is there hope for mankind? In several cases, the book recounts personal journeys that led from the anguish of despair to faith. I cannot help recalling the beautiful figure of Li Zhonghua, a sort of twentieth-century Nicodemus, who approaches Father Li Chang, his fellow companion in misfortune, after having guessed the secret: faith. The story, as told by Li Daoming, is remarkable for its simplicity and intensity.

> Li Zhonghua was an honest man and he quickly realized that there was something different about the way in which Father Li interacted with the other prisoners.... One day he took Father Li aside and asked him ...: "Am I wrong, perhaps, to think that you are a believer?"
>
> Seeing that he was sincere, Father Li decided to tell him the truth: "You are very perceptive, Li Zhonghua. You're right.... I believe in God. And I am a Catholic priest." ...
>
> "Father, would you be willing to teach me the Catholic religion?"
>
> "Certainly. If you'd like, we can even begin tomorrow. Instruction, mind you, like at school."
>
> The next day, Li Zhonghua began to learn the basic truths of the Catholic faith. He worked very earnestly and at times he would stop to discuss a particular point of doctrine for several days.. ...
>
> After about six months, Li Zhonghua asked Father Li whether he could be baptized. "Have you thought about this carefully, Zhonghua? To follow Christ requires great personal sacrifice.... Are you sure that this is what you want?"
>
> "With God's help, I want to try."

Li Zhonghua was then baptized. A few lines from Father Li Chang's diary convey the beauty of the occasion: "At the end of the celebration, Li Zhonghua was happy; he embraced Father Li and said to him, 'Thank you, today is the most beautiful day of my life. I feel like a new man.'"

And a little further on, Li Daoming observes:

After his baptism [Zhonghua] was more relaxed, more open and cheerful, more patient with the guards who treated him badly. Moreover, when someone asked him for a favor, he did all that he could to oblige. The other prisoners noticed the change and the comments began: "He has fallen under the influence of Li Chang." ...

Father Li responded with a shrug of the shoulders, for he knew well that no man can change another man. It is only by opening his heart to God that a man can truly be transformed.

The Fruitfulness of Martyrdom

Strictly speaking, the events recounted in these pages (except, as we said, for the ordeal of the Trappist monks) are not stories of martyrdom in the canonical sense of the term. They do, however, depict fierce persecution which has many features of "martyrdom", fragments of lives marked by suffering for the gospel. Today, after the great Jubilee Year 2000 and, above all, thanks to the teaching of John Paul II, the universal Church is very much aware that "it is always the age of martyrs", and that the twentieth century was an atrocious period of particularly widespread and intense persecution.

Well, in the case of China, it should be remembered that sufferings such as those described in *The Red Book of Chinese Martyrs* have characterized the underground Church as well as the so-called official Catholic community, though in very different degrees. Martyrdom, then, is not viewed as an occasion for rivalry (in a contest over "who has suffered more", which has little to do with the gospel), but rather as a sign of unity and a potential means for achieving further reconciliation, according to the hope expressed repeatedly by John Paul II. In speaking about the Jubilee, the Polish Pope never wearied of emphasizing that the grace of martyrdom ought to be interpreted as an occasion for reconciliation between Christians, united as they are in their shared testimony to Christ, even to the shedding of blood, transcending denominational boundaries.

In *Enemies without Guns*, we read the beautiful testimony of a Chinese guard following the martyrdom of Father Alphonse L'Heureux from the Yangjiaping monastery. "That man died in peace. He resembled that other man on the 'ten-shaped' wood (the Chinese character for ten is a cross) in the chapel in Yangjiaping." Just like the centurion in the Gospel who recognizes Jesus as the Christ ("Truly he was the son of God") at the height of his sacrifice, so this Chinese guard—an atheist—cannot help being moved by the startling witness of a violent death borne with serenity; he was unable to remain indifferent to the spectacle of a love that pours itself out to the utmost sacrifice. Martyrdom possesses an intrinsic and distinctive eloquence that transcends cultural boundaries of any sort, and it springs from a source that makes it ever relevant. This is why, after half a century, the life and death of these Chinese martyrs still speak to us today.

— Gerolamo Fazzini
Translated by Andrew Matt and Michael J. Miller

THE DIARY OF FATHER FRANCIS
TAN TIANDE

Introduction

*"While following the police out of the "Shishi"[1], I had abso-
lutely no fear. On the contrary, I felt honored. When I had
received the Sacrament of Confirmation I had promised that I
would be a brave soldier of Christ. . . . When I became a priest
I promised once again to offer my life for the Lord Jesus. . . .
Today I received the Lord's special grace to give witness to the
gospel. It was such a joyous event."*

*The few but incisive sentences in which Father Tan Tiande
recounts his arrest are sufficient to depict the human and spiritual stature of the protagonist. They also reflect the tenor of
his autobiography; by the intensity with which it is written
and the cruelty of many of the events which it narrates, it
reminds the reader of the* Acts of the Martyrs *from the first
centuries of Christianity.*

*Although extraordinary in many ways, the story of Father
Tan is one that he shares with many Chinese priests of his
generation. Born in 1916 in Shunde, in the province of
Guangdong, to a family that had been Catholic for many*

---

[1] The cathedral in Canton, dedicated to the Sacred Heart of Jesus, is com-
monly referred to as "Shishi" (i.e., "house of stone") because the walls and
columns are made of granite. It is a majestic building in the neo-Gothic
style. Its construction lasted twenty-five years and was completed in 1888.

generations, he studied philosophy and theology in the regional seminary for southern China in Hong Kong and in 1941 was ordained a diocesan priest in the "Shishi" cathedral in Canton. He carried out his pastoral ministry at first in Canton, then on the island of Hainan and then in Hong Kong, only to return again to Canton in 1951. Incarcerated in 1953, Father Tan Tiande was interned in a hard labor camp in the northeast of China. (He would be set free in 1983.) There he experienced all the harshness and the madness of that hell-on-earth. We read, for example, in his diary:

> I was locked up in an extremely small and narrow room. All day long the only thing I could do was to remain seated with my legs crossed. . . . I had to have permission from the guard if I wanted to go to the bathroom or even to clear my throat. . . . I was not allowed to speak with anyone at all, not even to get drowsy, otherwise I would be subjected to a painful tongue-lashing."

The following pages—in which the life and imprisonment of this courageous contemporary witness to the faith are summarized—were written in Canton in 1990, seven years after Father Tan Tiande's return to freedom.

Today Father Francis Tan is more than ninety years old, enjoys good health, continues to carry out his pastoral ministry in the cathedral parish and is dearly loved by the Catholics of the city. Father Giancarlo Politi, a PIME missionary and expert on the situation in China, has written the following about him:

> Anyone who knows him is impressed by his resemblance to the mental picture that one usually has of Saint Francis [of Assisi]. Almost thirty years of hard labor in the cold northern province of Heilongjiang, instead of breaking him or leaving him a

bent-over shell of a man, have made him a free and fearless man of substance. To encounter him is a blessing: one sees how fidelity to Christ and a complete and undivided love for Him can make a life beautiful.

I myself can vouch for this. I met Father Tan Tiande during a trip to China in the summer of 2005. Lean, with his face as though it had been worn smooth by the sufferings in his life, Father Tan struck me profoundly by the serenity which he manages to convey to his interlocutor, despite the severe trials that he has undergone, both physical and other. The power and authenticity of the witness to faith that Father Tan is prepared to offer with the utmost simplicity, and his extraordinary ability to speak about imprisonment, torture and inhumane privations without ever betraying the least trace of hatred or feeling of rage—which would be only too human—or a desire for revenge, leave an unforgettable impression on the interlocutor.

Anyone who meets him sees immediately in Father Tan a man "moved by the Spirit". He himself says in his diary, without bragging, "The word of the Lord has taken such deep root in me that the spirit of the gospel is in the very marrow of my bones. . . . All that I did and said demonstrated that I believed in God. . . . When I was in prison and in the labor camp, I always made the Sign of the Cross and prayed before and after meals."

There is something incredible about these admissions. Just as incredible is the strength to consider thirty years of prison in the terrible conditions of the Chinese gulag as a gift. "But I have always thought that our Lord was stronger than anything. Knowing that I was loved, being conscious that my life is 'precious in his sight', saved me from despair, from the *futility of the daily routine, from the fear of a meaningless life."*

The aged Chinese priest combines a passionate love for the Church with this ability to abandon himself to the Father. Only a man who senses within himself the strength of his vocation as a pastor can express himself as Father Tan Tiande does in the final lines of his diary: "Thus I received so many graces from God in all those years. What can I do in return? I would like to spend all my energies for His Church." At the moment of his longed-for liberation, his first thought was of his people, of "his" Christians: "What had happened to my flock while it was separated from me?"

In spite of the priest's granite-like faith, the interminable imprisonment put Father Tan Tiande sorely to the test. There were many moments of discouragement, even of anguish. He himself will tell you, and therein lies his greatness: he does not hesitate to show that he is vulnerable at the moment of the extreme trial. As for the prison guards, they missed no chance to torment that special, unusually determined prisoner. They tried to break down his resistance, subdue his courage, undermine his faith. They tested all three. We read in his diary:

> I could hear the roar of the crowd that was standing around the raised platform. . . . I was entirely calm. "Do you still believe in God?" the Party official asked contemptuously. "Why not?" I replied. "Why does he not come to set you free?" he said to taunt me. "God is free to save me or not. Whatever happens, I believe firmly in him." "See how these chains feel on your legs", he said, and went away.

Father Tan knows very well that, today as in the past, it is no credit to the apostle if he finds the strength to endure accusations, to oppose falsehood. He knows that if this happens it is by virtue of a special grace. "Man always wants to live and fears death. I am no exception. How could I have had that courage, then?" He adds: "For someone without faith, a day in prison is like a whole year. But I have faith. I was at peace with God and with myself. All the sufferings that I endured for the love of Jesus became a joy for me."

These words sound like a profession of confident trust in God, in the God of Jesus Christ, that unique rabbi who two thousand years ago chose a cross as the chair from which he would teach. Ever since his release, Father Tan Tiande has dedicated himself particularly to catechesis and the formation of catechumens. But his very simple room, on the second floor of the episcopal residence in Canton, is never empty: it has become an oasis for many people who sit and talk with him, drawn by his smile and his zeal.

His frail health and advanced age could be so many excuses to limit his apostolate and save his strength. But that would not be Father Tan Tiande's way.

> When I see so many people who want to know God and to learn the catechism, I feel an immense joy . . . that spurs me on to continue. My brother priests at the cathedral are either too old or too sick to work. . . . Therefore I must continue this righteous campaign. The love of God urges me onward. . . . Even if my daily workload is very heavy, I do not feel as overwhelmed as someone might think. Quite the contrary: I feel exhilarated every time my words of consolation or encouragement are able to help someone to rediscover confidence in life.

This same hope is ours as we present these pages to the reader.

A Choice of Life

In the past decade the Lord has accomplished marvelous works in me and, through me, miracles that are
difficult to explain. It seems that I am the only one to
know it until now. Having thus received so many gifts
from the Lord, I can now testify to His goodness. I
want everyone to praise the Lord with me, saying: "My
soul magnifies the Lord ..."

I returned to the Diocese of Canton after finishing
my studies at the regional seminary for southern China
in 1941. I was ordained by Bishop Antoine Fourquet:
this was the most sacred, wondrous and yet compelling gift that the Lord has ever given me. He chose
me to preach His truth and to lead many souls to salvation. In that period China was occupied by the Japanese. There is no need for me to tell about their
brutality or the sufferings that my compatriots endured
during their occupation. Everyone knows this. But the
strange thing is that I was able to travel freely through
the occupied territories, bringing comfort to my suffering brothers and sisters. I administered baptism and
prayed for the dying. And yet I was never mistreated
or hindered by the Japanese soldiers. I trusted completely in the Lord. In spite of the fact that I was thus
obliged to travel in order to preach the gospel, I never
had to suffer. On the contrary, I experienced a great
peace and interior joy.

When the Japanese occupation ended and peace
returned, one of my classmates from our days at the
regional seminary, Father Huang Zhongwen, who had

done missionary work on the island of Hainan, invited me to stay with him to help him evangelize that territory. I immediately accepted, although I felt no particular attraction to that island. I thought that by going there I would serve the Lord and bring salvation to many people. I prepared to enter into that barren island for the purpose of preaching the gospel of Christ.

Upon arriving (1947) I immediately set to work, traveling from north to south (from Haikou to Yulingang) and from west to east (from the district of Lingao to the district of Wenchang). Finally I went to the mountainous area inhabited by the *Limiao* tribe. At first I built a straw hut in which to celebrate Mass and hold meetings. Later it also served as our dwelling. I remained in the mountains of Hainan Island for three years. The air was unhealthy, the mosquitoes were troublesome, and eventually I contracted malaria. The local inhabitants urged me to return to my city to be treated, so I left.

From Canton I went to Hong Kong. I remember that I was then sent immediately to the Hospital of the Precious Blood on Castle Peak Road, in the Shamshuipo quarter. While I was recuperating at the hospital, the PIME missionary who served at Holy Rosary Church on Chatham Street, Father Orazio De Angelis, asked me to go to his church every Sunday to say Mass and to preach. The assistant pastor of the parish, Father Zhou Ruoyu, had just left for Rome to continue his studies. I substituted for Father Ruoyu during his absence. Thanks to the attentive care given to me by many nurses and friends, I recovered my health little by little. A whole year of convalescence passed peacefully before I realized it.

While I was preparing to return to Canton, Father De Angelis did his best to have me stay to help him in his parish ministry. He said to me, "There are so many Chinese Catholics in Holy Rosary parish. They need your pastoral care. Why are you so set on leaving? Missionary work is the same all over the world. Why do you have to go back? You are just looking for trouble!" I understood Father De Angelis' good intentions and his concerns on my account, but I excused myself, because I was already psychologically prepared to return to Canton.

"Persona Non Grata"

I returned to Canton in 1951 because I loved my flock, especially now that my people were going through difficult times. I felt closely united to them. I wanted to share their sufferings and I was even ready to die for them.

Once I had returned to the "Shishi" cathedral in Canton, I started again to train for athletic activities. (During the last seven years of my studies at the regional seminary, I had been the three-time overall champion of the annual athletic tournament and of the swimming competitions.) I made the rounds of all the parishes, preaching the Word and debating with those who were hostile to religion. I forged strong ties both with the Catholics and with those outside the Church. In May of 1953, the month of Our Lady, I organized a pilgrimage to Sheshan, the Marian shrine near Shanghai, something that had never been done before. This way of acting made me a "persona non grata" in the eyes of the authorities.

On August 5 of that same year, my "crimes" were published in the newspapers, both in the *Guangzhou Daily* and in the *Nanfang Daily*. I had never thought that the words spoken to me by Father De Angelis at my departure from Hong Kong would come true so soon.

When the Catholics of Canton read the notice in the two newspapers, they gathered in the "Shishi" to find out what was going on, whether or not I had been arrested. I realized that it could be the last time that I would ever see them. I quickly proposed that we should spend such a moment joyfully and have a "last supper" as a farewell. I told them, "If the worst is yet to come and it is possible someday for me to return to the 'Shishi' alive, then we will meet here once more; otherwise we will all be together in paradise!"

Those fervent Catholics kept me company and did not want to go away. At ten o'clock in the evening I forced them to return to their houses, saying, "I need a little time to gather my things and prepare to go to prison." They left reluctantly. Then I went to the quarters of Bishop Deng Yiming[2] and of my confreres to

---

[2] His Excellency Dominic Deng Yiming (the name in Cantonese is Tang instead of Deng) was arrested on February 5, 1958, and freed after more than twenty-two years of imprisonment, seven of which he spent in complete isolation. His prison diary, entitled *How Inscrutable His Ways! Memoirs 1951–1981*, has been published by Aidan Publicities and Printing in Hong Kong.

say good-bye. When I returned to my room I was so tired that I could scarcely move. No sooner did I lie down on the bed to try to get some sleep than I heard a rapid succession of knocks at the door. I knew that the hour had arrived. I went to open the door and found the police. They showed me the arrest warrant and asked, "Are you Tan Tiande?" I answered, "Yes." I followed them through the main door of the "Shishi". It was quite dark outside; I felt a chill in the air.

There was no precedent for this announcing the crime first and then arresting the criminal. The public safety authorities had first published my crime in the newspapers, giving me some time to prepare myself psychologically, and then they came to arrest me. It seemed that they were trying to be courteous.

While following the police out of the "Shishi", I had absolutely no fear. On the contrary, I felt honored. When I had received the Sacrament of Confirmation I had promised that I would be a brave soldier of Christ for the rest of my life. I would not hesitate to suffer and even to sacrifice myself completely. When I became a priest I promised once again to offer my life for the Lord Jesus: "To live for Him and to die for Him". I would never fail to keep my promise. Today I received the Lord's special grace to give witness to the gospel. It was such a joyous event. The Holy Spirit inspired me interiorly, giving me courage and wisdom. My brothers and sisters in China and outside of China were praying for me in the presence of the Lord, demonstrating a concern and a solidarity that was both tangible and spiritual. This was my great strength, and it would sustain me during all those years of imprisonment. Today, at a distance of more than thirty years, I have the opportunity to write these words and to praise the Lord.

"I Have No Silver and Gold"

A secret agent of the Nationalist Party was among my prison companions during my years of incarceration. He was forced to wear fetters on his ankles day and night because he was a soldier and a secret agent. He had also had to endure a tremendous amount of interrogation. His condition was far worse than mine. It pained me to see him so exhausted and depressed. I befriended him, but how could I have diminished his suffering, even by a little? I, who in the morning did not know what the evening would bring, was hard put to save myself. How could I have found a way to help others?

The words of Saint Peter in the Acts of the Apostles continued to come to mind: "I have no silver and gold, but I give you what I have" (Acts 3:6). I could truly say that the only thing that I possessed was Jesus Christ. I was goaded to act by something inside of me. Finally I decided to get to the bottom of the matter: I would speak about Jesus to my companion. I said to him: "You are suffering so much. I truly believe that only Jesus Christ can alleviate your pain." Then I briefly explained to him the teachings of the Church and taught him to make the Sign of the Cross.

With faith he accepted Jesus as his Lord. The following morning I watched as he made the Sign of the

Cross. In silence, I prayed with him, asking the Lord to strengthen his faith. Little by little he became more calm. One evening he said to me flatly, "Jesus Christ is truly marvelous! He has truly changed my suffering into joy!" Spontaneously we both began to pray, thanking and praising the Lord, for He was the one who changed my prison companion into a completely new person, giving meaning to his life. Before I left the prison, he promised that if he ever had the opportunity he would certainly come to the "Shishi" to visit me.

I was transferred to a hard labor camp,[3] a brick factory in Canton. One of the squad leaders always kept an eye on me. He continually looked for something to report on my account, so as to make things more difficult for me. Later, when he learned that I was a Catholic priest, he watched me even more closely. He tried to find out whether I had said anything against atheism. Then he would have his chance to denounce me to the captain of the section, and I would really be in trouble.

I was born into a family that had been Catholic for several generations. Moreover I had spent more than ten years in the seminary. The Word of the Lord has taken such deep root in me that the spirit of the gospel is in the very marrow of my bones. Believing in

---

[3] Hard labor camps, euphemistically referred to as "camps for reeducation through work", are in most cases uncultivated and peripheral lands that are to be cleared and tilled, or else factories with wearisome tasks. Besides exploiting manual labor at a low cost, the authorities intend to reform the mentality of those who are sentenced to the camps, overcoming their psychological resistance.

God is part of my being. All that I did and said demonstrated that I believed in God. This was my great
boast. When I was in prison and in the labor camp, I
always made the Sign of the Cross and prayed before
and after meals.

One day that squad leader could no longer control
his impatience. He said to me, "You are really stubborn. It is obvious that you are eating the food that
the Communist government gives you, and yet you
still want to thank your God. Do you not believe that
labor creates everything?" I was very happy that he
had asked me that. Now I had the opportunity to teach
him something. I spoke to him openly enough. "Work
can only change things", I said. "It cannot create them.
If farmers did not have seed, soil, sunlight, air and water,
what could their labor accomplish? What is the origin
of the grain? Perhaps you have heard the saying, 'It is
heaven that gives life and nourishes life.' " He went
away without a word, infuriated. That day I had sown
the seed of my own misfortunes.

Faith on Trial

It is very difficult for a Chinese person from the south,
accustomed to a warm climate, to endure the cold of
winter in northern China.[4] During the winter, when
the factory had to close, the authorities at the work
camp used the free time for the ideological formation
of the prisoners, in other words, for exercises that were

---

[4] Father Tan Tiande was transferred to the north of the country in 1955.

supposed to modify their personal convictions. The freezing weather of the northeast cannot be imagined by anyone who has never experienced it, and the experience of a prisoner who is being subjected to brainwashing during the most intense period of that horrendous cold is even more difficult to understand. Not only was I chosen to take part in those exercises, but I also had to be the principal actor in them.

My crime was my conduct itself: preaching religion while serving my sentence. Given that this was the most serious crime that a prisoner could be accused of, a public meeting was held in order to criticize and denounce the guilty party. All the prisoners at the labor camp had to take part in the meeting. I was the protagonist, the object of the criticism of all my companions.

The "director" had tied my hands behind my back. The "costume designer" hung a big rectangular sign around my neck which extended down my back; on it was written: "Counterrevolutionary". The "director" led me onto the stage and read my indictment to the audience: repeated preaching of religion in prison and no sign of repentance. The sentence was life imprisonment. When the sentence was pronounced, he made me lie prostrate on the ground in front of the thousands of people who were watching the spectacle. My legs were bent back at the knees, then bound with chains that weighed several kilograms. At that moment I could hear the roar of the crowd that was standing around the raised platform. I don't remember a single word of what they said. I only know that I was entirely calm. "Do you still believe in God?" the Party official asked contemptuously. "Why not?" I replied. "Why does he not come to set you free?" he said to taunt me. "God is free to save me or not. Whatever happens, I believe firmly in Him." "See how those chains feel on your legs", he said, and went away.

Among the prisoners present there was a Christian from Shanghai named Gu Xianfu, a member of a Protestant church. He used to come visit me and together we would spend the evenings discussing the differences between his church and the Catholic Church. The crime of which I was now accused had originated in those meetings in which I had explained to him the teachings of our Church. He was terribly upset and anxious when he saw how much trouble his meetings with me had caused me and how much I was suffering as a result. One day, after dinner, when I happened to be alone with him, I said to him: "Do you remember the Gospel passage where Jesus says, 'Blessed are those who are persecuted for righteousness' sake'?" Then I explained the eight beatitudes to him very simply and added, "Having the opportunity to witness to the gospel of Christ is a blessing. Really you ought to congratulate me!" I patted him on the shoulder with my hand. He smiled happily.

Thirty years have passed since that evening. I still see the radiant face of Gu Xianfu before my eyes. I have no idea where he is now. Nevertheless I believe that the gospel of the Lord has taken deep root in him. I pray that he might always remain faithful to the gospel and be a true follower of Jesus Christ.

The Girl with the White Hair

Winter in Northern China seemed endless. The ground froze and the river became solid ice. Not only people could walk and sled along the river, but even trucks and autos could travel quickly over the ice during their trips. There were few travelers; the countryside was white in every direction. For someone from the south of China, this scene was new and very strange. In winter people sealed up the windows and doors of the house and lit a fire to warm themselves. Most people did not go outdoors unless they had an errand to run.

One day I received an order to carry some firewood to a tractor driver's house in the commune. The order had come from the authorities. Although I would not have been allowed to object, I set out to do the job in good humor. Defying a cold, sharp and piercing wind, I hitched up the oxen, put the wood on the cart, and then set out on the road leading west. After a while I saw that the oxen were covered with frost. Icicles hung from their noses. Breathing heavily, they advanced laboriously and with difficulty against the wind.

After a debilitating fight against the cold for several hours, we finally arrived at the destination. I unloaded the bundles of wood, which were covered with ice. Despite an hour of demanding work, my hands and feet were still stiff and numb from the cold. I had almost frozen.

During the return trip the oxen, shivering and hungry, walked slower and slower, dragging themselves along step by step. There was practically no other traveler on the road. Just as the oxcart was going up a slope, a thirteen- or fourteen-year-old girl appeared. She had a woolen shawl wrapped around her head and neck, and it was completely covered with snow. She looked like the *Girl with the white hair* from the Chinese film. I looked at her sad face and asked myself what could distress her so, at her young age. I felt an unexpected compassion for her, so I plucked up my courage and shouted, "Little girl, it is very cold. Why don't you come here and get on the cart?" She raised her head and looked at me while I gestured for her to come closer. Frightened but in a way happy, she hastened her step and drew near to the cart. I immediately told the driver of the cart to go a bit more slowly. I jumped down and helped the girl to get on.

Once seated, she continued to keep her head down and didn't speak a word. Finally, after a while, we began to talk. She came from the province of Jiangsu. Her father, Chen Baojia, was a farmer. During one of the military campaigns the whole family had been exiled to northern China. From that day on, her father started drinking to forget his trouble. When he was drunk, he took out his anger on his family, insulting and beating everyone. There was not a single day of peace. The whole family regarded him as the devil in person and, whenever possible, tried to avoid him. When he wanted to drink, one of them had to go out and bring him some alcohol. Even if there was torrential rain or an Arctic wind blowing, they had to go, otherwise he would slap and beat them. In the midst of her tears the girl said, "I just returned from the store, but they had sold all the alcohol. I am terribly afraid of being beaten again." She let out a loud sigh, and she seemed like a middle-aged woman who had experienced life's many difficulties.

At first I did not know what to say to this girl who had already tasted the bitterness of life. In my heart I prayed to Jesus and his merciful Mother, because only they knew how to comfort her. We sat in silence facing each other, then I patted her shoulder and said with a smile, "Don't be afraid. I have just prayed to my God and have asked Him to change your father, so that he will not beat you." She looked at me very dubiously and said, "Your God cannot change my father." She changed her position and said softly, "Today I will not go home." Without waiting for her to finish, I interrupted her to say, "You won't go home? And what will you do then?" She pursed her lips and said, "Don't you worry. I won't bother you any more. Not far from this road there is a little noodle factory. My aunt lives there. She will take care of me." I thought that it would be a good thing for her to stay with her aunt until her father's fury had calmed down. Then she would be able to return home while avoiding a beating.

After a few minutes the signboard of the noodle factory appeared. I asked the driver to stop the cart. We got down, braving a piercing wind. Taking the girl by the hand, I walked forward hurriedly. "There's no need to go farther", the girl said. "It's all right here." She pointed out a door ahead of us. I knocked. I heard a voice from inside that asked, "Who is it?" "Aunt, it's me", the little girl replied. The door opened and a smiling middle-aged woman greeted us. We introduced ourselves. The girl's aunt, Liu, was very outgoing and friendly. She had me come in to have a cup of tea and to warm myself. I told her how it happened that I had met her niece. She clasped my hand and said, "Thanks for your help. I know how to deal with the child's father. I will keep her here for a few days. She can play with her cousin and amuse herself." I got up to leave and saw the girl, who was looking at me with gratitude. I patted her shoulder and said, "I hope to see you again." She smiled and said, "Your God is really great! Many, many thanks."

On the return trip the north wind was still blowing; it was an effort for the four oxen to go forward on the snow-covered road. The sound of their steps echoed rhythmically, while each hoof sank deep into the snow. Suddenly I felt quite relaxed and at peace. The surrounding fields, white with snow, were silent. I started to sing the popular Christmas carol: "Silent night! Holy night! All is calm. All is bright."

"But Not a Hair of Your Head Will Perish"

One day, a year later, I was called by a judge of the court for an interview. He told me brusquely, "You have improved a lot since last year. The court has decided to reduce your sentence. You no longer have to serve a life term but will remain in prison only for another year and a half. Do you have anything to say about the matter?" "Nothing", I replied coldly.

A year before, when they had condemned me to life in prison without a ruling from any official tribunal, I had made no objections but had willingly accepted the sentence. At that time I knew quite well that I had not committed any crime. Thus, my "voluntary" acceptance of my sentence had nothing to do with the question of my innocence. I only wanted to imitate Jesus to fill up what was lacking in the sufferings of the Church. To my utter amazement, a judge of the court filed an appeal for me and of his own volition reduced my sentence. I was completely baffled.

When my fellow prisoners heard the news about my reduced sentence, they were overcome with joy and hurried to congratulate me. My cool reaction surprised them very much. The group captains, the party leaders, the brigade captain, in short all the officials in the prison, seeing that my life as a prisoner continued as before, made fun of me and said that I was controlled by spirits, even possessed by them. And that, supposedly, was why I did not react at all to what happened in the outside world. My old friend, the squad leader who was always watching me, said sarcastically, "His whole body, down to the marrow of his bones, is filled with spirits! He is no longer a human being!"

I was extremely flattered by this "reputation" that the prison officials had pinned on me. All praise and honor be to the Father! I firmly believe that all the sufferings that I endured for love of my Lord were not in vain. The seeds of the gospel had already been sown in their hearts. I am sure that these seeds will germinate in the future, because God will change all that was evil into something good. I await impatiently the coming of that day!

Every time that the labor camp organized some campaign or "educational assembly", I was always the principal actor in the eyes of those who criticized or denounced others: a veteran player on the stage where all those violent meetings were held. At that time I felt honored to be chosen. The strange thing is that today, thirty years later, every time that I remember those meetings in which I was criticized and denounced, my knees begin to tremble involuntarily, to the point that I can hardly remain standing. A man always wants to live and fears death. I was no exception. How could I have had that courage, then? Where did it come from?

When I was a student at the seminary, I had to read the Bible in Latin. Because of the difficulty of the language, I was never very good at it. Despite that, every time that I was denounced, the words of Jesus suddenly came to mind: "They will lay their hands on you and persecute you, delivering you up to the synagogues and prisons, and you will be brought before kings and governors for my name's sake. This will be a time for you to bear testimony" (Lk 21:12–13). Those words are absolutely true, aren't they? The followers of Jesus cannot avoid persecutions. Therefore I accepted my sufferings joyfully, knowing that they were not in vain! The reward was simply "a time to bear testimony" to Him!

The disciple is not greater than his master. Now, if Jesus was prepared to suffer and even to die, should I, his disciple, avoid suffering? "Settle it therefore in your minds, not to meditate beforehand how to answer; for I will give you a mouth and wisdom, which none of your adversaries will be able to withstand or contradict." Jesus also said, "You will be hated by all for my name's sake. But not a hair of your head will perish. By your endurance you will gain your lives" (Lk 21:14–15, 17–19). Today, besides not having lost a single hair, my health is far better than the health of other men who are my age, even of those who are twenty years younger.

"God, Where Are You?"

During the thirty years in which I lived in the northeast, agriculture was my main occupation. Every year, when spring arrived, we had to try to fertilize a field that was as hard as steel. We used to use pick-axes to break up the earth. Once the ground had been softened, we would water it and plant the seeds. Today, as I describe all this, it does not seem that earth-shaking. In reality, at that time we were undernourished. All that work was beyond our strength, so that every minute of it was agony. Agriculture in a labor camp is much different from ordinary farming. Farmers have to work hard, but they do so with a certain hope. They know that their work is not in vain, because after a few months they will have a rich harvest. As long as a person can look to the future with hope, he can endure great labors. But people in labor camps know perfectly well that, despite their efforts, there will be no reward. They will have no share in the harvest that the camps produce.

And what is worse: no one recognizes that you had something to do with the harvest. In practice, they don't even consider the fact that you exist! This experience of not being recognized can ruin a human being. The suffering that it causes is more terrible than any physical toil.

There was a national famine that lasted three years. This intensified the privations in the labor camps, which already had inadequate provisions. Every day some of my companions died of starvation. During those years my job was to bury the dead. During the famine the government encouraged everyone to be very economical. Therefore it was a complete waste to use a wooden coffin to bury a prisoner who had died. Yet my companions did not feel right about simply throwing the corpses into a grave. Then someone thought of an ingenious way to solve the problem: a coffin was constructed with a hinged bottom. The corpse was placed into that coffin and then transported and positioned over the grave; the bottom of the coffin was released and the corpse fell into the grave; thus the coffin could be used again for another corpse.

People might wonder how I was able to survive in those horrific conditions. For someone who does not believe, that is a riddle without a solution. For someone who has faith, it is the will of God. Life is his most precious gift to mankind. I must take good care of this gift so as not to be an ingrate. Therefore, in order to survive, I ate wild herbs and tree bark. I even ate poultry that had been dead for several days. I also stole the forage intended for the horses and ate it. I would have eaten anything in those days. Only stones, mud and dung were not part of my diet. Someone who has never suffered hunger cannot possibly imagine the tremendous suffering that it causes.

A person can appreciate honors or disgrace only when he is clothed and fed. This is true. During those three years of severe famine I began to experience personally the brutal nature of man: egotism, cruelty, cunning, deceit. . . . What is an animal who has the power of reason capable of doing? I lived in such conditions as to experience the brutal actions of my companions and to discover what a brute can accomplish. This pain was even greater than the hunger. I would have liked to run into the fields and to shout in a loud voice, "God, where are You?" I don't know how many times I thought of putting an end to it all. But right at the crucial moment I saw Jesus on the cross looking at me with merciful eyes . . . and I would hear Him say, "O man of little faith, do you perhaps doubt that I love you?"

At the Mercy of the Waves

I spent decades in the labor camp, leading a monotonous life: work by day and sleep by night. There was never any change. We lived like machines, numb and indifferent. Rain or shine, snow or heat, we continued to work on empty stomachs. When I worked harder, I heard my stomach grumbling. One might almost think that it was thundering. It was a warning signal from the bowels of my body, which were telling me that there wasn't enough fuel and that I had to hurry to provide what was needed. The only thing that I could do in those moments was to ask my Lord and Master to help me. I meditated on His forty-day fast and heard Him drive away the devil's temptation. If the Master was tempted, so the disciple would be. I prayed for this and thus reinvigorated my spirit.

In the prison there were criminals but also gentlemen. Thefts, pilfering, fights and violent sexual acts often took place in the cells. And yet there were some who would never have done something wrong to the others for their own personal advantage. Most of these were "counterrevolutionaries" or "political" prisoners. Even though both types of prisoners lived together, one could quickly tell from their conduct who the criminals were and who the gentlemen were. While I was in prison I made many friends among the prisoners who came from all parts of China: from Shanghai, Shandong, Jiangsu, Beijing and Tianjin. This group of brothers in suffering would meet to chat whenever the occasion presented itself. We helped and supported each other. This was the sole pleasure that was given to us in prison. Unfortunately the happy days did not last long. Due to the prison regulations, the prisoners had to be moved frequently. Life there was like the fluctuating waves of the sea.

The Mirage of Freedom

In 1966, when my prison term expired, I was released. But I had to stay and work in the camp. I was a free man, nominally, but when I asked permission to return home for the New Year[5] or other holidays, it was always refused. Those of us who had to remain in the camp were referred to as "second-class workers". Some of them continually asked permission to return to visit their families, but often it was not granted. So they decided to go back home and then to return to the camp. At most, if they were discovered, they would be subjected to "criticism" and punishments.

As of 1975 I had already made many requests to return home to Canton to visit my family, but every time they were rejected. Finally I decided to follow the example of the other workers. I would leave without telling anyone. That day, early in the morning, I jumped on the southbound train. I thought to myself that I would soon see my family again, from whom I had been separated for more than twenty years. The joy that I experienced at that moment cannot be described in words. However "heaven disappoints us". The train had scarcely reached the district of Hulan (it was destined for Harbin) when I was arrested. Handcuffs were put on my wrists and I was carried off by two stout guards to the district prison. Thus I found myself once again in prison.

"Home Is Where Your Heart Is"

I suffered much more in that prison than I did in the labor camp.

---

[5] New Year's Day, reckoned according to the lunar calendar and therefore on a different date each year, is the principal holiday of the Chinese people.

I was locked up in an extremely small and narrow room. All day long the only thing I could do was to remain seated with my legs crossed. I could not stand up or stretch. I had to have permission from the guard if I wanted to go to the bathroom or even to clear my throat. Only after having received his permission could I get up. I was not allowed to speak with anyone at all, not even to get drowsy, otherwise I would be subjected to a painful tongue-lashing.

For someone without faith, a day in prison is like a whole year. But I have faith, and I was able to realize that our home is where our heart is. I was at peace with God and with myself. All the sufferings that I endured for the love of Jesus became a joy for me.

Finally I decided to have my case appealed to the People's Tribunal. I thought that, even though God has the last word on man's plans, I had to do everything in my power to resolve my situation. After eight years my case was like a stone thrown into the ocean: no one knew anything at all about it. One day in 1983, just as I was about to abandon all hope concerning my appeal, one of the officials told me to remain in my cell. He had also made arrangements to send me to the infirmary to rest. What was behind this "special treatment"? One of the older prisoners interpreted it as the first step toward my imminent discharge. And so it was. A few days later the section captain in charge of indoctrination told me, "Your case has now been reexamined. You are innocent and will be released." Later I discovered that my nephew, who lives in the United States, had been the one who took great pains to submit a petition in my name and to obtain my release.

Home at Last

I went through all the formalities required to leave the labor camp in the northeast. I knew that it would soon be possible for me to return to Canton. However I did not write immediately to notify the priests at the "Shishi" cathedral. Many changes could have taken place in Canton during the thirty years that I had been away, concerning both the personnel and developments in the Church. Moreover it seemed to me that I no longer knew anything about city life, having been confined to the country for thirty years. I needed a transition period before I would be able to adapt to living in Canton. I decided to go live with my sister, who worked at the naval shipyard in Huangbu. I would stay there for a while, seeking to understand what God wanted of me.

After resting for six months, I gradually readapted to the complicated life of the city. During that period the people from the "Shishi" cathedral came to visit me in Huangbu. They found that my general condition was good enough, and so they promptly invited me to return to the cathedral to serve the Catholic community. That was truly something that I had looked forward to for so long! What had happened to my flock while it was separated from me? How had they made out during those long and torturous years? Were my old friends still there? Would they recognize me?

Thousands of questions sprang up in my mind. I was more impatient than ever to know the answers.

I decided to return to the "Shishi" with them. As we were arriving, I saw from a distance my beloved cathedral towering over the rest of the city like a temple: it seemed exactly the same as it had been thirty years before, with its two tall spires that reached out like two big arms to welcome me. I automatically quickened my pace. I wanted to be enclosed within the embrace of my beloved Mother. I wanted to take refuge in her arms and let my heart speak. When I found myself in front of the discolored door, tears began to run down my face. I forcefully opened the door and saw the interior in ruins.[6] I felt a cold wind hit me from all sides, and my knees started to tremble. O, beloved Mother, what agony you have gone through! What sorrows and insults! Do you need me to tell you anything? You understand it all, because you have experienced it personally.

I don't know how long I remained kneeling in the cathedral. I remember only that when I finally stood up again, the great weight that had crushed me for all those years was gone. I felt liberated. I promised my beloved Mother that I would put the rest of my life to good use, so as to be a faithful servant of her Son, our Lord Jesus Christ.

[6] During the ten turbulent years of the Cultural Revolution, everything that was inside the cathedral in Canton (altars, chairs, pews, sacred vessels, statues of saints, etc.) was savagely destroyed and set on fire. Restoration work began in 1979. When Father Tan returned to Canton, obviously the interior of the church no longer looked like it had previously. On February 9, 2007, the cathedral was rededicated after being thoroughly renovated.

When I celebrated my first Sunday Mass after returning to the "Shishi" cathedral, I was so emotional that I could scarcely speak. After the liturgy I went out to greet the Catholics, who were so happy as they surrounded me. "Splendid! Father Tan has returned. . . ." "Father Tan, do you remember my daughter? Now she has two children. . . ." "Father Tan, my son is now studying at the university. . . ." These Catholic laymen, who were so affectionate, kept on talking. The deep creases on their faces and their lifeless gray hair testified to all the sufferings that they had gone through. My eyes were moist with tears. I felt a knot in my throat. I did not manage to say anything. I placed my hands on their heads and bestowed God's blessing upon them. Only the love of God could console them, encourage them and sustain them.

"Consumed" by the People

When the "Shishi" cathedral was reopened to the public, everything had to start over again from the beginning. "The harvest is plentiful, but the laborers are few" (Lk 10:2). The priests stationed there were old and sick. I myself was far from being young, and yet I was like a "little brother" to them. Obviously I took charge of the more weighty tasks, like visiting the faithful, administering the sacraments to the sick and teaching catechism.

Little by little the number of catechumens increased, young and old, from all social strata. They were workers, university students, doctors, nurses, engineers, teachers, household servants, even students from the elementary and secondary schools. They all wanted to receive instruction in Catholic doctrine and become members of the Christian community. For the catechumens' sake, I did not leave the house except for a serious reason. There were no set hours for the catechism lessons. They could come any time that was convenient for them, and I would give them a lesson. My work was so burdensome that finally I became ill. For the first time in my life, I had to be taken to the hospital. I experienced the suffering of being displaced without being able to do anything about it. After many tests, the doctors told me that I was suffering from exhaustion. I was extremely weak and would need a period of rest. I remained in the hospital for several weeks, receiving medications and injections. I didn't seem to recuperate completely. At the request of those who were close to me, I left the hospital for a period of convalescence in the Catholic church of Yunfu.

Yunfu, which is also called "Little Guilin",[7] was certainly a beautiful place in which to recuperate. The Catholic church in Yunfu was situated in the midst of rolling hills. The surroundings were very peaceful. The air was clean and fresh, filled with the perfume of the flowers and the singing of the birds. It seemed to be a paradise. The Christians grew vegetables and raised poultry. My old friend Father Ma kept me company. We chatted happily during meals. My appetite improved.

[7] Guilin (which means "cinnamon forest") in the province of Guangxi is considered to have some of the most beautiful scenery in China and to be one of the most picturesque landscapes in the world.

Every morning and every evening we rode around on bicycles or took a walk through the hills. Indeed, we amused ourselves and I recovered very quickly.

The Catholics who had grown fond of me sent letters telling me to get a good rest until I had completely recovered. They told me that there was no hurry about returning to the "Shishi" cathedral, declaring that my health was more important. Yunfu was truly a fine place to stay. And yet I heard a voice in the depths of my heart that urged me to go back. It seemed to say, "You are no longer young. Your days are numbered. A lot of work is waiting for you in Canton. Go back! Don't delay." I decided to leave the following day.

I informed Father Ma about my decision the next day, right away at dawn. He peered at me doubtfully as if to say, "Are you sure that you want to leave this enchanting place?" "Truly it is a magnificent land, yet it is not my land, and therefore it is not worth the trouble to remain here. . . ." These words from the famous classical composition *Denglou Fu* echoed in my mind. I wondered how I could remember that passage, which I had studied during my middle-school days.

The "Shishi" cathedral was just as it had been a month previously. The news traveled rapidly among the Catholics. Many of them came to make sure that I had really recovered. Some gently advised me not to overburden myself again with work, saying that I could reduce the number of catechism lessons by combining some of them. I was very moved by the care and concern of the people. I begged the good Lord to reward them for me.

"Every Ounce of Energy for His Church"

Thus I received so many graces from God in all those years. What can I do in return? I would like to spend all my energies for His Church, to the point of sacrificing my life. I sincerely hope that God will hear my prayer and accept my offering.

I am a frank and sincere person. I do not worry about details and do not speak in a disingenuous manner just to impress others. I suppose that my ways have been influenced to some extent by thirty years of working in the countryside of the northeast. People who mean well criticize me because I am brusque and stubborn. I must say that I still have not grown accustomed to city people's complicated ways of thinking. Friends who are concerned about me always advise me to try to adapt. My problem is this: How can I give in to people and things that don't have my sensibility? How can I change my ways so as to put others at their ease?

My days of working in the countryside of the northeast were days of austere poverty. Hunger was the greatest suffering. During that period I used to think that suffering would be over once I had had enough to eat. Now I realize that the pain of an empty stomach is not true suffering. The pain that breaks the heart comes from misunderstandings among people, from jealousy, mistrust and indifference. I am a simple man. I can't understand why people cannot treat one another openheartedly and sincerely. Is it because we don't want to do it, or are there other obstacles somewhere?

Fortunately, my boss is Almighty God, who is more generous and gentle. As long as I continue to be conscientious in carrying out my duties, He will be kind and will pardon my mistakes and defects. Why should I worry about criticism from other people and about the fact that they are dissatisfied in their dealings with me? Therefore, every time that I hear people's accusations, I lift up my heart to God. I offer everything to Him as a sacrifice and beg Him to accept my offering.

I am especially devoted to Saint John Bosco. The surprising story of his life is the source of great consolation and encouragement to me. He faced every difficulty and paid no attention to criticism as he befriended the abandoned, the downtrodden, the good-for-nothings and the marginalized. He listened to them and encouraged them to learn a trade. Gradually he converted them and led them to Christ. In the days when Don Bosco was trying to put his ideals into practice, he had to confront many obstacles and much opposition. Many people thought that he was downright mad and tried to have him locked up in an insane asylum. He had great faith in God: he knew that the Lord would take care of him and protect him.

What I am doing is insignificant, compared with the work of Don Bosco. I am sincerely concerned about the youth and the children. Every time that I encounter difficulties or feel downhearted, I ask Saint John Bosco for help, hoping that he might guide me along my path. Our Lord and Master Jesus Christ especially loved children. He said, "Let the children come to me . . . , for to such belongs the kingdom of heaven" (Mt

19:14). Not only do I love children, but I would also like to resemble them in their purity and simplicity so as to be closer to Jesus Christ.

The Seed of Faith

Speaking of children, I remember my childhood: I was a very lively little boy. I could not stay seated quietly, not even for a minute. I enjoyed running around all day. It was truly incredible that I should enter the seminary. I didn't understand a thing about vocations, the priesthood or what it meant to enter the seminary. I just thought that it would be very amusing to go to Canton to study. I felt very excited and considered it an honor.

The seed of my faith life was planted by my mother and also by the priest at my parish, Father Chang Qingqi. My mother was a very sweet and lovable woman. We very seldom saw her lose her patience. No matter how much we misbehaved, she never punished us by beating us or scolding us. She was, however, very strict about one thing: our duties and reverence to God. She would have punished us severely if she had discovered that we were not saying our prayers before and after meals, as well as our prayers of thanksgiving. Every time someone in the family had to travel, or when there was any sort of problem or difficulty, Mamma gathered us together to pray and entrust everything to God.

I was too little to understand why my mother was so faithful to God and had to turn to Him for everything. Now I realize that her deep faith had a great influence on me. It was because of her example and the formation that she gave me that I was able to keep my faith despite the terrible tortures and in all the crucial circumstances of my later years. Actually I did not spend many years with my mother because I entered the seminary very young. And yet every one of her gestures and smiles has remained deeply engraved on my mind. Even today I clearly see her gentle face when I close my eyes and remember days past.

Father Chang Qingqi was a priest whom I sincerely respected. Every year I went to Canton for a few days to participate in his annual spiritual exercises. I always returned with packages of cookies and caramels to distribute to the children of the village; I made no distinction between Catholics and non-Catholics. Every evening the children gathered around him and asked him to tell stories. Father Chang began by teaching the children to sing a hymn or two, then he would tell them some story from the Bible. All the inhabitants of the village respected him. For me, he was like Christ on earth. He was filled with the love of God his whole life long, and at the moment he died he was in church. Once he had come to visit us at the seminary in Canton and had brought us to the "Shishi" cathedral to attend Mass. After the liturgy, as we all got up to leave the cathedral, Father Chang remained seated there quietly, completely motionless. We thought that he had fallen asleep, so we tried to awaken him, only to notice later on that he was sleeping in eternal rest.

After his ordination in 1941, Father Chang had been assigned to do pastoral work in Tianyaomen, a locality near Ganzhu in the province of Jianxi. Every time that someone asked him for help, even if he was busy, he immediately put aside his work and welcomed the visitor with an open heart. All who had come into contact with Father Chang could not help but be struck by his gentle, pleasant and humble demeanor. Even the most wicked people were moved even to tears. Father Chang did not accomplish stupendous works, and yet his apparently ordinary life shone with an extraordinary splendor. He showed particular attention to me the times when I met him as a little boy; I am sure that he wishes me well even now. I hope that he is interceding for me in paradise, so that my love for God may be deeper and my faith in Him more steadfast.

My Seminary Years

I spent six years in minor seminary. It was a mixture of joy and sorrow. I went through some crises, but I overcame them. Several times I thought of leaving the seminary because I found the study of Latin extremely difficult. Thanks to the encouragement and help of my sister and my superiors, I stayed. After completing my studies at the minor seminary, I was sent to the regional seminary in Hong Kong to study philosophy and theology. At that time there were about seventy seminarians from various dioceses in the Guangdon, Guangxi, and Fujian provinces, and even some Chinese students from Borneo and Sarawak. Because of our different places of origin, we had very different languages and customs. We had heated discussions and even quarrels because of mutual misunderstandings. Fortunately we were young and unprejudiced and had not learned to harbor rancor in our hearts. Each time, after we had calmed down again, we were unhappy with our conduct and asked one another for forgiveness. We shook hands and were friends again. Forgiving one another is the foundation of love.

Besides acquiring a theoretical knowledge of philosophy and theology, we also learned at the regional seminary to put charity and forgiveness into practice in the everyday life of the community. It was very beneficial to combine theory with practice. Father John O'Meara, an Irish Jesuit priest who had just celebrated his ninetieth birthday in Hong Kong, was the rector of the regional seminary at that time. He always found occasions to speak with the seminarians, learning Cantonese at the same time. Every time that Father O'Meara spoke to me, I wished that he would express himself in his own language, because I was looking for an opportunity to improve my English. But he always started speaking in Cantonese, and I had to follow suit. Now that Father O'Meara speaks Cantonese so well, I think that we, his former seminarians, can be proud of the role that we played. I remember very well what he told me one time: "Your name is very significant. 'Tiande' means 'the virtues of paradise'. I am sure that when your father gave you that name, he wanted you to become virtuous like the saints in heaven. You should try not to disappoint your father." I was very little when my father died, and so I have only a vague recollection of him. Father O'Meara gave me a very effective way of connecting my name with my father. From then on I felt much closer to him. Every time that I think of my name, I recall the great hopes that my father had in my regard. I pray that when I am reunited with my father in heaven, he will be able to pat me on the back and say, "Tiande, you truly are my good boy. You have lived according to the name that I gave you."

A Sporting Spirit

Life at the regional seminary was much richer and more joyful than at the minor seminary. In the first place, I was older and more mature; I was beginning to grasp things that I could not understand at first. There was another, more important aspect: through the instruction and formation provided by all the devoted priests of the seminary, I deepened my knowledge of God. I was able to notice the presence and the love of God in my daily life. I was grateful to God for having called me lovingly. I made a firm resolution to serve God and His Church faithfully for the rest of my life.

I have liked sports ever since I was a boy. The regional seminary (now called Holy Spirit Seminary) is located on a little peninsula surrounded on three sides by the sea, with the mountains in the back. There are big athletic fields, and beaches that can be reached on foot. During the years that I spent there, I used to spend my free time taking walks, swimming or playing football or basketball. I had the honor of being the champion for three years in the intramural athletic and swimming competitions at the seminary. Besides a robust physique and good technique, a good athlete has to have above all great willpower and great self-confidence. Only now do I realize that the sporting spirit that I developed in those athletic exercises was essential in facing the challenges in the prisons and the labor camps in the northeast.

"I Have Fought the Good Fight"

Every time that I feel completely exhausted and have to lie down in bed, I like to close my eyes and meditate on these words of Saint Paul: "I have fought the good fight, I have finished the race, I have kept the faith. From now on there is laid up for me the crown of righteousness, which the Lord, the righteous judge, will award to me on that Day, and not only to me but also to all who have loved his appearing" (2 Tim 4:7–8). How I long to be able to finish my earthly task quickly and go before the throne of God to receive the crown that He has prepared for me! Once, while I was talking about this desire of mine with a dear friend, he took my hand affectionately and said, "Father Tan, I think that you are working too much. You have not yet recovered completely from your illness, and yet you keep working so much. Don't forget that you are already seventy-four years old. Other people your age are all at home enjoying a quiet, peaceful life. How can you manage to work even more hours than someone who is younger than you?"

I was unable to answer him. But when I see so many people who want to know God and to learn the catechism, I feel an immense joy. This joy is an interior stimulus that spurs me on to continue. My brother priests at the cathedral are either too old or too sick to work. We have no young priest to help us. Therefore I must continue this righteous campaign. The love of God urges me onward.... I know that God's crown is not too far off and that it awaits me. As Saint Paul said: "It is no longer I who live, but Christ who lives in me" (Gal 2:20). Therefore, even if my daily workload is very heavy, I do not feel as overwhelmed as someone might think. Quite the contrary: I feel exhilarated every time my words of consolation or encouragement are able to help someone to rediscover confidence in life. I think that it is worth the trouble to sacrifice my life, not to mention sacrificing my health.

Unworthy Servant

Allow me to recount one incident. Late one evening I was half-asleep in bed. The clock of the cathedral had struck ten. I heard someone knocking at the door of the rectory. Who could it be, so late? Perhaps it was a Catholic who was looking for a priest to go to his house to administer the anointing of the sick? I put on a robe and went down to the ground floor. I opened the door and saw an unfamiliar, middle-aged woman who seemed quite frightened. Before I could say anything, she had hurried inside, closing the door behind her. I had to jump back very quickly. "Are you a priest?"

she asked nervously. "Yes. What do you want?" "I am not Catholic, Father, but I would like to speak with you", she said haltingly. "Very well. Have a seat."

She sat down and told me her story. She was a pianist, married with three children. Recently her husband had suffered a nervous breakdown. He had turned the house into a chaos and caused her anxiety day and night. Instead of helping her, her parents and the neighbors made fun of her and gossiped about her. Fortunately her children were away from home as students. She had tried to address the situation, hoping to convince her husband to seek medical treatment. He had refused, and his mental confusion seemed to be worsening. Just an hour before he had taken a kitchen knife and threatened to kill her. She had had to escape from the house. She wept as she said, "I ran aimlessly along the street, wondering where I could go. There is no place for me to go. I stopped suddenly and saw a Catholic church ahead of me. . . ." What could I do for that poor woman? For that night I brought her to the guest house of the parish. The next day we would decide what could be done. Lord, I am your unworthy servant. I did only what I was obliged to do.

A Testimonial to Father Tan Tiande

We reprint the testimonial of Lin Suier, a woman who became acquainted with Father Tiande after he was set free. [When the original Italian edition of this book went to press in 2006, Father Tiande was the only one of the protagonists of this book who was still living.]

Father Tan Tiande is a priest at the cathedral in Canton; he is well-liked and highly respected by his parishioners. Today he is over eighty years old and has still dedicated himself, body and soul, to the truths of the faith and to the salvation of souls.

I am a disabled woman. Although I am more than forty years old, I have never even dared to think of marrying, like other people who are physically fit. I could only hope to live as long as possible in the care of my parents. However my mother died of an illness in 1980, and gone with her is all the tenderness and maternal warmth that had surrounded me from my childhood. In 1990 my father, too, who was always strict in bringing me up, died of cancer. I was completely crushed and felt that life had no meaning without the love of a family. While I was languishing in that state of confusion and bewilderment, a man, guided by the "Love" that rules the universe, brought me to Father Tan's parish. Thus I found myself in a large family made up of thousands of people.

Father Tan is able to apply maternal tenderness and paternal strictness in equal doses. He is generous with his time, and I very quickly became one of his regular visitors. He receives so many visits from his catechumens that his house is like a marketplace in which people are constantly coming and going. His friends come from different places and social strata and cover a very wide range of ages. All these people usually bring with them their own sorrow, hidden agendas, anger and regrets. They know Father Tan by reputation and come to listen to his instruction and to receive consolation. It doesn't matter who they are: millionaires, high-ranking officials, elegant gentlemen, poor laborers, disabled persons with twisted bodies, the terminally ill.... They all receive the same warm welcome from Father Tan. His little house (ten square meters) is always imbued with an atmosphere of fraternal equality, harmony and warmth.

Father Tan gives everyone a copy of the *Catechism*, a booklet that contains the most general and important teachings about our universe. He explains it attentively and indefatigably to his listeners. He speaks about philosophy and theology: God, the Holy Spirit, our ancestors, the Blessed Virgin Mary, hell and heaven, the resurrection, the Ten Commandments and the four precepts of the Church. Sun Yat-sen, the father of our country, once said that "religion can compensate for the inadequacy of the laws." Father Tan joyfully teaches people to keep God's commandments, to practice the virtues and to do penance by performing good works. He has a special charism for strengthening and encouraging people. After hearing his teachings, some feel that the burden of anger and sadness on their hearts is lightened, others find solutions to the complex problems in their relationships, young people who are tempted to immorality are revived, and corrupt officials decide to make restitution to those whom they have swindled.... With the help of Father Tan, they all return to their own work or studies with their spirit renewed and with greater enthusiasm.

Father Tan profoundly loves his country and his dark-eyed, black-haired, tan-complexioned people. Before the liberation [from Japanese occupation] and after the Cultural Revolution he refused on several occasions to settle in Hong Kong as the base for his evangelization work. He preferred to remain within the simple context of the cathedral parish in Canton. He used to say: "I am a pastor; I cannot abandon my sheep in Canton." Father Tan was interned in a labor camp in northeastern China for thirty years, at a time when the [political] Left had seized power. He learned "to have the heavens as a blanket, the bare earth as a bed, to drink from streams and to eat horse manure." He considers that adverse experience in his life as a trial assigned to him by God. With his faith and his will-power, he went through the dark night so as to meet the dawn, thus fortifying himself in the midst of those difficulties.

Father Tan always wears clothing of the same color and likes to walk barefoot. He has the physique of an old farmer in good health. He treasures the sunlight and the fresh air and labors tirelessly and energetically night and day.

(From *Kung Kao Po*, the weekly newspaper of the Diocese of Hong Kong, January 6, 1995)

THE DIARY OF FATHER JOHN HUANG YONGMU

Introduction

The following document compiles the memoirs of a Chinese priest, Father John Huang, who spent almost twenty-five years in prisons and a labor camp and died on October 7, 2005 in Hong Kong. During the last years of his life, after his release (February 5, 1980), he devoted himself with great zeal to the priestly apostolate and to catechesis. At the conclusion of his diary he writes, "I hope to do now what I was not able to do during the many years stolen from me by the Communists. I want to do all that I can to thank God for this second spring that He is granting me!"

The diary of Father Huang was published anonymously—a sign that, even at a distance of many years from the facts that are recounted in it, the author still perceived risks in presenting them straightforwardly. From the pages of Father Huang's account emerges, first of all, the great faith of the protagonist, his docility in accepting God's plan without any sort of fatalism. While telling about his arrest, which culminated in the death sentence, the priest writes:

> I thought that the Communists had arrested me illegally and that the trial and the sentence were certainly not according to the civil laws. Nevertheless I resigned myself, accepting God's

> plan as he willed it, even death. . . . A strange sense of calm
> and peace took possession of me. . . . Didn't our Lord say to
> Saint Paul: "My grace is sufficient for you"?

Father Huang relates that:

> During my trials I always tried to use reason and logic, entrust-
> ing myself to the Holy Spirit, so that He might make up for my
> weaknesses. . . . I recalled the words of Saint Paul: "We are afflicted
> in every way and yet we are filled with joy" (see 2 Cor 4:8).

Together with many other fellow prisoners and victims of
persecution, Huang shares one certainty: "The harm done to
the Church was serious, but we know from history that the
blood of martyrs is the seed of Christians." It is a genuine
faith which nourishes the untiring prayer that saved Father
Huang (and many other believers like him) from the danger
of despair.

> During the "Great Leap Forward" we worked shifts of twelve
> hours a day and often more, so that I was completely
> exhausted. . . . We were permitted to rest only five or six hours
> per day. Despite this, I always recited five decades of the Rosary
> each day and the litanies of Our Lady for the souls in purga-
> tory. Once I had been put into prison, I used to recite mentally
> the whole Mass from memory while lying down in bed.

The testimony given has a spiritual quality, and the text is
characterized furthermore by a number of keen observations
about Communism, the dynamics of the Revolution and political events in general. The priest does not attempt to offer
sophisticated analyses, yet his observations, combined with his
firsthand experience, lay bare many of the intrinsic contradic-
tions of the totalitarian Maoist system. Here is an example:

While I was in the prison in Haifeng, I lived through nine political campaigns: the reform of the farming cooperatives, the campaign against the bourgeoisie, the "Great Leap Forward", et cetera. Anyone who keeps abreast of the political scene in China knows very well that the object of every single campaign was to restrict the people's freedom of action and speech, so as to make them like slaves.

One of the most terrible control techniques devised by the Communists was the so-called "thought reform". Father Huang offers a brief description that nevertheless causes a shudder:

The purpose of thought reform was to develop our political sensibility, and so they tortured us diabolically in our thoughts, in the very essence of our freedom. . . . It consisted of subjecting our minds, imperceptibly, to an unbearable agony so as to bend them to their way of thinking.

Regarding relations with the U.S.S.R., Father Huang's account contains a significant passage that captures the climate of the era:

The Soviet Union was extolled for some time as our big brother . . . and the poor people were obliged to shout disgusting slogans of Communist propaganda. . . . After a while the Sino-Soviet friendship went to pieces. . . . All the previous praises ended up on the dust heap and the practice of following the Soviet model was completely abandoned!

The priest's comment is bitter:

It is quite true that in China one must never reveal one's own opinion with regard to politics, because what is considered right today by the Party can be considered wrong the next day. And they call this democracy of the people!

Also enfolded in Father Huang's account is the painful experience of the Christian community, whose members were subjected, with alternative outcomes, to the fire of persecution: there were those who were opposed and put up resistance, but there was no lack of those who gave in to the violence. The priest notes that:

> The Party leaders assembled all my parishioners every day so that they could confess all my crimes against the people. . . . They promised clemency to those who would confess their crimes and the utmost severity to those who refused to do so. . . . Hiding crimes was considered a crime in itself, and then every method imaginable was used to extort confessions.
>
> Under the pressure of threats and deceptions, a considerable number of Christians revealed things that caused trouble for me. For fear of being accused in turn, they sought to excuse themselves by reporting little things against me.

Even a man with steadfast faith like Father Huang, subjected to continual physical and psychological torture, at a certain point confesses his anguish:

> I often felt downcast by the terrible thought of never seeing my dear father again, of not seeing my beloved superiors, my parishioners, the people that I had instructed and baptized. . . . During those periods of the dark night of my soul, caused by the mental and physical stresses of the Communist persecution, I suffered so much that I thought that there could not be anything worse. . . . I could not have resisted if it had not been for the memory of Sacred Scripture, if I had not prayed using the psalms that I could remember. This gave me comfort, strength and the courage that I needed so much.

Nevertheless, like the other protagonists of The Red Book of Chinese Martyrs, *Father Huang, too, is able to raise his voice in a* magnificat, *despite the trials that he underwent and the tears that he shed.*

> *Thinking now about all that happened to me from the day of my arrest and through all those years of imprisonment, I can only thank God for helping me with His Providence and for consoling me with the promise made in Sacred Scripture that God rewards His faithful servants abundantly.*

The Beginning of the Persecution

I was born in 1914 in a village near Shantou in southern China. When I was born my father gave me the name "Yongmu", which means "brave shepherd". I remember that even when I was little my father told us that we were descendents of old Catholics who had received the faith handed down to them over many generations; that we were descendents of martyrs, because in one of the persecutions our ancestors had refused to venerate the pagan gods. Indeed, they were arrested and lined up to be executed, but the sentence was not carried out because the rifles of the soldiers jammed.

As a boy I was sent to the seminary in Shantou, but I missed my father so much that I ran away from school. Ten years later I reentered the seminary; I was ordained a priest in 1940 and was sent to minister in the district of Haifeng.

Those were difficult years because of the Sino-Japanese war, which lasted from 1937 to 1945, and then the civil war between the Nationalists and the

Communists, which ended with the victory of the latter and the proclamation of the People's Republic of China on October 1, 1949.

From the winter of 1949 until the beginning of the summer vacation in 1951 we were able to carry on our missionary work undisturbed. We were constantly being spied on, however, by disguised Communists who went into the churches and the homes to find out what we were saying. And everything was reported to the local police chief.

In 1950 the bishop, Monsignor Bianchi,[1] had permission from the police for himself and for his priests to make the rounds of the villages more or less regularly. This gesture was not as generous as it seemed; in reality the Communists let them do this so as to learn where we went, with whom we met and what we said.

At the beginning of 1951 our situation began to change gradually. Threatening clouds were gathering over us. First, the local authorities told us that in our visits to the villages no priest could travel more than seven or eight miles from the residence where he lived. Father Luciano Aletta, PIME, however, did not heed that order, and consequently they set an ambush for him. One day, while he was returning from a village

[1] Msgr. Lorenzo Bianchi, PIME, (1899–1983) governed the diocese of Hong Kong from 1952 to 1969. Right after his episcopal consecration in Hong Kong on October 9, 1949, he returned to Haifeng (where he had worked since 1923) shortly before the arrival of the Communists. Arrested on May 22, 1951, he was held in detention for seventeen months. In 1969 he voluntarily submitted his resignation as Bishop of Hong Kong, convinced that the moment had come to hand over the diocese to the local clergy.

more than eight miles away, he found himself surrounded by a band of men who beat him savagely and
carried him to the local police station. Several Christians hurried to bring us the news of his arrest; the
bishop and I went immediately to help him. The official in charge told us arrogantly that now the consciousness of the Chinese people was awakened and as
a result the Chinese despised all the imperialists and
their servants. From that moment on all activities of
foreigners in China were drastically restricted. With
the usual ambiguity, he told us that we ought to consider ourselves fortunate, because he was there to protect us, but from now on our activities would have to
be reported in detail. He then said that Father Aletta
would have to write a complete, well-prepared self-
critique. In order to regulate matters the bishop asked
me to write the self-critique for the priest, hoping that
that would settle the matter. That was the first time
that the Communists struck hard at the Catholic Church
in our diocese. In the following months the activities
of the foreign and Chinese priests were subjected to
ever more rigorous restrictions.

Around Easter of 1951 the bishop's health began to
deteriorate, and he asked me to write to the authorities requesting permission to leave China for medical
treatment. The authorities gave the bishop a curt negative reply. All the foreign missionaries of the mission
were ordered to meet in the city of Haifeng. They
were then arrested by the Communists and gathered
in a hotel. All the missionaries were thoroughly searched
and deprived of their freedom. Fortunately they could

say Mass secretly and even meet with any Christian who courageously came to visit them. In June of 1952, except for the bishop, all the foreign missionaries were expelled from China. The bishop, who had worked in that mission territory for almost thirty years, was left in prison and then subjected to the supreme ignominy of a popular trial; finally, in October 1952, he was also expelled.

Agrarian Reform

In 1951 the program for agrarian reform began. This was the first of the disastrous campaigns that followed one after another. It was a period of great suffering in a nation that was already suffering enough. The group that directed this program used the mission residence as their headquarters. In 1949 I had rebuilt my residence, which had been destroyed by the Japanese in 1944. I was allowed to live on the first floor of the premises. In June the authorities of the district sent me a notice saying that, in order to carry out agrarian reform better, it was necessary that everyone be organized, and so the Catholic Church, too, had to cooperate. So gradually all missionary activities, Masses, liturgies, et cetera, ceased. Our churches were turned into meeting halls, education centers and forums for heated discussions about the programs of the agrarian reform.

As long as I was not arrested, I was allowed to say Mass in my church only on the feasts of the Assumption and the Nativity. On all other days I could celebrate only in the houses of a few Christians who were strong in their faith and had no fear of the Communists. Since the common citizens also could not go far from home without permission, Sunday Mass was poorly attended. One could say that we already guessed the diabolical plan of the Communists against the Catholic Church. The first step was to control the Church; the second was to restrict its activities so as to destroy it completely. Some people did not see clearly what was starting to happen. They were too optimistic and inclined to say that Chinese Communism was unlike Russian Communism. But that was a fable told by foreigners.

The agrarian reform provoked an extremely volatile class warfare, pitting the Chinese against each other. The Communists wanted an egalitarian society and so began to reduce everything to the level of one single class. Rents and interest rates were abolished. The landowners were subjected to "popular trials" and ruthless criticism. The lands were divided and farmers could plunder the houses and properties of the owners. The "black sheep", in other words, those who were opposed to this terrible program, were exposed to the public and criticized. The poor farmers were regrouped into a single organization, the women on one side and the men on the other, so that they could be better controlled and manipulated.

In my parish the church owned some land, around two acres. In some years we received rent from it, in other years, nothing. Since the Communists could not stir up any popular indignation against the Church in this regard, there was no sort of class warfare or particular accusation against me. At the start of the program for agrarian reform the mother of a certain Christian, knowing that I had several rugs, aggressively asked to borrow them from me. I refused. The woman reported this to the director of the agrarian reform program, but the two members of the group criticized her. Then her son made an agreement with several directors who, for no reason at all, got into a fistfight with me. According to the Communist doctrine of class warfare, anyone who is rich is wrong and therefore has to be punished.

From the beginning of the agrarian reform until 1955 I had to put up with all sorts of harassment, threats, coercion and intimidation. All that notwithstanding, during that time I was fortunate because I was living by myself, and the work brigade assigned me two parts of the field for my livelihood, whereas I needed only one and a half. And so I started to work, cultivating the fields, planting vegetables and raising pigs. In this way I could share with my parishioners their welfare and calamities, consolations and difficulties, their joys and sorrows. My thoughts and feelings were more in sympathy with those of my Christian brethren. When I had a lot of work, some of my parishioners came to help me, as I in turn did for them when they were in need.

"Father, Forgive Them"

I continued my work in the name of the Lord, blessing marriages with the customary ritual, wishing the spouses long life and many children. By seeing to it that their children were baptized, by arranging for the sick to receive the last sacraments and consoling the dying with the hope of going to heaven, they would not forget their friends and their pastor. This was my life in those years.

In my parish there were two families of landowners. Many times they were forcibly subjected to crude denunciations in front of a "people's tribunal". Occasionally I gave them some sign of friendship. I was afraid to say to them some word of comfort, but I was able to give absolution to one of the two landowners as he was dying. Taking my hand, he said to me, "Father, I forgive them." This made me think of the other "Forgive them", uttered twenty centuries before by Christ on the cross. It made tears come to my eyes; I burst into tears, put my hoe over my shoulder and left.

When I had a little free time, I would go from house to house to baptize the infants, to bring Communion to the sick and to give Extreme Unction to the dying. Many times I put myself in danger by exceeding the limits on distance that the authorities had imposed on me. Following Jesus' teaching to help one another, every so often I went to pay a visit to Father Peng, who lived far away, beyond the permitted distance.

"Counterrevolutionaries" in the Crosshairs

In 1955 there was an unprecedented campaign throughout China to eliminate all the "counterrevolutionaries". For a long time Mao Zedong had been saying that the revolution had to be carried out through violence, that one had to respond violently to the counterrevolutionaries, putting aside dignity, gentility and humanity. Regardless of the wishes of the guests, even the gifts that are so appropriate to our Chinese culture were outlawed. The situation was chaotic!

From the very beginning of the People's Republic of China, the Communist Party had started a series of political campaigns, one after the other. That was Mao's policy. First there was the campaign against secret agents, bandits, landowners and everything connected with them. Thus the Communists liquidated more than ten million people whom they called "the scum of the old society". After that there was the campaign against the "Three Evils": corruption, waste and excessive bureaucracy in the government and in the armed forces. Then came the campaign against the "Five Evils": corruption, fiscal evasions, misappropriation of public goods, fraud in declaring the cost of labor and materials, and the use of information about the state economy for personal gain. These campaigns followed one after another with ever greater ferocity.

During the 1955 campaign to eliminate counter-revolutionaries, I had been very cautious, isolating myself and avoiding participation in Party activities. Like other persons from the old government, both intellectuals and religious, I sought to stay as far away as possible from the political upheavals.

The Communists, however, had already decided to liquidate all the counter-revolutionaries, who they thought were hiding behind the Church. Communism is absolutely materialistic, whereas the Church is essentially spiritual. These two ideas constitute the two philosophies of human life. The Vatican is considered to be the center of all reactionary circles, and so the Communists sought to mobilize an active campaign against the Church so as to destroy it. Initially the campaign was aimed at challenging organizations that were opposed to the Party. But soon the Party showed its real intention of destroying Catholicism. The Bishop of Shanghai, Gong Pinmei [known in the United States as Cardinal Kung] was arrested and thrown into prison. At that same time, again in Shanghai, many priests were arrested and put to death. It was actually a national-scale attack against the Catholic Church.

At that time I found myself in the Diocese of Shantou, where the vicar general was of the opinion that the violent storm would be of short duration. Meanwhile both the bishop and the priests were obliged to participate daily in the Party meetings. When I returned to the parish of my village, the Party leaders assembled all my parishioners every day so that they could confess all my crimes against the people. The method consisted of gathering all the faithful of the parish in a certain order, setting apart in one group those who had friendlier relations with the pastor. Often, with threats and incentives, they sought to obtain from them confessions of possible crimes committed by the priests. They promised clemency to those who would confess their crimes and the utmost severity to those who refused to do so. If we acknowledged our crimes, they would sentence us to lesser punishments. Hiding crimes was considered a crime in itself, and then every method imaginable was used to extort confessions.

Under the pressure of threats and deceptions, a considerable number of Christians revealed things that caused trouble for me. For fear of being accused in turn, they sought to excuse themselves by reporting little things against me. One Christian revealed to the agrarian reform that, while preaching in church, I had said that we must love one another, a phrase considered blasphemous in Communist jargon. This Christian also reported that I said: "It is not lawful to hate others; we must pardon those who offend us." All these expressions were contrary to the agrarian reform and to Communist doctrine.

Others accused me of having incited the Christians to collect and hide the propaganda leaflets that the Nationalists dropped from airplanes so that they could bring them out when the Nationalists returned. There was one man who really had collected and hidden the leaflets, and he showed them as proof of the charge against me in order to save himself. Another man accused me of having persuaded the people not to use fertilizers, with the result that the land did not produce enough to provide a large quota of rice for the State. Another accused me of having told them not to listen to what the Communists told them, because otherwise they would not enter into the kingdom of heaven. All these charges were silly and false!

While I was in Shantou, the police from Haifeng went to the village of Niupidi to requisition all that I had in my residence. A Christian woman, seeing the situation, went to the neighboring village of fervent Christians to find someone who would send word to me in Shantou, letting me know how matters stood. And indeed, as soon as I had arrived in Shantou, I learned that the vicar general of the diocese and all the other priests were on the brink of catastrophe. Then I understood, from what I had heard, that things were starting to go badly for me, too. Despite all this I felt at peace, ready to confront the danger that I had heard about. The pastor of the cathedral parish reassured me that it would be a good thing to spend a few years in prison. I did not foresee then that for me the years of imprisonment would be more than twenty.

In the Trap

In November the situation became tenser by the day. In the middle of the night on December 5, 1955, the police from Shantou suddenly surrounded the bishop's residence and arrested the vicar general and all the priests, together with other Christians. The other priests of the city were also arrested. The Communists embarked on a well-planned campaign to wipe out the Catholic Church in Shantou. All the Catholic families of the diocese, without exception, were subjected to thorough searches and annoying interrogations. The interrogations covered everything, even the most minute details of private life, and they were exhausting, continuing day and night in order to produce some result for the Communists.

When I returned to my village, I was arrested, too. As of December 16, 1955, I was isolated in the district prison in Haifeng, in a little cell measuring 2.5 by 1.7 meters [8 by 5.5 feet], which could scarcely hold two persons. This way of treating someone before he was charged with any crime, that is, throwing him into a small cell, was the Communist method of making sure that he would have time to examine his own life, in complete isolation, and to discover his own misdeeds. This little cell concealed a snare. When you are in a new setting, it is easy to fall into a trap. The Party places in your cell another so-called "prisoner". The two prisoners begin to confide in one another and thus to exchange their names and to make small talk to pass the time. Later I learned that that "prisoner", my cell-mate, was nothing but a Communist placed there with me to note what I said and then to report everything to the Communist authorities. I found out about this because one day I asked him how many prisoners had died in the prison in Haifeng since the day of the liberation. I asked him this question without realizing that he would report it to the Communist police. Later, during my trial, I was accused of having dared to collect, while in prison, information for the purpose of espionage, taking an interest in the internal affairs of the prison, inquiring about the number of prisoners who had died since the liberation. This was one of their deceitful methods of extorting information.

Before the trial the prisoners were not allowed to have any contact with their relatives. Thus, after I had been arrested and brought to Haifeng, my family did not know where I was. Many times my family tried to find out the locality where I was being held but did not manage to learn anything. Such was the iron rigidity of the Communists and the fear that they instilled in the people, who were afraid to talk against them. Therefore many months went by with my relatives uncertain as to whether I was alive or dead. The sufferings of my family, especially of my father, were unspeakable.

During all that time I was subjected to interrogation only once. From the start the Communist police sought to intimidate me, binding my hands behind my back and leading me to the house of a fervent Christian. This man of deep faith, confused and pressured by the police, said that once I had related that Our Lady had appeared in Europe, with tears in her eyes, requesting prayers for the conversion of Communists. The Communist police asked me whether that was true and whether I had incited the Christians to pray for the conversion and elimination of Communists. This was one of the principal charges during my trial.

On April 15, 1956, I was transferred from the prison in Haifeng to the prison in Canton. It was a large factory that had also been used by the Nationalists for political prisoners. I remained there for about six months. Other priests had stayed there as prisoners, too, among them a foreign missionary who could not withstand the rigors of prison and died in February of 1950.

That year, the month of July was extremely hot and humid. One day, while the door of the cell was partway open, I learned that in the cell opposite mine there was an old priest. We prayed together and exchanged absolution. Another day I heard the voice of yet another priest coming from a cell a little farther away from mine. Once I heard someone singing the *Ave Maris Stella*. From these incidents I understood that there were many Chinese priests in that prison. The judge finally called me and read excerpts to me from a book of confessions written by a Hungarian priest about his crimes against the State. This led me to understand that in Hungary, too, Catholics were suffering much under Communist rule.

The Humiliation of the "People's Trials"

I wish to relate some of the particulars of what happened in the people's trial, before I was brought to the prison in Haifeng. Exhaustive searches had been conducted in the houses of my parishioners and all the religious articles had been collected—rosaries, medals, statues, sacred images and vestments—which I used to leave in the private houses where I occasionally said Mass. When I was arrested, all these objects were piled up as proof of the charge against me. Then the Communists made every effort to get me to deny the faith, to abandon all ties to the pope and to join the Patriotic Church controlled by the atheistic government. Really, nonsense!

My first people's trial took place in my village of Niupidi. During this trial some Christian activists, at the Party's behest, reported their accusations and denunciations against me. Only they could talk to accuse me.

I could not defend myself and I was not allowed to speak. Some Christians bravely shouted, demanding a fair defense for me, and since the Communists noticed that this pleased me, they began hitting me with their fists. There were some Christians who courageously demonstrated a friendly attitude toward me; on the other hand there were those who, in order to camouflage their own misdeeds, took the occasion to box my ear and give me a kick. I protested, but the Communists told me to lower my head, to acknowledge my crimes and to be more sincere. Only then would my situation improve.

For my second people's trial I was brought to another village. For the third, I was hauled off to the city of Shanwei. Each time it was the same orchestrated procedure, that is, furious shouting and barbaric treatment. Only barbarians can devise and carry out this farce of the "people's trials". Even today I remember those who attacked me during the trial. Some were obliged to accuse me; there was nothing else that they could do. Therefore I harbor no grudge against them. In these trials the Communists sought to cause divisions between the faithful and the clergy and within the Christian community. Those who took part in the accusations against me were called activists, yet those persons were poorly instructed in religion. Therefore the Communists took advantage of them and used them against religion: the purpose was to put the priests in a bad light, so that the younger generations would not believe in them. The policy of the Communists in the diocese of Shantou was to show that the priests were reactionary, anti-social, so that little by little no one would approach them any more. But they did not succeed. During my imprisonment in the provincial capital I had to appear in court sixty-five times. The main charge against me concerned my opposition to the Patriotic Church's "Triple Autonomy Movement", which aimed at "liberating" the Chinese Church from the Holy See, thus giving it independence in its administration, finances and apostolate.

Before being put into prison I had already heard tell of the "Triple Autonomy Movement", but after leaving Haifeng I found that knowledge of this movement was not very widespread. In 1950 and even in 1951 the bishop had recommended that all his priests study carefully the "Triple Autonomy Movement". Monsignor Bianchi had seen at once that this movement was a plan to divide the Church and to make it a schismatic Church, and so he refused to accept the Patriotic Church. In reality the situation was not yet as serious as it would subsequently become, because the Communists had not yet formally revealed the complete physiognomy of the Patriotic Church. . . .

Moreover at that time the agrarian reform had not fully gone into effect and the Church had ceased all activity. Therefore there was not much to say on the subject of the "Triple Autonomy Movement". Nevertheless, during my court appearances, the judge subjected me to a severe examination with regard to the movement, and on my bill of indictment he wrote: "The thinking of Huang Yongmu is that of an inveterate reactionary under the papal cloak of religion; he has worked openly against the Communists, against the people and against socialism. Many times he allied himself with Bishop Bianchi and with the imperialists and opposed the 'Triple Autonomy Movement'. This is a truly serious crime."

Moreover I was also accused of having received donations from foreign countries, which is against the law. In 1954 and 1955 I received a sum of money from the Diocese of Hong Kong for my living expenses. In the Communists' view this was a serious crime. I told them that the Catholic Church is an international entity through which each country helps the other with what is needed, but the Communists were unwilling to understand.

The third charge against me was that I was very hostile toward the Communist Party and the socialist leadership of the country. With regard to government policy, they accused me of refusing to think as they did, of harming and scorning the Party. Furthermore they said that I cursed the advances in Communist military science and even Mao Zedong. They accused me of having called the Great Helmsman a "devil" and of having said that, even though Communism had subjugated the people using tyrannical methods, Communism would not prevail! Again, they accused me of having cursed the Communist government for allowing no freedom to the people, for calling what is black white and what is white black, and for ruining society and culture. In effect, the Party had invented a series of scandalous charges against the Church: it had made a film against the Church, entitled *Trimming the Claws of the Devil*.

Then I, with all my strength, responded that all this was an outrage against the Church. At that time one could buy books against the Church, in particular one by an Englishwoman who attacked it furiously. All that was part of a Communist campaign against us Catholics.

In the village of Niupidi there was a person who appeared to be Catholic but in reality was a Communist infiltrator who was secretly waiting for an opportunity to attack the Church. When we were on friendly terms, I showed him a book by a Russian author with the title *I Was a Communist* and another entitled *I Sought Freedom*. He saw to it that the fact that I owned those two books would be considered a crime against the Party. During my trials I always tried to use reason and logic, entrusting myself to the Holy Spirit, so that He might make up for my weaknesses. I tried to do my utmost to be logical. Consequently, when the sentence against me was finally pronounced, the judge added another special one, namely that I refused to confess my crimes and maintained an extremely negative attitude; I had incurred the people's wrath, and so I had to be severely punished.

Life in Prison

Once again they put me in prison. From May until October the heat was unbearable, even more so because I had been placed in a small cell. Every day I got up at six in the morning and had to endure the bites of the mosquitoes night and day. In the morning the guards opened the doors of the cell to allow the prisoners to go to the bathroom and to wash their faces. Each prisoner had a number and we were known by that number, not by name. In the cell there was a bed with a straw mattress, a bowl for rice and two chopsticks. That was it! At nine in the morning and at five in the afternoon we had meals, which were plentiful. We could eat as much as we wanted because the Communists hoped by that humanitarian policy to pressure us to collaborate. At ten in the morning we had gymnastic exercises and learned the rules of good conduct.

I remember that at that time we had to study the contents of the "first Five-Year Plan" in all its details. This "first Five-Year Plan" followed the Soviet program, given that the Soviet Union was extolled for some time as our big brother. How can it be that the Soviets are no longer our brothers today? In those days the Soviets were praised to the skies, and the poor people were obliged to shout disgusting slogans of Communist propaganda. The people were urged to praise uncritically everything that was Soviet. After a while the Sino-Soviet friendship went to pieces and torrents of insults were poured out against the Soviets. All the previous praises ended up on the dust heap and the practice of following the Soviet model was completely abandoned! When I was in prison in northeast China, I heard that the Soviet soldiers had caused the people a lot of trouble, stealing, harassing the women and so forth. At least initially, however, the Communist Party prohibited all discussion of these facts, and those who violated the order were arrested, accused of being anti-Soviet and punished with imprisonment.

While I was imprisoned in Haifeng, Khrushchev was considered the most important person on the political scene; I confided to someone that he seemed to be an anti-Communist. For that opinion of mine I was condemned as anti-Soviet. It is quite true that in China one must never reveal one's own opinion with regard to politics, because what is considered right today by the Party can be considered wrong the next day. And they call this democracy of the people!

On October 10, 1956, I had an unpleasant surprise. The prison supervisors told me that I had to be transferred once again to the prisons in Haifeng. I lost all hope. At that time in the region of Haifeng a true persecution had been unleashed against the Catholic Church. I sensed that in going back there I would have to suffer much, as indeed proved to be the case. In Haifeng I was locked up in a large warehouse along with twenty other prisoners. Since my trial had not yet been concluded, I was allowed for the first time to communicate by letter with my family. During that time I was forced to participate in the production crew, the so-called "reform through work". I remained in Haifeng for more than two years, learning to make fish baskets, manure baskets and other items out of bamboo. With these handmade items I earned a miserable pay each month, which allowed me to buy fruit, eggs, cigarettes and sweets.

The life of a prisoner in China is more bitter than death! While I was in the prison in Haifeng, I lived through nine political campaigns: the reform of the farming cooperatives, the campaign against the bourgeoisie, the "Great Leap Forward", et cetera. Anyone who keeps abreast of the political scene in China knows very well that the object of every single campaign was to restrict the people's freedom of action and speech, so as to make them like slaves. If the people cooperated, they became even more miserable, poorer and more forsaken.

Once the farmers saw that most of the grain that they produced was taken away, they began to work less. The fields and vegetable gardens were not cultivated. Because of this, the people began to abandon their own houses and to go surreptitiously into the colony of Hong Kong. From 1956 to 1958 there were so many people who fled in this way to Hong Kong that it seemed like a migration of fish to the south—so many that they could not be counted. Tens of thousands were intercepted by the police in Hong Kong and sent back, to their great disappointment and regret.

The prison of the prefecture of Haifeng was normally able to hold two hundred prisoners, but in 1957 it was crowded with over eight hundred prisoners. In one big room measuring sixty square meters [645 square feet] there were eighty prisoners, packed like sardines. If at night someone went to the bathroom, upon returning he would no longer find a place in which to sleep. All physical necessities (eating, sleeping, washing, etc.) were provided for in the same shed. In the winter, life was hard, but in the summer it was downright unbearable. In the province of Guangdong there were four large prisons and all of them held political prisoners. Besides these prisons there were also ninety-six labor camps; every camp held two thousand prisoners, for a total of around two hundred thousand. One could calculate that in all of China there were six million political prisoners.

There is an old Chinese proverb that says: "When you see the water freeze, you know that a wave of cold is sweeping over the earth. And so when you see the people immersed in great sufferings, you know that the Country is in dire tribulations." Because I repeated this proverb to a fellow prisoner, I was put in fetters for two months. These metal fetters are put around both ankles and joined by a chain that is so short that it prevents you from walking. To prevent the fetters from cutting my flesh, I took my shirt and cut it into pieces and bandaged my ankles, thus keeping them from becoming infected. Later, during the reeducation campaign, I told the authorities that this punishment by fetters was not provided for in the original sentence and that they had illegally changed my punishment. For saying that I was punished even more severely until the spring of 1958, when following a secret trial, the authorities notified me of my final sentence.

Sentenced to Death

The trial took place in a little room adjacent to the guard post. Only the judge and two assistants were there. I was sentenced to death. I was dumbfounded! When I recovered from the shock and began to protest, one of the assistants came up to me and shoved me violently, cursing me for my "dishonesty" and unwillingness to confess my crimes. At that point I thought that the Communists had arrested me illegally and that the trial and the sentence were certainly not according to the civil laws. Nevertheless I resigned myself, accepting God's plan as He willed it, even death, which would at least free me from the fierce claws of the Communists.

After the sentencing, the police led me away. They hung around my neck a large placard on which my name was written. They took photographs of me with that placard, just to prove that my crimes had been certified. Along the way, the police prodded me with the points of their bayonets. I wondered what all this meant. The judge had sentenced me to death, but he had added that the sentence did not have to be carried out immediately. That clause allowed me to appeal the death sentence. Finally I was brought back to my cell. A strange sense of calm and peace took possession of me and, with no fear whatsoever and without haste, I set about writing my appeal. Didn't Our Lord say to Saint Paul: "My grace is sufficient for you"?

In my appeal I protested: what I was being accused of was, essentially, of having grown up and lived in a capitalist environment, in an environment which, according to them, was lacking in freedom, equality and universal fraternity. Then with regard to Marxism-Leninism, I said that I had never studied it and had never had a clear idea of its fundamental principles. Therefore I accepted the viewpoints of the proletariat without elaborate discussion and asked to be excused for these errors of mine. The result was that the tribunal of the sub-prefecture of Huiyang accepted my appeal. And so another new trial started from the beginning. Since the sentence of the people's court was too severe, it was changed to long-term imprisonment. This happened in April of 1958. Finally, after so many years in prison, I had received my sentence. This was Communist justice!

To Hard Labor

I remained in the prison in Haifeng until August of that year. Nineteen of us prisoners were transported by truck to the Municipal Prison #2. We were held there for a month while waiting to be transferred to northeastern China, in Manchuria. There were one thousand two hundred of us prisoners, all packed into a special train that brought us directly to the province of Liaoning, to a place near Dairen. I was shut up in a cattle car, together with so many prisoners that there was no place to sit. The only ventilation possible came through a few little holes. The wagon was sealed from the outside. For the four days and nights that it took to reach the northeast, we never saw the sun. In Jing-zhou, a city of the province of Liaoning, they made six hundred prisoners get off the train, while the other six hundred continued the journey to another labor camp. I was in the first group, and my new prison was a machine factory. In my section there were around two thousand prisoners. We had to produce screws, metal plates and tires. I was rather lucky, if I can say so, that I had been sent to an industrial prison and not to the agricultural labor camps.

In the farming camps the living conditions were primitive; the inmates lived in straw huts without any necessities at all. Moreover the work was grueling and the hours simply incredible. Someone who was sentenced to more than twelve years of hard labor was not sent to the farming camps, because he would be dead before completing his sentence. In the farming camps there was only cold water for bathing and a little sponge, whereas in the industrial labor camps there was hot water for a bath every two weeks. And so I was quite set, condemned to a life sentence from which only death would free me, condemned for my whole life to an endless punishment in the cold of northeastern China, far from the balmy climate of my home in the south of the country.

A terrible sensation went through me. While I was a prisoner in Haifeng, awaiting trial, I used to think about the sentence which they would have inflicted on me. I wanted the trial to be concluded quickly, because I thought that at most they would give me three or four years in prison. Instead the verdict was the death penalty. Then, when this sentence was commuted to long-term imprisonment, I understood that the Communist Party had devised their plan to exterminate the Church once and for all and that I was a victim of that plan. The real reason for my sentence was precisely the extermination of the Catholic Church and not the crimes of which they were accusing me.

Proud to Be a Priest

During the twenty years in which I had to undergo a barbaric "thought reform through labor", many people came to know that I was a Catholic priest. All sympathized with me and wondered how a man could become a priest, live apart from his family, remain celibate, without starting his own family, and nevertheless find himself involved in endless woe. Without answering all those questions, my response was very simple. Everything depends on the aspirations, on the ideals of one's personal free will. Just as many people become farmers, merchants, et cetera, I wanted to be a priest so as to bring the good news to my people and to let them know about the love of God, the father of all peoples and especially of my people. With regard to celibacy, I said that, now that I was being subjected to this reform of my brain through work, I was very happy to be alone and celibate, since I was thereby spared the worries and sorrows of having a family. Being a priest and a celibate is the greatest and most sublime dedication, and therefore I am quite content to be celibate, since it is well suited to spiritual ministry. This is the most special and beautiful feature of the Catholic Church.

During that time I was thinking about another question: How could it be that the ecclesiastical authorities, before the Communist liberation, had not been able to foresee the stratagems of the Communists and to devise a plan for evacuating the priests to a safe place, to await the opportune moment to return? (That is what happened at the time of Henry VIII in England, when many priests emigrated to France.) At least they ought to have sent away from China the priests who were sick and frail. In my opinion this would have been an intelligent move, and the Church would not have suffered such great losses.

At the time of the so-called liberation, a small number of priests fled to Hong Kong but were called cowards. Consequently some of them returned to their positions in China. A group of seminarians escaped from Shanghai and Haimen, but had to return to their seminary; it closed soon afterward, and the seminarians were sent home. Nevertheless more than twenty seminarians went to Manila. Subsequently nineteen of them were ordained priests. After the liberation all the foreign priests, exactly 2,859 of them, were expelled from China. The 2,842 Chinese priests endured cruel treatment because of their faith. The harm done to the Church was serious, but we know from history that the blood of martyrs is the seed of Christians.

During those long years of imprisonment I came to think that the Church ought to include in the curriculum of philosophical and theological courses the study of practical matters and manual labor as well (such as repairing clocks, weaving, mechanics), according to each student's inclination. At a time of persecution such training would have been of great help in earning a living. Saint Paul was a tent-maker, even while dedicating himself to the apostolate. The first missionaries in China, such as Father Ricci and his companions, made use of their knowledge of the liberal arts to open the doors of China to Christianity. In prison, if a priest has technical skills, he is highly respected. After the "Gang of Four" was ousted and the country started listening to common sense, teachers of foreign languages were much in demand. While still in prison I was sought out as an English teacher for the sons of the directors, or even as a Latin teacher (the ultimate irony!) for the nurses and the pharmacy personnel of the prison.

The Prison in the North

When I arrived at my prison in northeastern China I had to deal with several problems. First of all, the food. In that region the people lived on millet which is ground and cooked together with maize, whereas I was used to eating rice. In prison every convict received a half-pound of meat or fish and a hundred grams of oil per month. On the occasion of the Chinese New Year or a national holiday, they gave us a half-pound of meat and fish. Otherwise we ate millet and noodles. On national holidays each prisoner received a *yuan* with which to buy something extra. Every two weeks, on Sunday, we had a day of rest.

The other major problem was the climate. I arrived in the northeast on September 19 and a few days later they gave me a blanket weighing twelve pounds (a little more than four kilos). The northeast is famous for its terrible cold weather and its frozen ground. For us who were used to the southern climate, a blanket was not enough protection from the cold. Moreover we had become accustomed to those working conditions. In the south we worked at temperatures that rarely dropped below 0°C. In the far northeast we had to work in cold weather many degrees below freezing.

Our hands and feet quickly became covered with chilblains!

A third problem was that between those of us from the south and those from the north there was an enormous difference with respect to language and customs, which caused many misunderstandings and difficulties of every sort. Added to this were differences in character, education and experience. Furthermore, we were all cooped up in a little space at that camp for "reform through work". A true Tower of Babel! Everything made it difficult to live in harmony. It couldn't have been worse! In that camp I happened to get hold of a book written by a French Communist who had been in a Nazi concentration camp during the last war. That little volume related many facts about the hard life in that camp, but my life in that Chinese prison, in comparison, was a lot harder! The Chinese Communist Party had a high degree of centralization and a rigid discipline. Our prison had to produce equipment made by several thousand convicts, optimally organized, with maximum discipline, and this demonstrated the Communists' organizational abilities and efficiency. The discipline was such that they forced us prisoners to work to the limit of our strength, with great physical suffering and mental anguish.

During the "Great Leap Forward" there were convicts who, because they had adopted a passive attitude, had their sentences prolonged or, worse, in some cases were summarily executed. I arrived in the northeast just as the chaos of the "Great Leap Forward" had been unleashed. The production in our camp had to be increased. We had to second the Party's call for greater production of iron and steel, so as to surpass that of England and America: we had to do in one year what would have required twenty years of time. The work shifts, initially twelve hours each, were then lengthened with other supplementary hours. It was grueling work with few evident results.

"Thought Reform"

At that time I used to think and worry about another problem. Being a priest, was I allowed to contribute to the rebuilding of my homeland while I was forced to undergo "thought reform through labor"? There were divergent opinions on the subject. Some said that, since Communists are atheists, we Christians had to assume a posture of resistance or, at least, had to remain passive with regard to the rebuilding of our country, avoiding collaboration with the Communist efforts to destroy the foundation of our civilization, so as to hasten the collapse of the Communist system. I am of the opinion that this way of looking at the situation is not right at all.

I am inclined, rather, to think that the policy pursued by the Communists does not please the people's hearts and that sooner or later that policy will be doomed to failure. Being Christian, one cannot have a passive attitude about rebuilding the fatherland; therefore in a labor camp it is absolutely forbidden not to work: all must work.

Thrown into prison like a criminal in need of a correctional facility, I watched a complete and unexpected change in my way of living and working occur before my eyes. Nevertheless I could still be confident in my Christian principles and hence, although staying in prison, I could resist that "thought reform" and survive. I must thank the Church, my former superiors and spiritual directors, my long years of Christian education, and especially the affection and concern of my aged father, which gave me courage and strength and allowed me, during that storm, to remain bold and steadfast in my convictions. For these reasons, and thanks to those gifts, I did not lose my head or my faith, even though I was subjected to severe tribulations. I recalled the words of Saint Paul: "We are afflicted in every way and yet we are filled with joy" (see 2 Cor 4:8).

Spiritual Crisis

As I just said, during the "Great Leap Forward" we worked shifts of twelve hours a day and often more, so that I was completely exhausted. My eyes were red from fatigue and, as I returned from work, I would feel my legs aching; we threw ourselves down on our mats to sleep with our clothes on, without even washing. They loaded us down with work beyond what we could do. We were permitted to rest only five or six hours per day.

Despite this, I always recited five decades of the Rosary each day and the litanies of Our Lady for the souls in purgatory. Once I had been put into prison, I used to recite mentally the whole Mass from memory while lying down in bed. At this point I can say, without boasting, that in the past there were many things in Sacred Scripture that I did not understand very well, but, by reflecting on them anew, I discovered therein inexhaustible treasures of truth and manifestations of God's love. These reinvigorated my heart and brought spiritual consolation to my weary soul. Finding myself oppressed by power-hungry non-Christians, I considered these inspirations coming from Sacred Scripture as gifts of God, which helped me not to harbor feelings of hostility toward anyone, and not to become pessimistic or to lose all hope.

After those long years in prison, I am able to have the courage to reveal all the thoughts that went through my mind, all the feelings that filled my heart, all the desires of my soul. In prison I meditated on the many things that happened to me each day and I used to think, during those long hours, days and endless weeks: I will always remember this terribly empty life.

My family lived very far away, in the south, and there was no possibility of receiving a visit from my relatives. I often felt downcast by the terrible thought of never seeing my dear father again, of not seeing my beloved superiors, my parishioners, the people that I had instructed and baptized. In a word, my whole life now seemed completely cut off and thrown into the river that flows toward the east and is lost in the vast ocean. Everything was completely lost!

During those periods of the dark night of my soul, caused by the mental and physical stresses of the Communist persecution, I suffered so much that I thought that there could not be anything worse. During those spiritual crises, only prayer gave me relief and the strength to persevere. If only I had been able to say Mass at least once! In all three of the prisons in which I was confined, many times I secretly made the Stations of the Cross, meditating on Jesus who suffered even unto death. I felt profound regret that I had not offered all my sufferings for the Church and for the souls in purgatory, as I ought to have done. Sometimes I thought of my seminary days, of the statue of the Blessed Virgin, imagining myself under the arbor that covered the shrine, praying to Our Lady of Peace, in the freedom and safety of the seminary, calmly reciting the *Salve Regina*. And then the old demon came over me again to torment me: Never again would I be able to see my relatives, my family, my father, my dearest friends. . . .

In that environment of hatred and terror there was nothing but enmity and cruel hostility. Oh, that oppressive and fatal Communist prison! But despite everything I was able to say: "*Salve Regina*, Hail, Holy Queen, Mother of mercy, our life, our sweetness and our hope!" A thousand thanks for this gift of having a Mother in heaven. What a great and beautiful truth. She had the power to save us from death. And this gave me hope and peace in the midst of my sufferings.

Sometimes I imagined that I was in Rome, in Saint Peter's, in front of the altar, and I ardently desired to be innocent and pure, full of love for God and for mankind; I imagined pressing my chest against the tabernacle door and interiorly begging Jesus, from the depths of my soul, to have pity on me. Then, after a while, I would confide all my cares to Jesus and ask Him to help me.

During those twenty years and more of life in prison which seemed endless, I could not have resisted if it had not been for the memory of Sacred Scripture, if I had not prayed using the psalms that I could remember. This gave me comfort, strength and the courage that I needed so much.

The prayer of Saint Ignatius, *Anima Christi*, together with the *Dies Irae*, kept running through my head and gave peace and confidence to my soul. During those miserable days that I spent in my unjust imprisonment—when my spirit was sinking into a fatal sadness—those short, pious phrases from Scripture, which before had not made much of an impression on me, reinvigorated me and swept away from my soul the thick fog of despair that oppressed me. They penetrated like gleaming rays into my bottomless abyss.

An Imperceptible Agony

That terrible psychological condition was due simply to the unceasing pressure of the "thought reform" to which we had been cruelly subjected. According to the Communists, this reform had the purpose of developing our political sensibility, and so they tortured us diabolically in our thoughts, in the very essence of our freedom. This way of reforming our thinking and mentality with violence, against all our will, was a way of stabbing us without our noticing it. It consisted of subjecting our minds, imperceptibly, to an unbearable agony so as to bend them to their way of thinking.

When I was in prison I had to participate in the campaign called "Open Your Heart": it consisted of manifesting to the Communists everything that went on against them in our minds and in our hearts. You had to confess openly all your thoughts about Communism, what you thought of their deceptions and plans, the political scene, their domestic and foreign policies. In short, you had to declare everything that you thought in the most secret recesses of your own mind. There was an infinite number of those confessions, one after the other!

Then came the campaign of the "Three Red Flags", the one of the "Three Years of Calamity", the one to "Win Back the Island of Taiwan". During that last campaign we prisoners had to launch a shameful campaign against Chiang Kai-shek, in order to make him lose face completely. Then came the campaign of the "Four Sanitary Rules". What did we poor suffering people gain from those campaigns? We were displayed to the whole world as a stupid, useless people.

During the campaign of the "Open Heart", the political instructor told me, "I have seen your file." Then he asked me whether I still believed in God. I answered him, "Certainly, I still believe in God!" He continued: "Suppose that I put you into fetters: does your God know that?" I replied, "He certainly knows it!" Then the instructor gave the order to bring the iron fetters and held them in front of my eyes, as though he were about to put them on my feet, and said to me, "How does your God know this?" I replied, "God knows everything! He knows everything that happens, near and far. He knows whether you intend to put me in fetters and also knows when you intend to take them off." At that point the instructor seemed somewhat alarmed, so that I took courage and quickly said to him: "The government of the people has published the Constitution, which guarantees freedom of religion. I believe in God and you threaten to put those fetters on me: that is unjust!" It seemed that a doubt was going through the instructor's mind as to whether God really existed, and so he replied, "I am giving you more time to think about it. When you have finished thinking, I will call you again." I felt completely trapped in those diabolical methods used by the Communists. I remember seeing once a fly caught in a spider's web: the more it struggled to free itself, the more entangled it became.

A Faith Purified by Persecution

In 1954, while they were making us study the origin and the historical development of socialism, the Communists—for reasons of their own and without presenting any proof—declared that man is descended from the ape. The instructor added that naturally this doctrine denied the basic assumption that Almighty God had created all things, among them the human race. While listening to this foolishness, I kept quiet, without protesting. Finally the instructor furiously turned against me and asked why I was remaining silent. I replied that it went without saying that socialism and its historical development originated from man, but that the human race did not come from the apes. I told him that that doctrine was completely devoid of any objective reason. He did not appear convinced by what I said, so I refrained from giving other proofs. I told him that if I had spoken again it would have been of no use to my companions, and therefore I kept quiet. I added only this: "I believe in God, the creator of heaven and earth and all things. You do not accept what I say, and so it is better for me to say nothing more." The upshot was that the instructor did not know what to say in reply and therefore, when there were other meetings, I remained mute and, strangely, was left alone.

The fundamental errors of Communism are the denial of God and of the soul. Communism takes into consideration only one half of man, the less important part, namely the body, while ignoring and denying the more important part, the soul. In every doctrine that it teaches, it tries to deny the spirit. For this reason Marxism bears within itself its own destruction. Thus one can understand why the Catholic Church is persecuted and why all the churches and every other material sign of religion in the country is being destroyed; the Communists do not grasp that true religion is not made of bricks and stones but rather lives in human hearts.

Despite this frenzy of destruction aimed at the material Church, she is still alive, and in many people the faith is even stronger than before. The faith is like gold refined in the fire, and my faith was refined and purified by that continual persecution.

The Conflagration of the Cultural Revolution

During the summer of 1966 the furious persecution of the "Cultural Revolution" spread throughout the country like an uncontrollable forest fire, with unprecedented acts of violence and revenge. Never in the history of China had such acts of cruelty been heard of: a persecution of vast proportions, which destroyed everything, with bloody floggings, tortures, killings. The whole nation was cast into an enormous whirlpool of immense sufferings. The so-called "Cultural Revolution" had nothing to do with true culture, but rather had the purpose of destroying the old Chinese culture. The Cultural Revolution was worse than common natural catastrophes such as plagues and earthquakes, because it was caused by men.

During that period the prison authorities took extraordinary precautions to prevent the prisoners from escaping. They transferred many of the political prisoners, who had been sentenced to many years of imprisonment, from the cities to the most remote areas of the west, in the province of Liaoning and in Inner Mongolia. The region in question was miserable and isolated. Our prison had been founded in the early days of the "Great Leap Forward", when the monumental plan of "thought reform through work" had first been conceived. This prison could be described as the "capital" of reforming prisoners through work. In a region forgotten by men, the Communists established their base of operations. There were various factories there: one for the production of electrical machines, one for steel, one for electric generators, one for the production of plastic, one for magnets, and also a laboratory for pharmaceutical products. The concentration of so many prisoners in such a remote region served to facilitate the supervision of the work and to make it more difficult to flee. Shortly after our arrival in that prison camp, the military took control of the region.

An Inferno of Torments

During that imprisonment we were subjected to various moral pressures. We had to expose the faults of others, reveal our own personal errors, make a sincere confession of past errors, and perform self-criticism and denounce others during the public meetings. At the same time we prisoners had to study the system of Mao so as to reform our thoughts and to apply the Maoist principles to our lives. In the midst of that vast tide of madness, Lin Biao and the "Gang of Four" were trying to overthrow the government and to usurp power.

In our prison the instructor insisted on forcing the prisoners' minds to accept the thought of Mao. From the time we woke up each morning until we lay down at night, we were compelled to assemble seven or eight times a day in front of Mao's image and to bow repeatedly as a sign of veneration. It was almost a religious act! Before this image we were obliged to ask forgiveness for our crimes, shouting, "We are all guilty!" And then, raising our heads up to his image, we had to cry out three times "Long live Mao!", respectfully wishing him a long life. Thinking back on it now, it's enough to make you laugh! But not at the time, because this comedy had some serious political consequences. There were in fact some prisoners who did not feel guilty and did not want to shout "we are guilty of crimes!"; just for that they were sentenced to all sorts of punishments.

If someone overturned or tore Mao's image or made a cynical remark about him, that action was regarded as a blasphemy and the guilty party was punished very severely. During those miserable, terrifying years, how many people committed suicide, throwing themselves into the void! Some took poison, others stabbed themselves with knives, just to free themselves from that inferno of torments. The prison had become for us a real hell.

One day—later in 1976—a prisoner found a cricket and, in order to amuse himself, decided to raise it. But the cricket died. Someone jokingly said that he ought to put it into a glass case: a veiled reference to Mao's remains, which had just been put into a glass case. We all laughed at this mild witticism. But this was immediately reported to the camp authorities and that prisoner was severely punished.

The fierce Red Guard came in great numbers to our prison as well, arresting prisoners, pillaging, stealing and completely shutting down production. The Red Guard seized anyone they thought was a capitalist and tortured him; finally the prisoner disappeared, and no one knew what had happened to him. In prison we found ourselves in a strange situation, almost dead and just barely living. When we returned from the factories, we had to sit down and study Marxism and Maoism. Day after day we had to put into writing what we had learned.

In those days I was disgusted with writing what I had heard and felt overwhelmed by great bitterness. That generation of vipers had not yet passed away, but the writings of Mao had already been forgotten. During that damned Cultural Revolution, it was as though a yoke had been placed on the people's neck which weighed more heavily upon it every day, and we who were in prison felt this even more. Usually the money that we received to buy something extra to eat was a very small amount. The pay—if it can be called that—which we received for a whole month of incredibly hard work was laughable. But during the Cultural Revolution it became even more meager and, worse yet, those little items that we were able to purchase before were no longer for sale because they simply could not be obtained. Food and clothing had become scarce even for civilians, and you can imagine what we prisoners were able to find. Our uniforms were dark blue so as to be more easily recognizable in the impossible case of an escape.

The political indoctrination was carried out more rigorously, with "thought reform" still firmly in place as the fundamental point. Many times I was summoned to help in the work of the camps to coordinate the collaboration between farming and industry, and this, of course, happened after my twelve hours of work.

Streaks of Dawn on the Horizon

Slowly we became older and older, and this grueling work each day pushed us slowly but surely into the arms of death. During that terrible time I knew that the Bishop of Shenyang had been paraded through the streets of his city, wearing the funny hat of a harlequin that they had put on his head, and that the people had been compelled to ridicule and insult him. I had learned that the Communists, when they wanted to profit from your time and your ability, were very nice, but when they had finished exploiting you, they kicked you around.

Even though our pay was minimal, some prisoners— good, honest folk—did not spend a cent on their own needs but sent all that they received to their families, who were in dire straits. To me this was a heroic gesture, and I admired those prisoners. Within the prison enclosure a black market had started, based on the barter system. There were some prisoners who, although they worked inside the prison, lived outside the camp. We who were incarcerated could acquire some article of clothing, or some other little thing at the prison shop and barter it for some other item that they found outside and brought in to trade. Naturally they did this for a little fee.

During the year 1970 I was assigned to a crew that specialized in construction. Thus I learned how to set pillars made of reinforced concrete and how to make the framework for roofs. I specialized in making those iron structures. It was a task involving responsibility that required some technical knowledge. In this new job I was promoted to crew captain and technician in charge and then to the regular supervisor of a small work crew, and finally to crew secretary. I assigned jobs and requisitioned construction materials, thus gradually earning the confidence of the government. For this I received a certificate of honor; my original sentence was modified and my conditions improved.

In 1978 my life sentence was commuted to a term of eight years in prison. Mao died in 1976. The "Gang of Four" succeeded him, then Hua Guofeng and finally Deng Xiaoping. Under Deng the whole nation started to smile again. It was during this euphoric situation that I received a reduction of my punishment.

The Longed-for Discharge

My dear father was already far advanced in years. At that time he wrote many letters to obtain my discharge: he wrote to the court of Canton, to the authorities in Haifeng, to the tribunal of Shantou and to a member of the Committee of Chinese Abroad. It was from the latter that he received the reply that he never expected. The committee member sent my father's letter to an official in the provincial police force. That official asked the authorities for a written report on my imprisonment that would highlight my progress in "thought reform", so as to make a decision. The moment this request came from high-ranking officials, my case was taken into serious consideration by the prison authorities. The Party arranged a meeting to examine my case. Finally it was decided that I could be released.

On February 5, 1980, I was set free. I cannot describe how excited I felt. My joy was boundless! I thanked God with all my heart, and the Virgin Mary, for the unexpected and miraculous change in my situation, for having helped me to escape from the diabolical claws of that dictatorship and to return to my family, to the Catholic Church. I felt extremely grateful to my father, to my brothers and sisters, to my bishop, to the priests, to all the Catholics who had prayed and done so much for me!

Before I finish, I need to say something in particular. My father had always led a truly holy life. He had offered me to the Church, to God's service, thus making a great sacrifice. Throughout his life he had faithfully observed the commandments of God and of the Church. All his life he had helped the priests and been kind to the faithful. Among the first memories of my childhood I remember that, during a great famine, my father gave bowls of rice to all the starving people who came knocking at our door. Every morning he went through the streets and alleys looking for children who had been abandoned during the night, so as to baptize them. He kept a list of saints' names to give them as baptismal names, and then gave the list of the baptized to the pastor.

As long as he could, my father went to Mass each day and received Communion. The priests and the lay people admired him for his great faith. During all the days of my imprisonment he prayed day and night to obtain my freedom. Thanks to his perseverance in prayer over a span of thirty years, his prayers were finally heard, like Saint Monica's of old.

When my father was no longer able to walk, my cousin took him into his house and cared for him. May God reward him for such a great work of charity! I do not know how to express my gratitude. Even now my father continues to pray with a faith that truly moves mountains.[2]

A Second Spring

But let us return to my story. Once I had obtained all the necessary permissions, I quickly left the camp and departed for Canton. It was June 22, 1980. When I arrived in the city I learned that the cathedral had been repaired, and I hurried to go there to visit that dear memory of my youth. As I entered and saw again that altar, those familiar and beloved details, I felt as though I were seeing a long-lost friend. I felt overwhelmed with emotion. I could no longer restrain myself and I cried like a baby. When I finally succeeded in composing myself, I looked around and on the other side of the nave I noticed a priest who was hearing confessions. After twenty-six years I knelt down and made my confession.

Thinking now about all that happened to me from the day of my arrest and throughout those years of

[2] This memoir was written after the author's release from the labor camp, when the father of John Huang was still alive.

imprisonment, I can only thank God for having helped me with His Providence and consoled me with the promise made in Sacred Scripture that God gives His servants an abundant reward. God had truly guided and protected me through difficulties and dangers of all sorts.

Many years have passed since my priestly ordination, but I still feel young, strong and—I hope—capable of spreading the good news and the love of God. And so I hope to do now what I could not do during the many years stolen from me by the Communists.

I want to do all that I can to thank God for this second spring that He is granting me, for all the help that He has given me, and to proclaim to everyone my most fervent thanks to God for having granted me the extraordinary grace of feeling as though reborn to a new life!

THE LIFE OF FATHER JOSEPH LI CHANG

Introduction

"Joseph Li Chang, the priest whose story we are publishing, passed over the land of China like a good spring rain, bringing comfort and peace of mind to so many distressed and suffering people whom he met during a tragic period in the life of his country." With these words Father Mario Marazzi, a long-time PIME Missionary who spent many years in Hong Kong and now in Canton (in southern China), introduced the diary of Father Joseph Li, which appeared in Italy under the title Pioggia di primavera [Spring Rain].[1]

Indeed, if there is one feature that characterizes Father Li Chang's life as a man and a priest, it is tenderness, combined with a typical pastor's care for his flock, which he managed to show during the tormented years that through which he was destined to live. The author of the biography is a cousin of the priest, Li Daoming, who was always close to him and, for that very reason, learned to appreciate him.

Father Li Chang died on March 13, 1981, during the first stage of the reforms of Deng Ziaoping, just when the Catholic Church, which had been severely tried by

---

[1] The life of Father Li was written by Li Daoming and published post-humously in Hong Kong in 1990. The original title, *Spring Rain*, comes from a work by Du Fu, one of the greatest Chinese poets (712–770). The little volume was translated into Italian in 1996.

persecution, at last began to breathe an atmosphere of relative freedom. He, too, had personally experienced the severity of the anti-religious hostility. Born in 1915, Father Li belonged to the Diocese of Jiaying (now called Meixian), in southern China, which was entrusted to the American Maryknoll Missionaries. After his initial studies in China, he completed his preparation at the Urbaniana University in Rome, earning a bachelor's degree in theology. And in Rome he was ordained a priest on December 20, 1942. He returned to his native land after the war. At first he was appointed instructor and spiritual director at the diocesan seminary of Meixian; subsequently he was assigned to pastoral ministry. In 1949 the Communists seized power, and the following years were for Father Li a time of suffering and trials, which he accepted with great dignity and courage.

Li Daoming, from time to time, captures the climate of those years in quick brush strokes. For example:

> As the Cultural Revolution progressed, only the most ruthless, the arrogant and the unreasonable succeeded at staying in power. The common citizens had to learn quickly to choose their words carefully and to be very cautious. . . . No one dared to take a personal initiative; everybody limited themselves to doing only what had been ordered or permitted by those in power.

Given that situation, the reader is struck even more by the frankness of Father Li Chang, his "parresia" (as the Fathers of the Church would say), that spiritual and moral strength that enables one to confront injustice head-on, to denounce falsehood without pride but also without any timidity. One page from his diary is, from this perspective, rather significant.

It is impossible not to feel admiration for the humble courage of this tenacious priest.

> *Among the older Catholics there were some who, for fear of the authorities, hesitated to get too close to him. . . . They were afraid of putting him at risk, and Father Li understood their fears. One evening he invited many of them to the church: "You all have the right to come here to pray to God. This is your duty and the privilege of every Christian. The Constitution of our country states quite clearly that all citizens enjoy freedom of worship. Why, then, must you be so reserved and cautious?"*
> *"We are afraid for you."*
> *". . . I know that you are worried about my safety, but it is my duty and my responsibility as a priest to serve you and to help you to carry out your duties as Christians. You understand this, don't you?"*
> *"We understand you, Father," an old man exclaimed.*
> *"Well, then, tomorrow is Sunday. Come to Mass."*

The circumstances were unfavorable, to put it mildly, and yet Father Li managed to treat the persecution as an extraordinary opportunity to care for his neighbor. From the pages that have become available to us emerges a personality endowed with an extraordinary vigor and an uncommon psychological equilibrium, but also a man with an innate ability to make himself "all things to all men". One marvelous passage describes the care and affection shown by Father Li Chang in his encounters with one of the many victims of the Maoist frenzy, an old priest who was close to depression and discouragement.

> *Father Li turned to his friend and said to him, "Old Zhuang, they told me that for a long time you have not gone out of the house. What happened to you?"*

"These last years have been very hard. . . . I think that my parishioners have forgotten me. . . . Sometimes I even think that God himself has forgotten me."

"That is what you think, my friend. If your parishioners had forgotten you, how do you think that I could have found you? Certainly they remember you! They are looking forward to your return. . . . Old friend, you must understand that you are not the only one to have suffered. We all have suffered in these last years. . . . Do not fear. . . . Hey, now we are old; why should we still be afraid?"

If he manages to be a traveling companion of those who have "lost heart" and to find words of consolation, it is because Father Li Chang, too, has passed through the fire of anguish and has been purified by it. He, too, experiences the abyss of the deepest existential solitude, the "silence of God". We read in Spring Rain:

Through all those years Father Li was continually being transferred from one position to another. He did not have a fixed abode and never ate a decent meal. His health began to fail. He became nervous and irritable. During one of my last visits to Jiaozhou, he complained to me: "Will it never end? . . ." While praying, he complained to God also: "When will you take this chalice from me? . . . I am so tired. I do not want to go on living. Be merciful to me, Lord."

The experience of "Let this cup pass from me" strengthened the faith of Father Li, made him docile to the mysterious designs of Providence. Thus he found a way of being a witness to hope and a source of encouragement for his prison companions. To one of them, Li Zhonghua, Father Li Chang explained: "This is exactly what happens when you put your life in God's hands: you live in the present, you do the best you can without worrying about what will happen tomorrow. Prison, for a Christian, is not the worst place to learn what it means to abandon oneself to Divine Providence."

What strikes the reader most about the life of this extraordinary priest is, as we have said, the intensity of his pastoral dedication; the tireless passion with which he spends himself for his flock sometimes seems downright excessive. And so it must have seemed also to some of the persons close to Father Chang who, it would appear, accepted the priest's ministrations almost with annoyance. Yet even in cases like that, the good-hearted Li Chang showed sympathy and concern for others.

One episode recorded by Li Daoming tells about the attentive welcome that two nuns gave to Father Li when they saw him weary and fatigued:

> "Father Li, you have worked ceaselessly for two days. . . . We have prepared some chicken soup for you. . . ." Father Li scolded them: "How many times have I told you that you must not worry about me? . . . I also know that your chicken soup is hardly enough for two persons. Take it away, I don't want any." At that one of the nuns exclaimed, "Well, who do you think you are? Jesus Christ, the savior of the world, since you are sacrificing your life to save us all? If you were truly attentive to people, you would allow them to take care of you. . . ." Then she burst into tears. Father Li was bewildered. . . . He went over to the nun and said to her, "Excuse me, Sister. . . . I am very insensitive. Are we still friends?" The nun took the priest's outstretched hand in hers and replied, "You are the one who must forgive me for saying all those things to you."

The whole biography by Li Daoming is filled with incidents like this that have a simplicity and power reminiscent of The

Little Flowers of Saint Francis. *This is not, please note, a chance remark: at one point in his account, Li Daoming writes that when Father Li had arrived "in exile" in a forest, he began to nickname each tree with a saint's name. . . .*

Father Marazzi rightly observed in his introductory note:

> *"In the west Father Li Chang is famous but unknown, even in Catholic circles; and yet, when one reads the account of his life, one is left speechless. His extremely human testimony is made up of simple incidents, having that evangelical simplicity that communicates the essential values of life with natural sincerity. And the lesson to be learned from these pages is that they are written in the same spirit as those that relate terrible acts of persecution. There is no hint of feelings of revenge, no accusation leveled against an oppressive authority; only a great serenity after thirty years of violent persecution and a great love for all, including the tyrants."*

Tireless Man of the Gospel

It was February 28, 1981, when Father Li Chang set out on a journey to the house of a priest friend, Liao Yuhua, where many Christians from the area had gathered to hear him preach. He continued to speak even after midnight. Finally, when the assembled Christians were getting ready to leave, he suddenly complained of a sharp pain in the chest. While they were helping him to lie down, blood started to issue from his mouth, alarming those who were trying to comfort him. When he had recovered somewhat, Father Liao administered to him the Anointing of the Sick. Father Li remained at his friend's house for five days, but the moment that he felt strong enough to attempt the journey, he began to insist that he wanted to leave. He promised that, as soon as he returned home, he would get some rest.

But once he was home, he did not keep his word. On the contrary, he used the occasion to reply to the letters, which had been accumulating in the preceding months, from many of his friends and which he had not yet got around to answering—a work that occupied him day and night, uninterruptedly. Until, on the afternoon of March 13, he gathered all his replies into a packet and headed for the post office. He would never again return. Scarcely had he crossed the threshold of the house when he felt a sharp pain in his chest and vomited more blood. The family immediately sent for a doctor, but before he arrived, Father Li had already departed in peace to be with God.

A few days later, in the parish church, a Mass was celebrated for the repose of his soul. It was a simple but very meaningful ceremony. More than five hundred people took part in it: priests, religious, relatives and friends, many of whom came from a significant distance. They had gathered to show, one last time, their esteem for a man who had been considered by all to be a loving brother, a faithful friend and a true pastor. With the assurance that only faith can give, they knew that he would continue, from heaven, to intercede for them and for those members of the Church whom he had loved and served so well in this life.

Shortly after the death of Father Li, Howard Trube, an American Maryknoll Missionary who had worked in the Diocese of Jiaying some time before and had been his lifelong friend, sent me a letter in which he asked me to tell his story in writing. And that is what I am about to do now. His life, the letter said, is a significant episode in the history of the Church of China, and it would be a great loss for future generations of Chinese Christians if it were not passed down to them.

Father Li was my cousin; since we grew up together in the same village, he had a great influence on my life. Of all the persons that I have had the opportunity to meet, he is the one most worthy of esteem. It is an honor for me, therefore, to be able to write his story.

At the time of his death, Father Li was sixty-six years old. His appearance was that of a common man; the casual observer might have thought him rather ordinary, but actually he was an extraordinary person. His was a life lived for one sole purpose: to give his best to fulfill the apostolic mission to which he had been assigned. And that is what he did.

Father Li had a character and talents which were truly special and allowed him to stay calm in times of great confusion, to overcome all adversity and to remain steadfast in the faith. He was vigilant in danger, always prudent and reserved in his relations, an indefatigable herald of the gospel driven by his love of God and neighbor. I think that it would not be out of place to compare him to the Apostle Paul, whose zeal and energy he mirrored.

Setting aside for the moment the admiration and respect that I have always had for him, I will attempt to acquaint the readers with the Father Li whom I have known and loved. If my account is lacking in style and not very expressive, if it sometimes seems vainglorious, I know for certain that Father Li, from paradise, will make up for my deficiencies, as he always did when we were both living on this earth.

Seminary Instructor

It was in 1946 that my cousin returned to China after his studies in Rome and his priestly ordination (1942); the bishop immediately assigned him to St. Joseph Seminary in Meixian as an instructor and spiritual director for the seminarians; I, having just entered that seminary, chose him as my spiritual director. Some of my classmates were surprised by that: "How can you choose a cousin as your spiritual director? Won't that be embarrassing for you?" "Well, why not?" I replied. "Who could know me better than he? He already knows everything about my character and my temperament. Where could I find a better guide?" Furthermore, of all the priests at the seminary, my cousin was the most down-to-earth and the most open. He lived with us, shared our food and lodgings and made no show whatsoever of his superiority.

He loved nature and liked to sing. At times we happened to surprise him while he was speaking with the trees and flowers; every so often he suddenly stopped and began to sing with the birds perched on the branches of the trees. He allowed himself to become completely absorbed in his singing and, when he was finished, we would jump out from our hiding places clapping our hands and shouting, "Encore! Encore!" He, without betraying the slightest hint of embarrassment, would take a bow and solemnly accept our applause, saying simply, "Thank you, thank you." Then he began to laugh with us. "The moment when I became a priest," he let us know, "the world lost a great singing star."

But at that point he became serious and explained to us how grateful he was to the Lord for having given him the grace to become a priest. And we realized how grateful we should be to the Lord for having sent him to us as our instructor and guide. "Organize your time wisely", Father Li never tired of repeating. "There must be time for work, for recreation and for rest."

This was his rule of life. He taught us to live in the present moment, to walk in "God's hour", to be aware of his presence at every moment. We should not consider prayer and silence a wearisome obligation, as one more thing to add to the already lengthy series of duties that crowded our days, but should integrate them into the fabric of our life, and make them the heart, the essence of it.

My cousin was a good teacher. He was enthusiastic about conveying his knowledge to us, and therefore he prepared his lessons conscientiously. He corrected our assignments with extreme care. Once he had finished his presentation he always left time for questions. But if no one asked him anything, he would begin to question us; if we were not able to answer, because we were not prepared, he scolded us. He could not tolerate laziness. With him you had to work hard.

Father Li had little patience with "yes men", that is, those who always nodded. "A head that nods", he used to say, "shows that it has nothing inside. Use your brain! It is a precious gift that the Lord has given us." And he admonished us not to waste any of our talents. To encourage us to think critically, he organized debates and meetings in which we were invited to speak in front of everyone present.

Life at the seminary was in no way monotonous. Even during free time there were always many things to do. Besides the public debates, we had founded a theatrical group and printed a little newspaper. In those days we were a very close-knit family, and Father Li was the artisan who shaped our intellectual and spiritual formation.

My cousin was rather small in stature, but his gracious demeanor made him seem taller than he actually was. He had fine features and wore heavy glasses with dark frames and thick lenses.

He was generous to a fault. Whatever he had, he shared it, and he always managed to discover persons who needed his help. Therefore he never owned anything. On the other hand, his lifestyle was so simple and basic that he required very little. When people made remarks about his poverty, he limited himself to saying: "I have a bed and a blanket. . . . Jesus didn't even have a place to lay his head. How can you say that I am poor?" And he dismissed any reference to his virtues, saying, "I am unworthy to be called His disciple."

He had a frank and honest way of acting; he did not get lost in thickets of verbiage but called things by their names and always went to the heart of the matter. Putting into practice the Gospel admonition, he said "yes" when he meant "yes" and "no" when he meant "no"; all the rest he considered superfluous. Yet he was not arrogant. He taught us to be direct in speaking, without ever being discourteous. "Courtesy", he used to say, "is a way of expressing charity, and if something that we have said has offended against charity, it would have been better if we had not said it."

He wanted to make us understand that courtesy is not the fruit of hypocrisy or of calculation, but rather springs from an honest, gentle heart. I remember another one of the examples that he would cite to show us how we ought to behave in the case of a misunderstanding. He told us how Father Cai Zhenshan had arrived late one day at the bishop's residence, where a meeting of priests was being held. Father Cai was a man who paid no attention to his appearance, and so, when he presented himself at the door of the chancery, the porter (who was new) did not recognize him. Thinking that it was just the umpteenth beggar who was coming to ask for alms, he scolded him, saying, "Go away, and don't come back until after dinner, when all the other beggars are received." Father Cai just shrugged his shoulders, turned around and went away. About an hour later, Father Li happened to look out the window and saw Father Cai standing near the chancery. He went out and said to him, "But what are you doing here? You are already late for the meeting." When

Father Cai explained the incident, Father Li asked him, "And why did you not say who you were?" "He didn't give me the chance; and even if he had, it was too late: I would have just embarrassed the poor man."

The Parish in Linzhai

Father Li had brought a breath of fresh air to the seminary community. In a very short time he had earned the affection and the respect of everyone. He managed to make a real contribution to the formation of the young men who were preparing for the priesthood, and he felt at ease among us. He was happy with our enthusiasm and was proud of the diligence that we displayed in tackling our studies.

In the winter of 1948 the political situation was worsening. People started to abandon Meixian.[2] Then, unexpectedly, the bishop gave Father Li a new assignment: he had to leave the seminary and transfer to Linzhai as the local pastor. Father Li did not want to go, but, on the other hand, he knew that the promise of obedience that he had made at the moment of his ordination left him no alternative. Our reaction was immediate and vehement: "Father Li, we will send a petition to the bishop right away asking him to relieve you of your new position. Indeed, if he knew how much need there is for you here, he would surely change his decision."

[2] This was during the final phase of the civil war. Southern China was still under the control of the Nationalists, but it was evident that the Communists would occupy the whole country. In that situation it was natural to feel fear and apprehension.

After allowing us to vent our feelings, the priest spoke to us about his duties, the relationship that binds priests to their bishop, the absolute priority of the needs of the diocese, and about how we should all collaborate for the good of the Church. He promised to come visit us when his new responsibilities permitted; he assured us, moreover, that if one of us was having particularly difficult problems and would like to speak with him, he would be welcome in Linzhai.

Three days later Father Li gathered his few belongings and left the seminary to travel to his new destination. The parish of Linzhai was located in a mountainous area in the northeastern part of the Diocese of Jiaying.[3] It had a rather numerous Catholic population and a reputation for being difficult to manage. Indeed, the priests who had been assigned there previously had soon given up, discouraged and overwhelmed by the work of solving its pastoral problems, and had asked to be transferred elsewhere. Father Li, who knew the situation well, made use of the journey to prepare himself psychologically to confront what awaited him.

The main problem of the parish was of an economic sort. Indeed, neither the preceding pastors nor

[3] The Diocese of Jiaying (originally an Apostolic Prefecture and then an Apostolic Vicariate) was split off from the mission of Shantou in 1925 and entrusted to the American Maryknoll Missionaries. It comprised a mountainous territory of around 22,000 square kilometers (850 square miles) in the eastern part of the province of Guangdong (southern China), with a population of 2.6 million inhabitants, of whom 17,700 were Catholics (statistics from 1938–1939). The ordinary of the diocese was Msgr. Francis Xavier Ford, who was arrested by the Communists and died in prison in Canton on February 21, 1955.

the parishioners had ever managed to get a clear under-
standing of the accounting methods of the two treasurers, and it was known to everyone that the two men
slipped part of the parish's money into their own
pockets.

The custom was for the two treasurers to host a ban-
quet so as to welcome the new pastor. Ostensibly it
was an act of good will, but in reality the dinner had an
entirely different purpose: to intimidate the new arrival
with this show of their power, and to let him understand, by veiled threats, that it would be better for him
if he left things as they were. But with Father Li things
did not go according to form, for the simple reason
that he did not notify the two men of the date of his
arrival. Hence, on the afternoon when he arrived, he
was able to slip quietly into the parish house and unpack
his few bags. Only then did he send for his two administrators. Thus, instead of their usual dinner, Father Li
was the one who organized a meeting, during which
he explained very clearly that the parish belonged to
everyone and that its smooth operation depended on
coordination among the various services rendered by
the individual members of the community. "The priest",
he said, "cannot run all the business of the parish by
himself." Then, staring at the administrators, he added,
"Not even with the help of two laymen."

Then he invited those in attendance to discuss with
him the various problems of the parish with a view to
solving them. It wasn't long before someone raised the
question of the financial situation, and the administrators were accused of being unqualified and dishonest,

because they had abused their power and hidden the truth for their own personal gain. The proposal to relieve the two men of their positions was approved by all, and a commission was immediately formed which would thereafter be in charge of the parish's financial interests. The two men remained seated the whole time, silent and indignant, which did not go unnoticed by Father Li. When the meeting concluded and everyone else had gone, he said to them, "Be careful about your future moves. There are so many proofs of your misconduct that it would be enough to bring you before the magistrate. The only reason why I do not intend to hand you over to the authorities immediately, is that I think that we should give everyone the chance to put the past behind him and to start a new life. Think about it." This was a typical trait of Father Li: unshakable, intransigent, but never vindictive. When he was still teaching at the seminary, he urged us to adopt the same attitude as Jesus, who hated sin but loved the sinner and treated him with mercy.

A few days later, Father Li went to the house of the two men. He went there in order to become acquainted with their family situation and to offer practical assistance. The two men began to understand the sincerity of the concern that Father Li showed in his meetings with them, and so he became first their confessor and then their friend. Thus the two administrators ended up becoming the most active and loyal supporters of his pastoral work.

The Catholics of Linzhai, with the passage of years, had acquired some bad habits; for example, no one asked the pastor to borrow money; they demanded it without paying it back, and that was that. They were not really in need; they were just accustomed to taking advantage shamelessly of the fact that the priest was kind, compassionate and much more well-to-do than they. Moreover, since the sum requested was always trifling, they were sure that the pastor would not bother to ask for the money back.

One morning a man named Simon went up to Father Li as he came out of the church; he had had some misfortune and asked whether the priest could perhaps lend him a few dollars. It was not the first time that Simon asked for money, but he had never repaid any of it. "I have no money with me, Simon," the priest said, "but if you come to my house, I'll see what can be done." They entered Father Li's house and he took a large register down from a shelf, opened it to a blank page, took his pen and began to ask Simon all sorts of questions about the reason why he needed money and the deadline for repaying it. He carefully noted his answers in the register, explaining that the money belonged to the people of the parish and that, while they all would be happy to lend it to someone who needed it, the money naturally should be repaid. "After all, the money comes from the offerings of every parishioner, and so we must consider carefully how it is to be used."

Father Li handed the register to Simon, inviting him to read what he had written to check whether everything was in order, and to sign it, making sure to write the date. Simon's face had turned all shades of red; he could not look the priest in the eye and just stared at the floor. Finally, Father Li put a hand on his shoulder: "Take the money, Simon, and pay it back when you can." Simon raised his eyes, looked him in the face and replied, "Father, to tell the truth, I don't need money; I was simply trying to take advantage of you. Please forgive me. I promise that I will give you back also all the money that I asked for before." Simon kept his word, and his example was followed by all the other Christians of the village.

Within two years from the arrival of Father Li, the parish of Linzhai was brimming with new life. The renewed fervor and unity of the Christian community began to attract many other inhabitants of the village. Soon many, many people began to attend the catechism lessons, inspired by the hope of joining a community that was so united by bonds of charity, peace and harmony.

Although the life of the parish was changing for the better, the political situation was worsening from day to day. Gradually the Communist authorities had begun to expel all foreign missionaries and nuns from the country. The bishop saw a progressive reduction in the number of religious personnel at his disposal. And so the moment came for Father Li, also, to be assigned to another position.

Daoyuan School

Daoyuan Catholic Elementary School was located in Changbu, near the native village of Father Li. The school was small but well built and, most importantly, permeated with the spirit of Christ. Since it had the reputation of being a very good school, both for the caliber of instruction and for the educational method, middle schools throughout the province were eager to accept its students.

Great changes took place throughout China beginning with the establishment of the People's Republic of China in October 1949. Politics permeated every sphere of civil life. The local authorities sent into the schools various instructors who were specialists in political indoctrination. Their job was to teach the teachers and the students the new ideology. Some teachers allowed themselves to be so enchanted that, in a short time, they ended up radically modifying their way of thinking and started arousing in the children an attitude hostile toward religion, the West and the foreign missionaries. The children, for their part, started to organize "campaigns for thought reform" within the school, and then went on to boycott their lessons. Finally, after the arrest of the principal and the escape of the priest in charge, who feared for his life, the school was closed.

When news of what had happened was reported to the bishop, he thought of sending Father Li in the hope that he might be able to normalize the situation. As soon as he arrived he immediately gathered the teachers and the students in an assembly, inviting both groups to express openly their opinions about the state of the school. He pointed out to them how the situation had by then developed farcical elements, with teachers who did not teach and students who did not go to their classes, and proposed that they together evaluate the situation, with each one expressing an opinion—according to his conscience—on what was going well and what was going badly.

All the teachers were Catholic and many of them knew Father Li from their childhood, respected him and considered him a friend. During their meetings, the priest emphasized several times the need to remain united and urged them to make use of their influence to convince some of the teachers to take a less rigid attitude in dealing with the problems of the school. Gradually he convinced them of the damage done to the school by excessive politicization. Finally, after long discussions and the consistent application of friendly persuasion, Father Li obtained the consent of all and the school was reopened, with great joy and relief on the part of the local people.

Moreover his presence in Changbu had made it possible to reopen the church for worship and for other community activities. The inhabitants of the village began to think that it was possible to trust the government authorities after all.

Nevertheless, scarcely a year later, new rumors started to circulate concerning an eventual closing of the school. When the parents went to Father Li to find out more information, he advised them not to worry and told them, "Bring your children to school every day, as always. I am the one responsible for them, and no one can force me to close our school." But even he was worried. Indeed, he knew very well that there was a basis for those rumors; he noticed that tension was increasing day by day and felt completely helpless.

The authorities started to exert increasing pressure on the Church. Every day the mail brought new governmental forms that had to be filled out. Father Li perceived that many of the requests for information violated personal freedom, but when he went to the officials to ask for explanations, they did nothing more than repeat that all the forms had to be filled, threatening court proceedings and imprisonment for anyone who had concealed any information. Father Li understood that any discussion whatsoever was useless and—after thinking it over for a long time, carefully weighing everything—decided that, for the good of the Church and the salvation of his people, he would comply with the government's requests. That decision caused him great distress, because he was obstinate by nature and could be inflexible when matters of principle were concerned. With a heavy heart, he provided in writing, in detail, all the information that the government wanted concerning the Church, his Catholics and their material goods. When he submitted the forms to the authorities, the officials praised him for his efficiency and his cooperation: "We need people like you to work for us. We hope that you continue to serve the government in the future as well."

Having had to endure silently the further humiliation of being praised for his efforts, he walked back home with his heart pounding with anger. When he arrived there was a man waiting for him: he held in his hand another envelope of governmental forms. He said, "Read these papers. I will return in a few days for your answer."

Father Li took the paperwork; he didn't need to read it to know the contents. The government wanted to "borrow" the property belonging to the Church so as to put it to the people's use. He could not refuse. The method that they followed was always the same: first they "borrowed", then they confiscated. When the government was installed on the Church properties, Father Li was subjected to continual ill-treatment. He was confined to his bedroom and was not allowed to receive visitors. Every day they sent persons to "reason" with him: they suggested how wrong his life had gone and urged him to "repent" of his countless crimes.

Toward the end of 1951, during the campaign to repress counterrevolutionaries,[4] the government confiscated all Church property throughout the national territory: religious buildings, parish houses, convents, schools, orphanages, hospitals. Father Li became ill with a serious form of hepatitis.

The Temple of the Huang Family

As soon as Father Li became sick, the authorities ordered him to leave. Since he had no place where he could settle, some Christians offered to take him in at least

[4] On February 20, 1951, the Communist government promulgated the "Regulation for the Suppression of Counterrevolutionaries". The campaign of persecution that followed terrorized all of China and caused many deaths. In the Constitution of the People's Republic of China, being a counterrevolutionary is still considered as an extremely serious crime, tantamount to treason.

until he had recovered. But he was forced to refuse their generous offer. If he really had to leave, he wanted to take with him whatever he could of the church furnishings, including the statues, the vestments, the chalices and the prayer books. But it was not possible to crowd all those things into their tiny houses.

Then he remembered an ancestral temple[5] located about half a kilometer from the church. Once it belonged to the Huang family, but it had been abandoned for many years. He sent some Christians to investigate to find out what condition it was in. When they returned they told him that it was impossible to live there: the exterior was a labyrinth of undergrowth and thistles, the interior was completely covered with cobwebs, the floor was damp and covered with moss and the only inhabitants of the place were mice and bats.

"Really, it would be impossible for you to live there. Even if you were not sick already, in a place like that you would certainly become sick."

Father Li was undeterred and simply asked, "Has the roof fallen in?"

"No, but the door is gone, and the windows are shattered."

"What about the walls? Are they still standing?"

"Yes, but . . ."

---

[5] The ancestral temple is connected with ancestor worship, which plays an important role in the life of the Chinese. Those clans that have the opportunity build a little temple in which the prescribed rituals in honor of the forefathers are carried out in front of the so-called "tablets of the ancestors"; gatherings are celebrated to strengthen clan ties and genealogical registers are kept up-to-date.

"Do you want to help me or not?"

"Of course, but ..."

"Well, then, I am content. Now find me a young man who will clean the temple for me. I will turn the front part into a church, while the back will serve as my office and residence. If all goes well, I will be able to move on Saturday. And tell all the Catholics that Mass on Sunday will be celebrated in the ancestral temple of the Huangs." Then he leaned back in his chair, closed his eyes and went to sleep.

A few days later, Father Li went in person to see how the work was proceeding. His parishioners had done a great job and he decided to move into the temple immediately. He asked them to help carry all his baggage, and they joyfully complied. Then they erected inside the temple a very simple altar, put the statues on either side and placed the tabernacle and the candles on it.

Father Li was quite satisfied with the final result and invited them to return that evening for the celebration of a Mass of thanksgiving to the Lord because he had given them a new place of worship just when it seemed that all was lost. During the Mass he asked the Lord to make them stronger in the faith and spoke to them of how it is necessary to trust always in Divine Providence.

Father Li gradually recovered his health and resumed his custom of going every day to the homes of the Christians to help them and to solve their many problems. He also organized an evening catechism course, in which a considerable number of catechumens participated.

Among the older Catholics there were some who, for fear of the authorities, hesitated to get too close to him. Moreover when a member of their family was on the point of dying, they sent for Father Li only in the middle of the night, when it was possible to escape indiscreet looks under the protection of darkness. They were afraid of putting him at risk, and Father Li understood their fears. One evening he invited many of them to the church: "You all have the right to come here to pray to God. This is your duty and the privilege of every Christian. The Constitution of our country states quite clearly that all citizens enjoy freedom of worship. Why, then, must you be so reserved and cautious?"

"We are afraid for you."

"You see, the purpose of my life is to help you to be good Christians and good citizens. If I should have to get into trouble for that, well, so be it. And even if I were to be sentenced to death, my life would have been spent worthily. I know that you are worried about my safety, but it is my duty and my responsibility as a priest to serve you and to help you to carry out your duties as Christians. You understand this, don't you?"

"We understand you, Father," an old man exclaimed.

"Well, then, tomorrow is Sunday. Come to Mass."

Then he accompanied the little delegation to the door and wished them good night. A cool breeze wafted through the darkness, and he stopped to heave a deep sigh. He experienced a sense of great happiness which filled his heart: he was at peace.

The temple of the Huangs, until just recently deserted, was swarming with new life. The Christians, leaving their fears behind them, went there openly and with a new sense of freedom. Day and night they called on Father Li and the priest's work continually increased.

The First Arrest

Just when everyone thought that everything was now running smoothly, the unforeseeable happened. The officials notified Father Li that he had to return immediately to his house, because that was in keeping with the new government policy concerning the agrarian reform. This was in the spring of 1953. And the priest knew that there was no way to ignore orders from the government. He assembled those who had responsibilities in the parish and exhorted them to keep things as they were when he was present: "I hope that my departure will be only temporary. As soon as I have settled this matter, I will return to you. Support and encourage one another. Be strong and united in the faith." The people in charge of the parish assured him that they would follow his instructions to the letter and would await his return.

When they had gone, Father Li said to me with a smile, "Do you think that you can find something decent for me to wear and someone who would be available to cut my hair? If I have to return home, I want to arrive there in order. It would not be right to greet my relatives in such a sorry state, would it?"

"You are right. If we have to 'return in glory', let us at least try to fit the part." We both did our best to make light of the situation. In reality we were worried and depressed, and we wondered what fate had in store for us. Neither of us wanted to speak about it, or more precisely, neither of us dared to do so.

Early the following morning we prepared the baggage, put on the new clothes and set out on our journey. We had scarcely left the temple when a man drew near. He said that he had been asked by the authorities to take Father Li. My heart skipped a beat. "They are toying with us", I thought to myself. But Father Li took the news calmly and said to the messenger, "I was ordered by the government to pack my bags and return home, and that is what I am doing, as you can see. What need is there for anything else?"

"I am only carrying out orders."

Father Li turned around and gave me a pat on the back to reassure me. "It is better for me to go with him. I don't think that it is anything serious. Wait for me here."

As soon as the priest had gone, my eyelids began to tremble. . . . It was a sign of bad luck. I waited all day, but he did not reappear. The same thoughts kept hammering in my head: Will he be in danger? What should I do? Where can I go to look for him? The Christians who were accompanying me kept spouting suggestions: "Brother Li, we must call the Office of Public Security. He has been away for ten hours now. . . . We have to call the police."[6]

---

[6] The Office of Public Security in China is roughly equivalent to police headquarters, whereas a police station is a lesser entity staffed by a few policemen responsible for neighborhood patrols.

It was already dark when we went together to the public security authority. The office was closed. Through the door we heard voices. Not long afterward two men came out. I hurried toward them and asked, "Comrades, by any chance did someone remain inside?"

"Of course, by the hundreds!" one of them replied dryly.

"Is Li Chang perhaps among them?"

"How do I know? Besides, what does that matter to you?" After saying that, he went away.

We kept knocking, but no one answered. Finally we went to the police station and reported his disappearance. We were exhausted and had eaten nothing the whole day. We found a place to lie down but could not sleep.

At dawn we went out again to look for him, but without success. Then we returned to the temple to eat something, but we had no appetite. We couldn't do anything but walk back and forth in expectation. It was evening when I went out without any precise destination. Everything was enveloped in the bright light of the moon when suddenly I saw a figure approaching. Could it be he? I quickened my pace. It was indeed Father Li; he was strolling along in a carefree way, whistling a happy tune. Thank God, he was safe! I was seized by a sudden rage. I turned on my heels and went back into the temple. The others saw the change in my expression and were baffled by it: "What happened, Brother Li? Did you perhaps lose your temper?"

I did not answer. Meanwhile the priest appeared at the open door. When they all saw him, they could not contain their joy. "Father Li, Father Li, where have you been? We were frightened to death. Couldn't you have sent us some news? We couldn't sleep a wink all night and have not been able to eat anything since you left us."

The priest quickly noticed that I was upset. He came up to me and put an arm around my shoulders, saying, "Your cousin has returned safe and sound. Why are you so downcast? Did they harass you? Come, tell me."

The others were annoyed by my strange behavior. "What's wrong now? Aren't you happy that your cousin has returned?"

"And why should I be? He seems to have had a good time."

Then I turned to him. "Why didn't you at least send us a message? Weren't you concerned that we could be terribly distressed about you?"

"Please forgive me. I am sorry to have caused you so many problems ... even worse, on an empty stomach! But believe me, I could not communicate with you in any way. They kept me locked up in a room and told me that I was there because they were giving me 'ideological' instruction. Many people came in groups and in successive waves to give me lessons ... all day and all night uninterruptedly. But can you imagine that? All those teachers and me, their only student. They posted a guard to accompany me even when I had to go to the bathroom. How could I have sent you a message?"

When he had finished, all that I wanted to do was weep. He took me by the hand and gently asked me, "John, are you all right?"

"Forgive me, cousin, I was worried, and when I heard you whistling calmly ... bah, I thought ..."

He started to laugh. "And why shouldn't I whistle? I have a clear conscience. I did nothing that could cause offense to God or to my neighbor. Isn't that a good reason to whistle? Come, now, let's go eat and tomorrow we will face the return trip home."

The next day, when we had arrived, our two elderly relatives were beside themselves with joy. My father, who was very fond of my cousin, followed him everywhere full of pride. As for my aunt ... well, her happiness was boundless. All day she walked up and down through the kitchen, frying foods and preparing one dish after another so that her son could regain his strength.

The authorities had used the pretext of the agrarian reform to make him return home. Now that he had returned, they gave him no assignment. Yet Father Li always managed to find a way to keep busy. When he realized how large the farmyard of his house was, he began to raise chickens. Very soon he included also a group of geese and some rabbits. He was well enough and was content with himself.

The authorities always sent someone to watch over him, but no one dared to speak to him directly. Finally he decided to take the initiative himself and went to the local officials to tell them that if they did not assign him to a job he would return to the temple of the Huangs. The officials immediately assigned him to a factory. The experience that he had gained in the farmyard of his house was very useful in his new job. He found working in a factory very interesting and was convinced that God himself had seen to it that he would end up in such a position. He carried out his work with the utmost care and diligence, so that very soon he earned the affection and the respect of almost all his fellow workers (there were more than two hundred, thirty of them Catholics). Father Li actually managed to carry on his pastoral mission during his free time, but he had to do this inconspicuously and in absolute secrecy.

The official in charge of running the factory did not look kindly on Father Li's popularity and could not stomach the fact that the other workers turned to him to solve their problems. Therefore he began to harass and mistreat Father Li and to take advantage of the slightest pretext to do him harm. The priest endured every affront in silence until something happened that no one could have foreseen. One day the official's son was running a high fever. They brought him to the doctor, whose diagnosis was that the boy had an acute form of hepatitis and had to take certain antibiotics. The official and his wife combed the whole city but could not find the medicine. When they had arrived at the brink of despair, Father Li managed to find the medicines that they needed. The official could not believe his eyes; with tears running down his cheeks he took Father Li's hands between his and said, "You have saved the life of my son and I have treated you so badly."

The priest, placing one hand on his shoulder, consoled him, saying, "Don't be sad; the truth is that we are all brothers and sisters and each of us needs the other's help." From that day on they became friends.

Father Li worked at the factory during the day and returned home in the evening. The Public Security Authority ruled that whoever left the village had to ask permission first; anyone who was found going somewhere without permission would be punished.

At first the new rule caused no problems, but later the authorities claimed that the inhabitants of the village would have to ask permission even to visit their neighbors and that anyone who received a visit would have to report it. Father Li refused to stoop to compromises about a rule patently contrary to the rights of the human person and told the officials that, since he had committed no crime, he had no intention of letting himself be treated as a prisoner, that he would instead come and go as he saw fit. He ignored the regulation, and the authorities took no punitive measure against him.

In other cases, however, Father Li was more cautious and tried to take the proper precautions. When they called him to the house of a Christian to administer the sacraments or to celebrate Mass, he disguised himself as well as he could and slipped out of the house when there was no one around, at dawn or in the middle of the night. The Catholics, too, were very careful about how they welcomed him in their houses. Normally they addressed him using the title "Doctor", which was true anyway.

One day he had gone to administer Extreme Unction to an elderly Catholic woman, and she, without thinking, exclaimed in a loud voice, "Li Shenfu (Father Li)!"

Some non-Catholic neighbors, who were sitting outside the house, heard her and asked him, "Hey! Are you by any chance a priest?"

"I am a doctor, Doctor Li Shenfu."

"Oh ... well, in that case, welcome, Doctor Li Shenfu."

The Palace

One evening in the autumn of 1953, a man with a gun in one hand and an envelope in the other came to our house asking in a loud voice for Li Chang. He was a grim-looking character, and my aunt feared that he might do her son some harm, so she replied that he was not home. "I was ordered to notify him that he must go to the Palace immediately."

Father Li, who had heard everything, came out and said to the man: "I am Li Chang; why are you asking for me?"

"I don't really know; they will tell you when you show up at the Palace by eight o'clock this evening. Excuse me, but now I must attend to other business."

"What is the Palace?" my aunt asked anxiously after the man had left.

"It is a large building in the Western style located outside of Wuhua that used to belong to a very rich family. The edifice is so impressive that everyone calls it 'the Palace'. Now it is government property."

"But will they hurt you if you go there?"

"Don't be alarmed, Mother. You'll see: everything will be fine. When they ordered me to go back home, I did so without any objections. When they commanded me to work in a factory, I became a model factory worker. Why, then, should they hurt me now? I have always complied with their wishes."

He looked at the clock. "It is already seven. I had better be on my way."

"At least wait for me to put a few things in your bag and to prepare something for you to eat along the way." It was becoming increasingly difficult for her to conceal her growing anxiety.

"Would you please stop worrying, Mother? I will pack something for the night in a bag. I am sure that they don't intend to detain me for long. Come on, be brave; lean on my arm, and I will go with you to your room; you need to rest a little. I can fend for myself very well."

He accompanied his mother to her bedroom, wrapped in a wide handkerchief the few things that he had decided to take with him and set out on the way.

It was exactly eight o'clock when Father Li entered into the Palace. Once he had passed the threshold he found himself in the middle of a big crowd. A message on the blackboard explained that he was there to take part in a group educational program especially for laborers. The notice continued, saying that, whereas lodging was free, the students of the course would have to provide for their own food. Many had brought food with them, but not Father Li. Fortunately some men offered to share their provisions with him, at least until supplies arrived from his family.

He felt oppressed by a great sadness at the thought that thus far he had caused nothing but trouble to his family, while he knew that he would have need of still more help from them. How could he ask them, now, to provide food for him, too?

The educational program at the Palace imposed a very strict routine. Besides having to attend classes in the mornings and evenings, the students had to do very hard and tiring work during the day. First, they had to read books, study some newspaper articles, attend classes and participate in group discussions which, for the most part, were geared toward self-criticism. All this took place in an atmosphere of intimidation and mistrust, with a constant sense of imminent danger. Furthermore, the interns had to carry heavy loads of bricks from one place to another. If someone dared to slacken his pace, the guilty party was beaten on the spot. The students were forbidden to do anything alone; everything was done in pairs, even going to the bathroom. These measures were necessary to assure that everything, at every moment, would be subjected to strict surveillance.

Father Li had already suffered for several years from gastritis. Once he was at the Palace, the lack of adequate nourishment aggravated his condition in the extreme and he began to suffer from diarrhea. Those in charge mistook his frequent trips to the bathroom for a sign of rebellion against their authority and decided to make his life even more difficult. One morning he remained in the bathroom longer than usual. When he finally came out, he was immediately attacked and beaten senseless.

Many years later, remembering those days, he said, "The cramps were painful enough, but the most terrible thing to endure was the embarrassment." And smiling bitterly, he continued, "Those bathrooms were indescribably repulsive. What person in his right mind could ever have decided to remain sitting in a place like that as a sign of protest?"

Alone in the Forest of Wuhua

The mountains of Wuhua are very beautiful, covered with pine forests. Father Li was very attached to that land; he had grown up there and loved every rock and every tree. When, finally, the course of instruction was finished, his job assignment was to cut the bark of the trees to extract their resin.

He had always loved the simple, peaceful life of the countryside: "Far from the madding crowd", he used to repeat, citing a poet. In those mountain groves he used to work alone, but every so often he brought a relative with him, and so he could earn some extra wages to add to the family's income. Occasionally, in the forest, he met some Christians: he heard their confessions and explained to them how to make progress on their journey of faith. When no one was there, he prayed continually while doing his daily chores. "From a material perspective I was poor, but I was rich in spiritual joy. I felt very close to God, and I had become a good friend of all the saints in heaven."

Sometimes he allowed himself to walk to the edge of the forest and went to visit the Christians who lived in the vicinity. As he took leave of them, he would invite them to come visit him.

"The forest is so big that we will never be able to find you."

"While I work, I sing. All you have to do is follow the sound of my voice."

The news spread quickly and from then on it was difficult for Father Li to be without visitors. The Christians took the precaution of disguising themselves as woodmen or hunters, so as not to attract attention.

Everyone thought that Father Li, living such a secluded, solitary life, was cut off from the world. Therefore they were very surprised when they realized that, instead, he had the latest news about everything. Some years later I asked him whether the solitude had been a problem. He answered, smiling, "How could I feel alone? It was the happiest and most peaceful time of my life."

Father Li knew how to appreciate the simple joys: he loved familiar conversation and he had made friends with the flowers, the plants and all the animals of the forest. Once he confided in me that although he had always been a great admirer of Saint Francis, he only understood him completely after having lived for a long time in the woods. Father Li assigned names to the trees according to their height, circumference and the quantity of resin that they could give. He called one Saint Peter, another Saint Michael, and so on. He even went so far as to introduce them to the Christians by name and told them to look for him "under Saint Paul" or "near Saint Mary Magdalen".

There were more than three hundred pine trees in the section of the forest reserved for Father Li, and every day he had to check on them all, walking along trails covered with thistles, clambering up rocky hills and down again by difficult footpaths. He went through a pair of straw sandals every five days. Every single time that he began to work on a tree, he was accustomed to saying a short prayer. In that way he never let his thoughts go far from God. "Repeating those brief prayers keeps you close to heaven", he used to say.

One day, while Father Li was cutting the bark of a pine tree, a stranger appeared. He introduced himself in a refined way as Comrade Huang from the United Front of the province of Guangdong, sent expressly by the central Department of Culture to track him down.

"I have never had any contact with the Department of Culture; why should they be looking for me?"

"They know that you studied in Italy and that you earned a degree. And so it is a waste to leave you here. Therefore they have decided to send you to teach at the university."

"But you are joking! Do I look like a university instructor to you?" Indeed, his worn-out appearance had nothing of the dignity of a professor.

"Please tell them that I appreciate the offer, but I am happy to do what I am doing. I prefer to remain here."

"Comrade, I made such a long trip to find you; why would I be joking? See, I brought with me your appointment." As he said this he drew from his jacket an envelope and handed it over to him.

Father Li examined it attentively and thoughtfully for a moment, then gave it back to him. "Comrade Huang, perhaps you do not know who I am and what sort of history I have. I am a Catholic priest. In Italy I studied theology. All my academic competence is limited to that field. I think that someone has made a mistake. You have found the wrong person."

"The members of the Department of Culture know all about you, Li Chang, and know your qualifications. Go ahead, sign this document and get some decent clothes. I myself will introduce you to the director of the Department."

"Please don't think me an ingrate, but I cannot come with you. I have a sick mother and, as you know, it is the duty of every son not to abandon his parents when they grow old. Tell them that I thank them, that I am flattered by the offer but that I cannot accept."

Comrade Huang understood that the priest had already made his decision and changed his tone: "You are an intelligent man and ought to know what the consequences of your refusal could be. Those who do not serve the Revolution are counterrevolutionaries— the intellectuals more so than the others. Listen to my advice: accept the appointment and go meet the director of the Department. I promise you that you will be able to live in peace."

"Comrade Huang, you are very kind, but I cannot agree with you. Who can demonstrate that running a factory is not advantageous to the Revolution? I did not come here of my own free will to cut pine trees. How is it possible that the government should assign me to counterrevolutionary jobs?"

Comrade Huang could tell when he was dealing with a more intelligent man; he put the appointment back into his pocket and left Father Li among his pine trees.

The Incident of the Eyeglasses

"Without them, I am not so different from a blind man", Father Li used to say, referring to his eyeglasses with the thick lenses and the black frames. During the time he spent in the Palace, he always wore them, even when he was performing the humblest tasks. One day, during a self-criticism session,[7] he was put in a position of being accused vehemently of some misdeed. Not knowing what pretext they should think up, they started on the eyeglasses, maintaining that they were a sign of vanity and Western decadence. Therefore they ordered him to take them off immediately. The priest turned a deaf ear, but they would not admit defeat. Indeed, the following day, while he was cutting wood, a group of persons gathered around and started to tease him about his eyeglasses. Suddenly one of them rushed at him to snatch them away. Father Li jumped back, stared at him furiously and shouted, "How can you demand that I work if I can't see? It is no crime to wear eyeglasses, and if someone tries again to take them away from me, I'll split his head in two with this ax."

[7] Self-criticism, through forced confessions, has been one of the methods used by the Chinese Communists at all levels to oppress and control individuals.

Surprised and favorably impressed by this reaction, some took his side. "You are right! Leave him in peace." To tell the truth, in his whole life he had never come to blows with anyone. But the incident had served to inspire in the other interns a new feeling of respect.

A few days later, the man who had tried to snatch his eyeglasses was assigned to his group. Before starting work, Father Li approached him. "I know that you are still convinced that eyeglasses are useless and harmful. Here, put them on, and if you can walk ten paces without falling, I promise that I will not put them on again." The man took the eyeglasses and examined them: they were nothing but two thick pieces of glass held together by two circles. Without a word he returned them to the priest. It was not long before Father Li and his adversary started to work happily side by side.

Many years later, my cousin and I were in a railroad station when a man ran up to us: "Comrade Li, don't you recognize me? You saved my life! Do you remember? It was at the Palace .... I had horrible pains in my spine and you gave me some medicine. Then you convinced the officials to send me to the hospital. When I was discharged and did not have a cent, you gave me some money to buy food for myself. Without your help, I would not be alive today."

"Yes ... yes ... You are Comrade Mui. That was more than twenty years ago. How good it is to see you again!"

"You know, I also remember the incident with the eyeglasses. That day you were a hero. I looked for you after I was discharged from the hospital, but they told me that they had taken you away under strict surveillance."

My cousin laughed. "Those eyeglasses caused me a heap of trouble. Just think: some time later, in another labor camp where I had been sent to build a bridge, the officials began to insist that I take them off. For five days I couldn't do anything. I even had to be accompanied. Finally they stopped wasting time and gave them back to me."

Camp 101

One day in the Spring of 1955, Father Li disappeared suddenly from the pine forest. We made some inquiries but were unable to obtain any information. As soon as the news spread, the Christians began to be alarmed, because they were concerned about his safety. We began to comb through all the labor camps in the region to see whether we might be able to find him. Three months later, a Catholic man discovered by chance that he was working in a coal mine outside the city. He had also managed to speak with him, without being seen by the guards, so that Father Li had been able to tell him what had happened.

Four armed men from the Office of Public Security had arrived in the forest with an arrest warrant. Without so much as a word of explanation, they loaded him on a truck which sped off. After several hours it stopped in front of a large gray building, surrounded by high walls. Father Li could not imagine why they had brought him to a prison. Sure of his innocence, he decided to confront the situation calmly and to limit himself to awaiting subsequent developments in the matter.

They led him into a dark room, with a table in the middle that had a pair of seats on each side. They left him alone, but he did not have to wait long before the door opened, admitting a small, fat man who sat down, put his feet on the table and started to peer at the ceiling. Suddenly he began to scream:

"Are you Li Chang?"

"I am Father Li Chang."

"Don't talk nonsense! This is a courtroom! Speak! What crimes have you committed against the Country?"

"Everything that I do, I do for the good of my Country. Those who know me can testify to that."

"Nonsense! We know that you are a liar and we have proofs of your misdeeds. Nevertheless I am willing to give you a chance. We are merciful with those who confess their crimes and severe with those who disobey us. Therefore be reasonable and admit your offenses." The fat man took a pen out of his pocket and held it suspended in the air, as if he were on the verge of writing something.

"My conscience is clear and I have nothing to confess."

The fat man leaned over from his chair and pounded his fist on the table. "You clever little liar! We know that you secretly hoarded many things in the dwelling of Zeng Qingdao. Admit it, confess it! What did you hide?"

Father Li remembered that Zeng Qingdao was an old Catholic man to whom he had, indeed, given custody of some of his personal effects. "I don't see how that fact can be of interest to you. I can leave my stuff where I want and to whom I want. It is not necessary to ask for any permission."

The priest was locked up in a little cell where he remained for ten days. Two times a day they brought him some food, and two times a day they came to take him to the bathroom. These were his only encounters with other human beings. On the morning of the eleventh day they came for him and sent him off to a labor camp.

The labor camp had the number "101" and very strict rules. The prisoners started work at 4:30 in the morning and were not brought back to their cells until 3:00 in the afternoon. Moreover, they were subjected to very strict surveillance. The workplace was an open area upon which many extern laborers converged also, but they were forbidden to fraternize with the prisoners, who wore large numbers on their backs. If a prisoner was caught speaking with an extern, he was immediately punished. The punishments could be of various sorts: a day without food, two days of seclusion in a dark room or a severe beating.

Once the Christians finally discovered that Father Li was at that place, friends and relatives began to disguise themselves as laborers so as to visit him. They took advantage of the moments in which the guards were not looking in their direction to slip into his hand packets with a bit of food or news about what was happening outside the camp.

Father Li spent a year in Camp 101. During that time he was able to meet old acquaintances, among them the former district official from Changbu, the one who had made him fill out those forms. When he ran into Father Li, he was rather embarrassed. But Father Li did not hesitate to approach him and to shake his hand warmly: "Welcome, Officer Chang. If I can be of help to you, please let me know. Here we all suffer in the same way, and therefore we must help each other."

"Comrade Li, I thank you, but I ask you not to call me 'Officer' any more. Now I am one prisoner among many."

"Don't be so sad. We are living in difficult times, but if we can look at the world and ourselves with an upright conscience, it does not matter where we are. Try not to take things too much to heart and you will feel better."

Fire on the Mountain

After spending a year in prison, Father Li was sent back to work in the pine forest. He got up every day at 4:00, celebrated Mass and then did his chores. The oily resin was less viscous before dawn and flowed out more readily, and for that reason he started cutting as early as possible so as to gather a larger quantity of the product.

One fine winter day, in freezing weather, after finishing his morning's work, Father Li sat down to rest under a tree. He rolled a cigarette and started to smoke it, leaning back on the soft pine needles. In the forest everything was peaceful and silent, and he fell asleep. It wasn't long before he was awakened by an acrid odor of smoke; he started, jumped up, and realized that the cigarette, which remained lit while he was sleeping, had set fire to the woods. What could he do? He knew that he was too far from the river to be able to use the water, but on the other hand he could not stay there, either, and watch the fire destroy his forest. He took up a fallen branch and tried to put out the fire by beating it, but in vain. Exhausted and desperate now, he fell to his knees imploring the help of the Lord and asking Our Lady to intercede for him: "I place everything in Your hands, O my God, because You alone are the Lord of the universe." The prayer restored peace to his heart.

When he finally stood up again, he looked around and saw that a column of fire had been climbing slowly up the side of the mountain but, strangely, the trees on either side of the flames had not been touched. Then, suddenly the fire went out, leaving behind a black scar that began at the foot of the mountain and reached the peak.

Saved by a Miracle

In 1958 the government started a campaign entitled "Let a Hundred Flowers Bloom". During that period Father Li found himself involved in various public debates with some progressive members of the Church on the question of papal primacy. His arguments always got the better of his opponents—until the authorities, for lack of arguments, first accused him of being a reactionary, then confined him to house arrest and finally interned him in the Penal Institute for counterrevolutionary elements in Shuizhai, where he was assigned to a work crew on a bridge construction project.

One day, while he was plodding with his heavy load of stones on the ladder that led from the riverbank to the bridge, suddenly one of the ropes that anchored the ladder broke and Father Li fell into the void from a height of about thirty meters [100 feet]. The laborers who were working on the riverbank fled in all directions, while those who were observing the scene from above starting shouting for help. Afterward the priest admitted that he had felt like a leaf suspended in the air that had landed on a bale of cotton. The laborers ran to the site of the fall, thinking that they would find him dead. They were therefore disturbed to see him get up again as though nothing had happened.

"Heaven protects its own."

"The gods read hearts and reward virtue", they exclaimed in astonishment.

"If I had not seen it with my own eyes, I would not have believed it", said someone in the crowd, expressing what everyone was thinking.

As for Father Li, he was almost scared to death. After his fall he got up slowly, touched his head and inspected the rest of his body to see whether everything was in order. Then, walking through the middle of the crowd, he withdrew to a quiet corner where he thanked the Lord.

The Clandestine Mass

After some time, Father Li was transferred to the Huie-liu labor camp. The detainees worked at a land reclamation project near the hydroelectric plant on the Jiaozhou River. Their job was to extract earth from a mountain and to put it to productive uses. It was a work done with pick-axe and shovel, which involved an enormous expenditure of energy, yet the daily ration of food allotted to the laborers was hardly enough to keep them from dying of hunger. There were visible signs of serious malnutrition: the men had bloated stomachs and stiff joints.

When we found out that the relatives were allowed to bring something to the detainees, we wrapped up in a bundle some food and other provisions, including the hosts and the wine for Mass. It was up to me to bring it all to my cousin. Our meeting was very moving. We embraced for a long time. He stared at me with swollen eyes, and he was so pale and tired that I could not keep back the tears. He tried to make light of it by teasing me. "Big boys must not cry; what will the neighbors say? Hey, dry your tears. Aren't you happy to see your old cousin in this shape?"

Yet, looking at his forced smile, I guessed how much he was suffering.

According to the rules of the camp, a visitor could ask permission to spend the night with an intern, and we longed to do so. That evening Father Li and I did not go to the refectory; we two remained in the dormitory eating the food that I had brought from home.

We had the whole dormitory to ourselves. It was enormous, wrapped in complete silence. But the silence didn't matter to us. We just wanted to be together.

As the others began to return from dinner, Father Li asked me when was the last time I went to Mass and received Communion. So much time had gone by that I didn't remember. . . . Certainly not since he had left.

"Would you like to tonight?"

"I would like that very much."

"Well, I will grant your wish; just trust me."

I looked around, but I saw no sufficiently secluded place in which to celebrate Mass; moreover the number of workers was rapidly increasing. "Of course I trust you. . . . You're a priest, aren't you?" To be honest, I was a little annoyed because he kept smiling at me like someone who has a secret but does not want to tell it. "Only I don't see where . . ."

"Let's go to bed soon. Don't undress, just lie down quietly and try to sleep a little. I will wake you when it's time." At that point he lowered the mosquito-net and slipped onto the cot beside me.

"Could you hear my confession?" I asked him.

"Better wait until everyone has gone to bed."

I don't know how many hours we were lying there, but it seemed to me an eternity. My mind was occupied with so many thoughts that I was unable to fall asleep. Finally Father Li sat up; he did not need to call me because I was already awake. I sat beside him, on the cot, and made my confession. We recited together the Act of Contrition and clasped each other's hands. I felt very relieved and at peace.

Then he brought out from under the cushion a little parcel, opened it and took from it everything necessary to celebrate Mass: a corporal, a little Mass book, a small chalice, a little tin containing the hosts and two vials with the wine. He arranged them very carefully on the blanket and lit a flashlight. When he had finished, he put on the surplice and began the Mass: *"In nomine Patris, et Filii et Spiritus Sancti. Introibo ad altare Dei. . . ."*

We had to whisper for fear of awakening our neighbors. I acted as the altar server. It was a clear night and the moonlight, filtering through the windows, illumined our little altar. At the Elevation, when Father Li raised high the Body and Blood of Christ, I was so excited that my heart seemed ready to burst from my chest. Then, at Communion, while I was receiving the Body of the Lord, I could not hold back the tears. Then I remembered Jesus' words: "Blessed are those who mourn, for they shall be comforted." Looking up, I noticed that my cousin was weeping, too.

When Mass was over, Father Li put everything back in the handkerchief, tied up the parcel and put it under the cushion again. We slept soundly for the rest of the night.

"How Much Longer?"

Through all those years Father Li was continually being transferred from one position to another. He did not have a fixed abode and never ate a decent meal. His health began to fail. He became nervous and irritable.

During one of my last visits to Jiaozhou, he complained to me: "Will it never end? How long must I still wait? My patience is running out." While praying he complained to God also: "When will you take this chalice from me? Haven't I suffered enough? I am so tired. I don't want to go on living. Be merciful to me, Lord."

But the Lord had not abandoned his faithful servant. Just at the moment when he believed that he had hit rock bottom, news arrived that he would be transferred to a labor camp near his native village. The living conditions in the new camp were much better. If he behaved well and carried out orders, he could ask permission to return home for a few days. He was also allowed to leave the camp after work to visit friends. Taking advantage of these opportunities and of the new freedom that he enjoyed, he very soon resumed his pastoral ministry, visiting the Christians and bringing them the Sacraments. All this served to reinvigorate his spirit; even his health improved noticeably.

In the meantime, I had become his assistant: he would tell me which families to visit and send me to bring Communion to the Christians who lived far away. I then brought them his greetings and his blessing.

Because of the difficult situation, many Christians had not gone to Mass for years. Therefore Father Li went to their houses, starting with the elderly, and celebrated the Eucharist for them. The people spread the word and, by the time he arrived, the house was always so crowded that many people had to remain standing outside the door. He often heard confessions until after midnight, then celebrated Mass. Most times he did not return home before dawn: he splashed a bit of water on his face, quickly ate a frugal breakfast, then hurried to return to the camp to begin the new day's work.

His pastoral ministry absorbed a major part of his time and energy, but the fervor and appreciation of the Christians helped him to forget his weariness. "They do my heart good; for me, they are like a shot in the arm", he used to say about the Christians. "Every time that I meet them, they fill me with new strength; for me they are an inexhaustible source of joy. When I feel depressed and alone, seeing even one of them is enough to cheer me up."

We were both very busy, but our work was very rewarding. Father had turned into the joyful, optimistic man he was before. One day I heard him say, "How good the Lord was not to listen to my prayers when I asked Him to let me die. He has restored me to health and has made me happy again. I will show Him how grateful I am by trying to serve as well as I can."

Nicodemus in the Labor Camp

Almost all the prisoners confined in the camp as "right-wing elements" were intellectuals. To them was assigned the task of building a bridge across the Shuizhai River. That bridge proved to be one of a kind, just as its builders were: long, wide and very high, it was built entirely by hand, with stones held together without the help of reinforced concrete. Among the intellectuals of the camp there were neither engineers nor technicians who could give them a hand, and yet they succeeded in finishing the work. And the bridge was considered a monument erected in memory of the blood, sweat and tears of some of the most cultured men of the country.

Father Li used to speak at length about his life in the camp for the "right-wing elements", because there he had had the opportunity to make deep and lasting relationships. In particular he remembered his friendship with Li Zhonghua, a fellow who had been born in the same district as he and in the same year and had the same surname. Li Zhonghua was an honest man, and he had quickly realized that there was something different about the way in which Father Li interacted with the other prisoners and about how they behaved with him. One day he took Father Li aside and asked him what sort of work he did before he was thrown into prison.

"I was a teacher; I already told you this a while ago."

"Why then do I continue to have the feeling that you were something else, other than a teacher?"

Father Li smiled, "So you find me that complicated?"

"No, no. It's only the way you act and how you deal with others. Am I wrong, perhaps, to think that you are a believer?"

Seeing that he was sincere, Father Li decided to tell him the truth: "You are very perceptive, Li Zhonghua. You're right, I am a believer. I believe in God. And I am a Catholic priest."

"A priest? A Catholic priest?" Li Zhonghua smiled. "I remember that when I was a student in Shanghai, once I went with some friends to visit the cathedral of Xujiahui.[8] I am sure that you know it. A place full of peace."

"Full of peace", said Father Li, and his mind began to wander. . . .

"Father, would you be willing to teach me the Catholic religion?"

"Certainly. If you'd like, we can even begin tomorrow. Instruction, mind you, like at school."

The next day, Li Zhonghua began to learn the basic truths of the Catholic faith. He worked very earnestly and at times he would stop to discuss a particular point of doctrine for several days. Naturally, there were no Bibles or religious texts in the camp. The prisoners were not even allowed to have newspapers or magazines.

After about six months, Li Zhonghua asked Father Li whether he could be baptized. "Have you thought about this carefully, Zhonghua? To follow Christ requires great personal sacrifice. . . . You will have to give up much. Are you sure that this is what you want?"

"With God's help, I want to try."

Father Li was radiant. "An answer like that proves that you are ready. Now let us choose a suitable date." They had joked about the "suitable date". The truth was that in prison all sense of time was lost and the only thing that one remained aware of was that the

---

[8] The cathedral of Xujiahui (literally "place of the Xu family"), dedicated to the Mother of God, was built in the neo-Gothic style at the beginning of the twentieth century. It towers over land donated more than three hundred years ago by Xu Guangqi, a famous Chinese layman who was converted to the Catholic faith by the Jesuit priest Matteo Ricci.

day ended with sunset and the next day began with sunrise. No one remembered what day of the week it was, or what month, or what year, because no one cared what would happen in the future.

Father Li told Zhonghua, "This is exactly what happens when you put your life in God's hands: you live in the present, you do the best you can without worrying about what will happen tomorrow. Prison, for a Christian, is not the worst place to learn what it means to abandon oneself to Divine Providence."

And so the day for the baptism came. The sun in the sky shone very brightly. The other workers were resting in the shade of the trees or were in the dormitory. After lunch, Li Zhonghua went with Father Li to the other bank of the river. The two men sat down beside each other at the river's edge, and there the priest baptized him.

That evening, before dinner, during a moment of calm, Father Li led Li Zhonghua behind a tall pile of rocks, near the place where he had been baptized. They looked around to make sure that they were alone. The priest said, "We can celebrate Mass."

"Are you sure that we are safe?"

"Yes, I come here often."

Father Li untied his parcel, took out the articles necessary for the celebration, arranged them on a little stone altar and celebrated Mass in the light of the sunset. At the end of the celebration, Li Zhonghua was happy; he embraced Father Li and said to him, "Thank you; today is the most beautiful day of my life. I feel like a new man. I have decided to become a good

Christian, you know ... for the rest of my life and you will be my witness."

Now that Father Li had his own flock, however modest, he no longer felt alone. Li Zhonghua prayed with him and, whenever he could, participated in the Mass. Even the time seemed to pass more swiftly.

Zhonghua was truly changing after his baptism: he was more relaxed, more open and cheerful, more patient with the guards who treated him badly. Moreover when someone asked him for a favor, he did all that he could to oblige. The other prisoners noticed the change and the comments began: "He has fallen under the influence of Li Chang."

"Those two are always together; that's why he's not the way he used to be."

Father Li responded with a shrug of the shoulders, for he knew well that no man can change another man. It is only by opening his heart to God that a man can truly be transformed.

Zhonghua was set free a year before Father Li, and during that year he returned a few times to visit his friend. Life outside was not easy for him. It was difficult for him to find work and he did not enjoy good health. His situation, in many respects, was worse than before. But his faith did not waver. He even spoke about it to his family and friends in the hope that they too, one day, would have themselves baptized.

Shortly after the priest was released, Zhonghua became seriously ill. Father Li went to visit him regularly and brought him Communion. But the political situation made another of its sudden changes and the two friends were separated. It appears that Li Zhonghua died soon after the outbreak of the Cultural Revolution.

The Miracle of the Peanuts

In the early 1960s the Chinese population did not have enough food, and those who had been sent to prison or to the labor camps particularly felt the effects of the shortages.

In 1961 Father Li was assigned to a farming commune. A ration of rice was provided each day to its members, but they had not seen a drop of oil for over a year. That scant ration of food was not sufficient to ease their gnawing hunger, and all the prisoners were seriously malnourished.

Father Li was a man of prayer, but also a practical person. He liked to quote the old monastic motto, *"Ora et labora"* ["Pray and work"], to which he used to add, "God gave us hands, feet and a brain. He expects us to make good use of them."

One winter day, while he was coming back from work, he happened to walk by a barren field that was used by the commune to cultivate peanuts. The priest knew that beneath the arid surface there were surely some little plants that had been forgotten during the harvest of the preceding summer. If he planted them in the soil next to his cabin, the peanuts could constitute a precious source from which to extract the oil that was so much needed. However, when he began to dig, he found that the earth was as hard as rock. Tired and hungry after several hours of useless attempts, he decided to return to his cabin. He would wait for the spring rains.

In spring, some peanut sprouts peeped out of the dry earth. Father Li was struck by the beauty and power of creation. How could those fragile, delicate little plants break through such a hard soil and thus make their graceful appearance?

After an abundant rain fell for two days, the priest knew that he had no time to lose: indeed, the sprouts would be cleared away as soon as the workers began to prepare the ground for the spring sowing. He filled a basket with the little plants and carefully transplanted them to the plot beside his cabin.

Very soon he noticed that his little plants were weak and that the soil was of the poorest quality: he would have to fertilize it, but how? There was nothing else to do but to gather each day the manure left by the draft animals belonging to the commune. He made himself a small container out of bamboo and went around with it gathering manure for his little plants.

That was how Father Li began to cultivate peanuts in his spare time. Later, when people noticed that his little plot of ground yielded a harvest twice as large as that of any other in the commune, he used to answer those who asked for an explanation: "By the power of prayer, naturally."

"Is It a Crime, Then, to Believe in God?"

The Cultural Revolution had thrown the country into complete and utter chaos. No one worked any more.

Young and old, without distinction, spent all their time either in "mass meetings" or in "struggle sessions". People were dragged by force[9] onto platforms where they endured barrage after barrage of accusations and abuse by the crowd. It did not matter that the charges were contradictory and baseless: they had to stand up there anyway, motionless, while every detail of their private lives was put on display and made known to all. Among the many who were unable to endure the violence of this moral lynching, some later developed symptoms of mental imbalance, while others committed suicide. It is not far from the truth to say that in those years the whole country had turned into a colossal insane asylum.

Father Li, who had already passed through a very difficult period before the Cultural Revolution, was sufficiently well prepared. Every time he was thrust onto the platform and forced to endure the endless series of accusations and insults, he put up with it in silence, closing his eyes and praying, asking God to pardon his accusers and to free the country from the terrible disorder into which it had fallen. His calm and balanced comportment always ended up baffling his accusers, who would let him go after a few minutes. And the priest went back to conversing with his friends as though nothing had happened. The people, who wondered how he could maintain such complete calm under such difficult circumstances, asked him to let

[9] According to the jargon of Chinese Communists, "struggle" means a session during which, by a decision of the authorities, all present form a coalition against the victim, who is not allowed to defend himself.

them know his technique. But the priest replied: "If you are sure of your innocence and have done nothing wrong, you will have peace of mind. If your mind is at peace, then, even if other people speak nonsense about you, it won't be able to disturb you."

Easier said than done! Indeed, when the accused were dragged onto the platform and bombarded with accusations and insults, it was almost impossible not to be deeply shaken by it. Assemblies of that sort were held to the bitter end, and the number of persons who went mad or committed suicide continued to grow.

One day Father Li learned, only a half hour in advance, that he would be subjected along with seven other persons to a people's trial in a crowded stadium. When he arrived, he was seated in the first row. Later he recounted that he felt somewhat excited, as though he were one of the finalists in a competition.

The trial began according to ritual with the celebratory slogans which the crowd directed toward the "Great Helmsman", the "Red Sun". The first two of the eight defendants were pushed onto the platform and accused of corruption and fraud, then they were beaten while the crowd—increasingly intoxicated by its own frenzy—shouted, clapped their hands, spat on them and insulted them with vulgar epithets. Father Li, who was the third on the list, was filled with a profound sadness by the behavior of the crowd. What grieved him most of all was the fact that all his accusers had lost their reason and had become slaves to their baser instincts. When the second defendant fainted as a result of the blows, someone announced over the loudspeaker that he had confessed his crimes and that he would be taken back to prison to await sentencing.

When it was his turn, the priest recollected himself in prayer, asking God for the strength to withstand the trial. Seeing him absorbed in thought, a man sitting behind him hit him on the shoulder, saying, "Hey, wake up! How dare you sleep at a moment like this?" Two other men took hold of him to drag him onto the platform, but the priest resisted them and, looking them in the eye, said in a loud voice: "Take your hands off me! My name is Li Chang and I will go onto the platform of my own free will!" His comportment disconcerted the two men, who were dumbstruck, while the crowd started to ridicule him, saying, "You sure are brave, Li Chang!"

On the platform the presiding official tried to regain control of the situation. After repeated requests over the loudspeaker, order was finally restored and the trial began. Someone started to shout, "Li Chang, you are nothing but a jail-bird. Don't pretend to be on a par with us! Kneel down when you speak with us!" But Father Li stood there motionless, looking up, beyond the crowd, in silence.

"On your knees!" the official shouted. The two men turned and stepped forward to force him to kneel down. The priest recoiled and, after looking them in the eye again, said, "Didn't I already tell you once not to lay hands on me?"

At the priest's words, the two men hesitated and the crowd started again to mock him: "You're a hero! Li Chang is a hero!" Someone on the platform tried to oppose the crowd by making more serious accusations: "You are no hero! You are a spy, a dog in the pay of the imperialists. Acknowledge your offenses, confess!"

Finally Father Li began to speak. "Of what crimes am I guilty? Show me some evidence and I will confess." A child in the crowd spoke up and said, "There's one crime that he's guilty of: he believes in God!" The crowd roared: "The child is right. That is his crime."

The man at the microphone asked the priest: "How do you plead, then, guilty or innocent?" The priest smiled. "It is true, I am guilty because I adore God, but is that really a crime?" Suddenly he burst into a roar of laughter that carried to the end of the stadium. The public fell silent. Finally one of the officials shouted, "Make him get down! Make him get down this instant!"

Father Li climbed down from the platform, passed through the crowd and left the stadium through a side door. He was still laughing when he recounted the incident to us. "The boy was the one who made the difference. Imagine all those people who dared to say that it was a crime to adore God."

"I Think That God Has Forgotten Me."

One day, shortly before dawn, a youth arrived at Father Li's house; he came from Liusha, a center of the neighboring diocese of Shantou. One of his relatives was dying and he asked the priest to come right away to administer Extreme Unction. Seeing the anxiety written on his face, Father Li followed him immediately.

They walked for five hours before they reached their destination. The sick man made his confession, Extreme Unction was administered to him, and he received Holy Communion. The family members, happy to see their relative at peace, could not stop thanking Father Li as they were accompanying him to the door. He bowed to the family and went off again, still accompanied by the boy who had called on him that morning. Along the way, the priest asked his traveling companion why he had not contacted Father Zhuang Yili, his old friend, who lived only three kilometers from the village of Shangshan.

"Father Zhuang used to come and visit the Christians often, but about a year ago he became ill and we have not seen him since. They say that he was transferred to the mountains and no longer leaves the house."

"Ill? What illness does he have?"

"They say that he has become a bit crazy." The youth shrugged. "My father claims that his brain must have been deranged by something serious and that he is still in shock."

Father Li remembered how timid Father Zhuang was and imagined what a terrible trial it must have been for him to be subjected to "struggle sessions" and "mass assemblies". He decided to go visit him.

A Catholic man from Shangshan offered to accompany him. As he climbed the side of the mountain, the man pointed out to him a mud hovel. "He lives there. Wait for me, I will ask him if he wants to see you."

"Don't force him. Just tell him that his old school friend, Li Chang, has come to visit him. If that should cause problems, let him be. I will return another day."

While waiting, Father Li looked around: the panorama was enchanting and the air was fresh. He thought that that would be the ideal place to recuperate. The Christian returned rather quickly, saying that Father Zhuang wanted to see him. At that moment his friend appeared on the threshold of the house to welcome him. They embraced emotionally for a long time. Father Li was the one to break the silence: "Old Zhuang, how are you?" But he could see for himself the condition that he was in: he was pale and thin, with clouded, lifeless eyes and unkempt hair that fell to his shoulders.

Father Zhuang, who had read in his friend's eyes all his sorrow, quickly turned away his glance.

The guide said, "Father Zhuang, why don't you invite Father Li into your house?"

But Father Li took his friend under his arm, saying, "It would be a sin to waste this splendid day. Let us go take a nice stroll."

At those words, Father Zhuang shook off Father Li's arm almost violently, withdrawing toward the door of his house: "No, no! It is dangerous out there!"

He raised his eyes toward his friend imploringly and said, "Wouldn't you like to come into my house, even if it is quite dirty?"

"But of course I would like to. Come on, let's all go in."

The house was very small. There was only one room with a table, a stool and a folding cot beside the wall. The guide went to the table and poured a cup of tea for the two priests. "It is still hot. But now excuse me. I have other things to do." As he said this, the guide walked to the door and went out.

Father Li turned to his friend and said to him, "Old Zhuang, they told me that for a long time you have not gone out of the house. What happened to you?"

"These last years have been very hard.... I think that my parishioners have forgotten me.... Sometimes I even think that God himself has forgotten me."

"That is what you think, my friend. If your parishioners had forgotten you, how do you think that I could have found you? Certainly they remember you! They are looking forward to your return."

The reassuring words of Father Li did not seem to have dispelled the doubts of Father Zhuang, who remained silent. Then Father Li approached him again and took his hand. "Old friend, you must understand that you are not the only one to have suffered. We all have suffered in these last years. Can you tell me the name of one person who has not suffered as much as we have? And many have suffered even more. Do not fear.... Hey, now we are old; why should we still be afraid? Look at our Christians: they are wandering through the countryside like sheep without a shepherd. Just this morning a boy from your village traveled more than thirty kilometers on foot to find a priest who could hear the confession of one of his relatives who was on the point of death. If you had been available, you would have spared him that long journey."

Father Zhuang shook his head in silence.

And Father Li gently went on speaking. "My friend, now you are doing much better; return to them. They need you."

Father Zhuang was becoming alarmed. "They will come again.... They will give me more trouble.... I will not be able to endure it...."

"As far as I know, we have done nothing wrong and no one can point a finger at us. The worst that can happen is being sent back to a labor camp, but we have already been there and have survived."

"You can say that because God has granted you a special grace. You are never afraid.... You are never depressed."

"God bestows a special grace on every single person, my friend; it's just that your heart is so full of fear that there is no room for Him."

Father Zhuang became pensive. "I have not left room for Him...."

It was late; Father Li stood up and said good-bye. "Trust in the Lord, and let us pray for each other."

Then Father Zhuang threw himself into the arms of his friend. "Old Li, I am grateful for your visit and... pray for this sinner."

Father Li went over to the door, turned again toward his friend and said, "The Christians of Shangshan greet you with affection."

Long afterward Father Li learned that Father Zhuang had resumed his ministry.

"Big Brother"

In 1974 disorder and confusion continued to prevail unabated in the country. As the Cultural Revolution progressed, only the most ruthless, the arrogant and the unreasonable succeeded at staying in power. The common citizens had to learn quickly to choose their words carefully and to be very cautious. People tried to hide their own opinions, even from their closest relatives. No one dared to take a personal initiative; everybody limited themselves to doing only what had been ordered or permitted by those in power. The Cultural Revolution spread such a climate of mistrust and suspicion that it threatened to suffocate entirely the modicum of natural goodness that is inherent in every human being.

In that climate, Father Li was considered a dangerously recidivistic element, the slave of false ideologies, and therefore someone to be reeducated. This reeducation could be carried out in various places and take various forms: there were the endless interrogations; the mass assemblies for "struggle sessions"; the indoctrination courses; the humiliating parades; the public condemnations followed by long confessions submitted in writing. The most violent forms of reeducation that were reserved for the recidivists included internment in a labor camp or exile to remote and deserted areas where the convict had to live in complete isolation.

After having been subjected for more than twenty years to all these "mental reeducation programs", Father Li was still a tough nut to crack, and the authorities no longer knew which way to turn. Finally they decided to send him to a "study center". Actually the "center" was a labor camp for "thought reform". The "students" assigned to that special school consisted of around fifty men and women, ranging in age from twenty to seventy, who belonged to every social class. Among them there were merchants, retirees, domestic servants, but also university professors, physicians, landowners and a thief who was kept in prison as a preventative measure.

There was neither a fixed schedule nor a definite program for the classes, and the length of the term varied from one student to the next. Some attended only a few lessons and then disappeared, while others obtained a diploma in one or two months. Father Li, who was a slow student, remained there for two years, during which he said farewell to many classmates and met many others. Consequently he admitted to us that they were the most incredibly meaningful years of his life.

Life at the "study center" was less harsh and freer than at a labor camp. The only obligation was to attend classes, and once that was done each one could spend the time as he thought best. One was also allowed to meet with one's own classmates to chat and exchange opinions.

Father Li became the "big brother" of the course because he knew everyone and welcomed the new arrivals very considerately, trying to alleviate their initial uneasiness. But his classmates called him "the big brother" for another reason also. During the indoctrination lessons, while everyone remained passive, Father

Li argued openly, becoming involved in heated debates with the instructors. Although no student dared to admit it openly, they all admired him and, in private, praised him for his courage and honesty. And because he said things that they too thought but were afraid to express, they considered him a sort of official spokesman, indeed, their "big brother".

Every time they had problems, his comrades came to him for advice. In that atmosphere of suspicion and mistrust, they sensed that Father Li was different from the others and that he truly cared about them. Therefore they felt that they could trust him.

After he had returned home, Father Li liked to reminisce about those years when he was staying at the center, and most of all he remembered the people whom he had met: all of them capable individuals who were of necessity involved in a difficult situation. He also spoke about his instructors without rancor, even with a lively sense of pity for their narrow-minded approach to the wealth and variety of choices that life offers to everyone.

During those years many interns at the study center became his good friends and several of them, after leaving the center, became Catholics.

A Meeting with Old Friends

The year 1976 was a memorable one in the history of China: first Zhou Enlai died, then Mao. Shortly afterward, even the "Gang of Four" was arrested. The political atmosphere suddenly changed and finally a "diploma" was awarded to Father Li. Thus it was possible for him to return to his village and to his home. He began to raise chickens and cultivate a garden for a living. In his free time he went to visit the Catholic families in the surrounding areas and, when circumstances permitted it, celebrated Mass in their houses, baptized their children, heard their confessions and gave Extreme Unction to the sick. He was always busy.

Often his visits brought him to the neighboring villages, and sometimes he made his way as far as the mountainous regions of Huayang, Dengche, Meilin, Longchuan and Anlin. The Christians of those regions were for the most part farmers and hence had not suffered particularly from the government repression of those years. Nevertheless, they too had endured the consequences of the Cultural Revolution: their fields had gone to ruin and now they were trying to get through a difficult time. Furthermore, during all those years they had not been able to profess their faith freely. Those who had been born in the 1950s (and who were now twenty years old) had never seen a priest.

Therefore the farmers were thrilled to see Father Li. The older ones remembered him and insisted that he stay for the night. The warm welcome by those Christians almost made him forget the weariness of the journey. They told the priest about their sufferings in those years, when bands of constables pounded on their doors in the middle of the night, made the whole family get up and drove them out of the house while they looked for religious objects. They threw crucifixes, rosaries and sacred images on the ground and trampled them violently and forced the Christians to blaspheme. Anyone who refused was beaten.

Pastors in the Fog

During the political campaigns in the fifties, the priests of the Diocese of Jiaying had all had to go through the same troubles as Father Li. Indeed, as a group they were one of the prime targets of the government's repressive policies; they were subjected to every sort of abuse and treated very harshly. The mistreatment perpetrated by the authorities reached its climax during the Cultural Revolution. Many died in prison or in the labor camps.

In 1976, when Father Li was released, he tried to learn about the fate of his confreres. Upon hearing that Father Liao Yuhua had been set free in 1970, he went to his native village with the hope of finding him there. What joy he experienced when they were able to embrace again! Together they celebrated a Mass of thanksgiving for the special grace of fidelity, granted by God in the midst of the trials of those years, which had enabled them to continue serving the Church.

Lan Guorong, who in 1956 (the year of his arrest) was substituting for the Bishop of Jiaying, spent the next twenty years in jail. After his release in 1976, he continued to be subjected to strict surveillance. In the winter of 1977, Father Li, after many unsuccessful attempts, managed to make contact with him. He was anxious to see him again, because ten years earlier word had reached him that his seminary classmate had died in prison; if he had not received a letter in his handwriting, written in Italian, he would never have been able to believe that he was still alive. However, when he tried to go see him, they told him that Father Lan was still under house arrest and that he was not allowed to receive visits. Father Li was grieved by this. Two years later he tried again and this time succeeded in meeting his old friend. The joy that they experienced was immense.

Father Li Hanzhong was originally from Wuhua, but he carried on his pastoral work in the Diocese of Canton. In 1966 he left Canton and returned to his native region, where he lived in complete seclusion. Father Li sought him for a long time in Shuizhai, Sikeng, Shuanghua, Caidong and in the adjoining regions, but no one had ever heard of a priest by the name of Li Hanzhong. Finally he decided to give up. But one day, while walking through the village of Hekou, he met an old man on the street and asked him whether he could show him the way to Caidong.

"Caidong? And who in the world could you be looking for in Caidong?"

"My uncle lives there; his name is Liu Yangxian."

"I know him; I myself will go with you to see him." After a brief pause he spoke again, "May I ask, whether you believe in God?"

"Yes. And you?"

"I do, too. I am Catholic, and you must be Father Li."

"That's true, but how do you know that?"

"Your uncle often talks about you. When you said that you are the nephew of old man Liu, I immediately understood that you must be Father Li Chang."

They resumed their walk and chatted happily all along the way. Suddenly Father Li remembered that Father Li Hanzhong was originally from that area, and he asked the old man, "How far is Zikao from here? I heard that a priest lives there."

"Zikao is not far away, and it is true that a priest lives there. To tell the truth, he has the same surname as you. I know this because just a few days ago my niece told me that she lives near a priest named Li."

"What luck! It must surely be Li Hanzhong. Could you take me to him? I can go visit my uncle later."

The meeting was emotional. Indeed, they had been classmates at the regional seminary for southern China in Hong Kong before Father Li Chang left for Rome. Father Li Hanzhong invited his friend to his house, where they spent the afternoon talking about the events of recent years. They recounted their bitter experiences, but above all they spoke about how God had sustained and encouraged them in those dark moments, for which they were immensely grateful.

Suddenly Father Li Chang turned to Father Li Hanzhong and said, "The times have changed, and the authorities are more lenient. We must no longer live in fear." Then, looking at him steadily, he continued gently: "Our flock has scattered, and therefore it is time for us to go back to being shepherds."

When it was time for him to leave, he warmly embraced his friend and told him: "If you ever need anything, just let me know." Father Li Hanzhong resumed his priestly life, carrying on his ministry in the Christian communities of Beidon, Huayang and Shuizhai.

Even Saints Make Mistakes

Father Li had always had rather delicate health, and his physical condition had certainly not been improved by the years that he spent in prison and in the various labor camps. He suffered from a whole series of ailments: fevers, headaches and a chronic gastritis combined with serious respiratory problems. He was frail and had a heart that could have stopped beating at any moment. But he was endowed with a will of iron, which kept him constantly active and determined to carry out his duties fully.

There were so many pastoral problems as yet unresolved that Father Li felt that he could not allow himself even one day of rest. For this reason he refused to consult with a doctor, because he foresaw that he would tell him to rest, and he already knew that he would not heed the advice. Since he had a good knowledge of medicinal herbs and knew how to use them, he himself prepared medicines whenever he felt the need of them.

He never spoke with others about his health problems; when they noticed that he was pale and fatigued, he joked about it: "Stop worrying about me. I am healthy as a horse, strong as an ox and as ready to fight as a tiger."

One day he went to Beidouzhai, to the house of two elderly nuns, where a large number of Christians had gathered for Mass and confessions. The Christians of that area had not gone to confession for years and some had forgotten how. Therefore they asked Father Li to refresh their memories. The catechesis lasted for several hours. When he finally began to hear their confessions, it was already very late. He heard confessions until morning, and then administered baptism to more than a hundred children. Then he went back to hearing confessions, continuing until sunset, when he began to prepare for Mass. When it came time to distribute Communion he was so exhausted that he could no longer remain standing.

When Mass was over, the Christians were very concerned and gathered around him. By an extraordinary effort of his will, Father Li managed to compose himself, assuring them that he was well. When they had left, he rested for a few minutes then got up to prepare his suitcase. But the two nuns stopped him. "Father Li, you have worked ceaselessly for two days; you must get some rest. Stay here for the night, and you can go back home tomorrow morning. We have prepared some chicken soup for you." Father Li scolded them: "How many times have I told you that you must not worry about me? Besides, who are you to talk? I know very well how much you have worked during the last few days: you contacted the Christians and prepared everything for my arrival ... and all that despite your age! I also know that your chicken soup is hardly enough for two persons. Take it away, I don't want any."

At that one of the nuns exclaimed, "Well, who do you think you are? Jesus Christ, the savior of the world, since you are sacrificing your life to save us all? If you were truly attentive to people, you would allow them to take care of you. How do you think they feel when they see you ill because you have overworked yourself for them? Do you think, perhaps, that they feel at peace? Why do you insist on seeing things only from your perspective? And you call that Christian charity?" Then she burst into tears.

Father Li was bewildered and did not know what to say. He thought about it for a moment and then admitted that the nun was right. Without being fully aware of it, he had never shown appreciation for their good intentions or respected their wishes. He had hurt their feelings and only now was he realizing it. He went over to the nun and said to her, "Excuse me, Sister. . . . I am very insensitive. Are we still friends?" The nun took the priest's outstretched hand in hers and replied, "You are the one who must forgive me for saying all those things to you."

The other nun, who had witnessed the scene, was very happy and said, "Good, and now let us eat this chicken soup."

"We Have Not Seen a Priest for Thirty Years."

Father Li cared especially for the sick. When he learned that someone was ill—it didn't matter whether that person had caused him trouble—he quickly went to visit him to examine personally his state of health and to offer his assistance. Sometimes he brought medicinal herbs to the sick and, when necessary, made arrangements for them to recuperate in the hospital. He never refused money to anyone who asked him for it in order to help a sick relative. If he had none, he borrowed from a friend.

A woman had borrowed a certain sum of money from Father Li in the past. Since she was poor, she had never been able to repay it. One day her son became seriously ill, but she could not call the doctor because she did not have the money to pay for a visit. As soon as Father Li heard about it, he quickly went to the woman's house, had her prepare the child and brought them both to the hospital, assuring the administration that he himself would cover the expenses.

When the child was in bed, Father Li scolded the mother: "You should have brought your son to a doctor immediately. If irreparable harm had come to him, you would never have forgiven yourself!"

"How could I have asked you for help? I still have to repay the money that you once lent to me."

"And so the child would have to die because his mother felt embarrassed? Look, I know that you don't have any way of repaying the money, but you must promise me that from now on you won't let a problem like that upset your life. We are all members of one family and must help one another. That is what brothers and sisters are for."

After the child had recovered, the woman and her husband brought him to the priest to thank him. After a while, the entire family asked to be baptized.

Since the parish entrusted to Father Li's care covered a vast territory and included many villages, he devised a plan so as to be able to visit them all systematically. The Christians of Huayang, aware of this plan and tracing its course, understood that at least six months would pass before the priest came to their village. But they were anxious to see him and could not wait that long; therefore they held a meeting to discuss how they could convince him to change his itinerary. During their discussion, someone recalled the particular care that Father Li showed to the sick. "If we send someone to tell him that in our village there's a very sick man who is asking for Extreme Unction, surely the priest will hurry here."

No sooner said than done. When the messenger had left, all the Christians in the area were invited to meet at the gates of the village to welcome the priest. Indeed, thinking that someone was actually at the end of his life, Father Li immediately set out for Huayang. When he drew near the village he was astounded to see so many people.

At first he feared that it was a group of ill-wishers who wanted to prevent him from entering the village, but when they began to sing, "Welcome, Father Li! Welcome, Father Li!" and crowded around him and accompanied him joyfully to a large house that they had prepared for his arrival, the priest was speechless. Recovering from his amazement and remembering the sick man who must have been waiting for him, he said, "Well, I am pleased with this welcome, but first I must administer the Last Rites to the dying man, then I will return and we will celebrate Mass."

One of the leaders, with some embarrassment, stepped forward and hesitantly confessed: "Father, you must forgive us, for we were not honest with you. No one in the village is dying; it was only a trick to make you come quickly to us. We were too anxious to see you and could not wait so long!"

An old man, his eyes moist with tears, added, "We have not seen a priest for more than thirty years. I am already more than eighty years old, and I don't know whether I would still be alive six months from now, when you were supposed to come visit us." Another old man said, "Father, my son and his wife gave me a new grandson, and not one of them has been baptized."

Father Li was torn between joy and sorrow. He looked around, observing them attentively. "I understand you and I don't dare scold you for being unable to wait. But you must not come all together to the village gates: it is still too dangerous to attract attention in that way."

As though the priest's words had anticipated what was to come, another inhabitant of the village came running into the house: "Ahniu is on the way, and a large crowd is following him." Ahniu was a renegade who tried in every possible way to cause trouble for the Christians of the area. Father Li interrupted: "If you think it prudent, I will leave immediately so as not to cause you any more problems." But everyone responded, "We aren't afraid of him or of his band."

When Father Li understood their resolve, he suggested that they close and lock the doors of the church. "Keep them outside. They will not dare to beat down the doors. First I will hear your confessions, next we will celebrate Mass, and then I will baptize the children. By that time it will be dark and you will be able to go back home undisturbed." And so it happened; when they reopened the doors, Ahniu and his men had gone away.

The Memorable Christmas of 1979

With Father Li as pastor, little by little the Christians of Beidouzhai returned to their former fervor. They often met to pray in their little church and seriously endeavored to put into practice the commandment of love. The joy and sincere affection that united them began to fascinate and attract the other inhabitants of the village, who asked to be instructed in the Catholic faith and to join the community. Father Li's work, which was already demanding, continued to increase.

Christmas of 1979 was a memorable day for the Chinese Catholics: for the first time in thirty years they were permitted to assemble publicly for a religious celebration. On Christmas Eve all the churches, which had been reopened for the occasion, overflowed with people. So many showed up that volunteers had to provide crowd control. Even the little church in Beidouzhai was packed, but Father Li, anticipating that, had taken all the necessary measures in advance.

Three days before Christmas he began to hear the confessions of those who were already starting to pour in from the neighboring villages: he remained in the confessional for two days and two nights and continued to hear confessions until the beginning of the midnight Mass. Participation in the liturgy was so massive that it took more than an hour to distribute Communion. When his parishioners asked him where he got so much energy, the priest replied, "The people are my medicine."

The Christians of Beidouzhai, too, had worked intensively to prepare for Christmas. They began to organize and to assign tasks a full month in advance. Some went about the villages to explain the schedule; others, who lived near the church, prepared places to sleep for those who came from a distance and, because it was winter, also saw to it that they were furnished with blankets and quilts. Everything was prepared with meticulous precision so that it would be a memorable Christmas. Such generosity and willingness to work without reward provoked more than a few questions among the non-Christian villagers, who could not conceal their amazement.

A large part of the work was devoted to beautifying the church, which was first cleaned, then decorated with a crèche on one side and a Christmas tree on the other. Moreover the Christians thoroughly cleaned their houses, decorating the doors with colorful ribbons announcing "Joy to the world" and "The Savior is born." Those who had some money repainted the house as well. As Christmas drew near the village had an increasingly festive atmosphere. The people under thirty years of age had an additional reason to be elated: it was their first Christmas. For the others, the older ones, the smiles were mixed with tears: of consolation, of course! They had almost abandoned the hope of ever being able to celebrate again the birth of the Savior in their little church.

The Christmas Mass was also an opportunity for many to embrace again relatives and friends whom they had not seen for years. Never had embraces been so intense, and never had hearts been filled with such spontaneous gratitude to the Baby Jesus who had arranged such a special Christmas. And everyone, in the recollected silence of the night, promised to remain faithful to Him, not only in word but with their whole lives. When the traditional Mass at dawn was over, a salvo of firecrackers exploded over the door and a cloud of confetti fell to the ground, spreading a gleaming red carpet.[10]

After a short rest, Father Li baptized a group of eight catechumens. They did not wear the traditional white robe of baptism, but all put on their best clothes, carefully washed and pressed for the occasion. After the baptism the new Christians posed with the priest for a group photo in front of the altar. For Father Li it was the most beautiful moment of that unforgettable Christmas: he had been sent to preach the Gospel, to proclaim the kingdom of God, to care for the flock of the Good Shepherd; nothing, therefore, could have brought

---

[10] In China red is the festive color par excellence.

him more joy than to receive those new sons and daughters into the house of the Father. At the moment when they received their First Communion, many of the newly baptized, and many of their godparents, wept.

The concluding ceremony on Christmas took place at three in the afternoon with Benediction of the Blessed Sacrament. While taking in his hands the gleaming gilded monstrance, Father Li remembered how a few years earlier, during the persecution, while an enraged crowd was sacking the church, an elderly Catholic risked his life in order to salvage the monstrance from their fury and buried it in the farmyard at his house. Just two years ago the man revealed this to his son on his deathbed. And when the son, together with Father Li and a group of Christians, went to dig it up, they found it, covered with a layer of rust and filth.

"Too bad that it can't be used any more", said one Christian. But the priest said that it should be brought to his house and carefully cleaned with lime. "It will look like new." Although they doubted his word, the Christians did as Father Li had suggested. The next day they surrounded him, all excited, holding over their heads the monstrance which was now gleaming.

To the priest, at the moment when he took the monstrance in his hands and turned it toward the crowd to bless them, the whole event seemed like a miracle. What he saw before his own eyes could only be the result of the divine power and mercy. The altar boy rang the bell, and he raised the Body of Christ. He was moved. How much he had desired to be able to bless the people in this way! And not only those who were kneeling there, but also the multitude of people who had yet to know and love the Lord.

The Final Blessing

Those days that preceded and followed Christmas in 1979 were perhaps the happiest days in Father Li's entire life. Certainly the busiest. His determination and enthusiasm enabled him to overcome all limits in giving of himself for others.

But when the Christians had gone back home and life returned to normal, he had a complete physical breakdown. He lay in bed, motionless; he seemed to have aged all at once. He stared into space absentmindedly and, if he tried to speak, managed only to whisper. He alternated between moments of lucidity and complete lack of consciousness.

When several physicians came to visit him, they could only confirm the seriousness of the situation. The Christians turned to God as a last resort. Day and night they stormed heaven with their prayers. They reminded the Lord that Father Li still had much to do and that He could not take him away from them so soon.

God heard their prayers and granted their request. By the end of the week, indeed, Father Li began to get better. By the time spring arrived, he could move about and was again eating regularly. Little by little he regained his strength. As soon as he had the energy, he resumed his activities: he said that he had thought of a series of new pastoral projects and that he had to speak about them with his parishioners in the different villages. It was time now to go back to work.

However, when he spoke to his parishioners he could not help making many references to the fact that he had only a little time left and that it was necessary to make good use of it. And when he quoted in his homilies with increasing frequency the words of Jesus: "Watch therefore, for you do not know on what day your Lord is coming . . .", many understood that he was not directing it to them but to himself.

Everyone was worried about his health and tried to relieve him in every way possible. Father Li knew this and tried to cheer them up, saying, "Stop worrying about me. Do you perhaps think that the good Lord intends to allow me to go enjoy eternal happiness just now when I still have so much work to do here below?" He continued to travel from one village to the next to preach, to celebrate Mass and to administer the Sacraments. He labored to leave firm foundations so that, when they were left without a guide, the Christians could nourish their faith by themselves and hand it on to their children.

Often he gathered the little ones and told them how much Jesus loved them, with a great love, and invited them to follow Him. "The harvest is great, but the laborers are few", he used to say to encourage them to give their lives for the good of the Church; when he met a Christian in the vicinity of the church he would invite him to go in and pray a moment before the Blessed Sacrament that "the master of the harvest will send laborers into his harvest".

He encouraged his people to pray for vocations and asked the parents to instill the highest ideals into the hearts of their children. He invited young people to be docile to the guidance of the Holy Spirit and to listen attentively to the voice of God speaking within their hearts, so as to be able to discern whether Christ was calling them to serve Him.

As months went on, Father Li's health again deteriorated. It was now December, time to celebrate another Christmas. And the parishioners knew that their priest was not capable of repeating what he had done the previous year. He knew it, too, and so he allowed them to assume complete responsibility for the planning. He would limit himself to hearing confessions and celebrating Mass.

After Christmas, his health rapidly deteriorated. Father Li was visibly losing weight and complained more and more often of sharp pains in his chest. But despite everything he was always cheerful. When people urged him to rest, he replied, "I thank you for your concern on my behalf, but now God has numbered my days and every minute that I have left should be dedicated to working in his vineyard."

During the final weeks, after allowing himself a day off to meet his relatives on the occasion of the lunar new year, Father Li went to Huayang, Shejing, Jiulong, Meilin, Dengche, Longchuan, Mianyang, Beidou, Anliu and Changbu. Everywhere he went the Christians welcomed him joyfully and gathered around to hear his words. Then, when he had to leave, they accompanied him to the gate of the village. They sensed that this was the last time and that "they would not see his face again". Seeing their sorrow, the priest tried to console them: "We are all pilgrims on this earth and this is not our real dwelling place: our home is in heaven. We must not be sad to leave each other; if we do not meet again in this world, certainly we will meet in the next."

Then the people knelt and asked him for a final blessing. Father Li then looked for an elevated spot and from above traced in the air a large Sign of the Cross, because there were so many people to whom he had given his heart, and he wanted them all to be blessed by the Lord.

Father Tan Tiande (left) with Father Mario Marazzi, a PIME Missionary, photographed in a Canton hotel in the summer of 2005. Father Tan Tiande spent thirty years in hard labor camps (1953–1983). Originally from Canton in southern China, he spent long years in the far north of the country in extremely harsh conditions.

Left: The façade of the cathedral in Canton, which during that time (1973) was used as a meeting hall and warehouse. The sign reads: "Do not enter." The cathedral in Canton was reopened for worship in 1979. After being completely renovated, it was rededicated on February 9, 2007.

新 天 新 地　　　張弗作

〔我看見了一片新天新地，因為先前的天地已經過去了。〕

Left: A gigantic photograph of Mao looms over the entrance of the cathedral in Canton (mid-1970s), an image emblematic of the attempt by the Communist regime to transform Maoism into a religion.

The drawing depicts representatives of various social classes, united by the new ideology. The caption, paraphrasing the Book of Revelation, says: "A new heaven and a new earth, for the first earth is gone."

Kaifeng, view of the cathedral.

Left: Close-up of Gertrude Li, a young teacher at a Catholic school in Kaifeng, who was arrested and tried because of her friendship with the missionaries and her fidelity to the Church which refused to compromise with the regime.

The autobiographical memoirs of Gertrude were smuggled out of China on cropped pieces of paper (right) which Father Giovanni Carbone, a PIME missionary, slipped into his shoes when he was expelled from the country (1952).

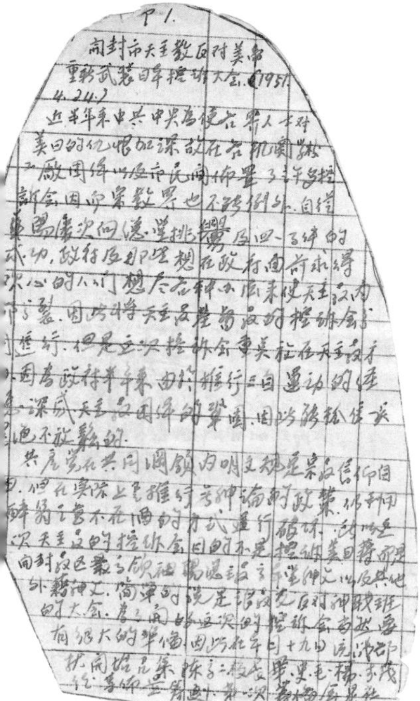

View of the imposing monastic complex of Our Lady of Consolation in Yangjiaping. When the Maoist troops arrived in 1947, the monastery was flourishing and had started the priory of Our Lady of Joy, also in Hebei Province. (The photo below depicts the latter community.)

After sacking the monastery, the Communist troops arrested the monks and subjected them to interrogations, humiliations and torture. Finally they forced the survivors to make a *Via Crucis*, a Way of the Cross that lasted several weeks. By the end of it, thirty-three victims were left dead by the wayside. Upon regaining their freedom, the monks who survived formed another small community in Beijing.

Below: The document sentencing one of the surviving Trappist monks, Dom Maur Bougon (inset, above).

Three pictures of three typical moments in the persecutions regularly conducted by the Maoists. The "counterrevolutionaries" were brought before popular tribunals and often accused of horrendous crimes that they had not committed; as a result they were detained in inhuman conditions at the whim of their captors. Finally, in some cases, they were executed in cold blood.

A Maryknoll missionary (above) celebrates the Eucharist in a village. In the early 1950s, when the anti-Christian persecution broke out, Catholic parish life was rather vibrant, especially in rural areas. The number of Catholics was around three and a half million. More than three hundred seminaries had been opened. There were more than five thousand foreign missionaries in the country (three thousand priests and two thousand nuns); within the course of a few years almost all of them would be expelled. Some of them led dioceses, as in the case of Monsignor Gaetano Pollio, a PIME missionary and Bishop of Kaifeng (left).

聖母的旗號

文陳詩·張譽著

為母的旗號
神不住你們寶院的面目，
的髮的外名
不讓你的掃空的喘裕。

大聖共的偉人如己，
你們如殺人不眼說：
大聖全世界和平，
你們卻望關了頭。

你們是全世界人民的敵人，
你們是耶穌基督的反教。
聖說你們是天主的信徒，
聖才顧是於天主手掌！

The Legion of Mary was a particularly widespread Catholic association in China. The photo above shows a group of Legionaries from Kaifeng (with them are Bishop Pollio and Fathers Georges Chatel and Amelio Crotti, PIME Missionaries).

Deliberately misinterpreting the term "legion", Maoist propaganda portrayed this association as a dangerous, militaristic group.

One of the accusations most frequently leveled against foreign missionaries was that of "imperialism". Above is a drawing used in propaganda: the bishop bears a dollar sign on his miter and wears a robe with stars and stripes, a sign of his collusion with the Americans. On this charge many missionaries were arrested and expelled from China in the early 1950s.

Above: Two missionaries at the train station in Hong Kong—one a Spaniard, the other Argentinean—expelled after undergoing duress and torture.

Left, right: A group of Canadian nuns who, after they were set free, reproduced the conditions of their imprisonment.

Above: Watercolor by the Chinese painter Guo Mingjiao illustrating the violence and devastation wreaked in a house of worship; such scenes were particularly frequent in China around the mid-1960s.

Left: September 3, 1953: the profanation of the Church of the Immaculate Conception in Hankou, documented by Father Giuseppe Carrà, a PIME Missionary.

The Bishop of Hong Kong, Cardinal Joseph Zen Ze-kiun, one of the more prominent figures in the Church of "Great China". A promoter of freedom and human rights, he has fought tirelessly in recent years to defend Chinese Catholics.

Sources: PIME Archives in Milan, the book *Monaci nella Tormenta* and USIS.

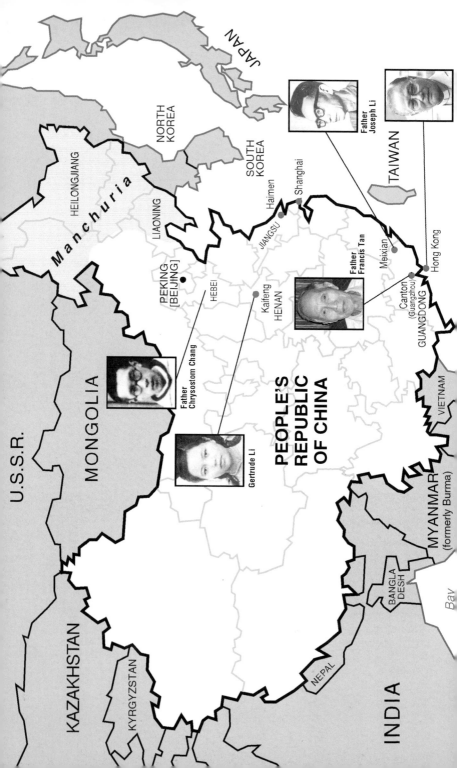

THE PRISON DIARY
OF GERTRUDE LI MINWEN

Introduction

Toward the end of 1952, when the PIME Missionary Father Giovanni Carbone was expelled from China, he brought with him a "souvenir" that was peculiar, to say the least: indeed, sewn into the soles of the missionary's shoes were hidden around twenty pages filled with tiny, almost illegible Chinese characters. They were written by hand by a young Catholic woman: Gertrude Li Minwen. They recount the physical and spiritual sufferings of the author and of other young women who fell into the hands of the Communist officials because they were affiliated with the Legion of Mary (a lay apostolic association which was especially active in China during those years and was considered a counterrevolutionary organization) and were opposed to belonging to the Patriotic Association.

The text—written in Kaifeng and dated September 17, 1951—describes the insidious techniques of the persecutors to induce Gertrude and her companions to submit. The cocktail of flattery and threats, however, did not obtain the expected result: at the end of the stream of interrogations, after spending several days in prison, Gertrude was judged "hostile to the course of indoctrination" and even "a loyal dog of the imperialists".

Midway between confession and autobiography, this text, in its simplicity, provides yet another fragment that helps us to reconstruct the mosaic of the persecutions of Chinese Christians during the first years of the People's Republic. The following pages tell about arrests, detainments, interrogations, people's trials and so on: the gears of the tremendous "machine" devised by the Party and its men to resist the threats of the "counterrevolutionaries", headed by the missionaries.

Gradually, as the account of the harassment and oppression experienced by Gertrude and her companions unfolds, an equally clear and contrasting portrait emerges of the protagonist's spiritual depth. Hers is a simple but steadfast faith which is not afraid to defy an arrogant, cruel authority: a faith that knows moments of doubt, crisis and also betrayal. A real faith, therefore, mixed with sufferings and humiliations.

All these elements make the diary of Gertrude Li a precious testimony. While Father Giovanni Carbone physically brought it to Italy, the one who publicized it was Father Amelio Crotti, another PIME missionary who spent many years in China. He arrived in Kaifeng in 1937 and was expelled in 1951 by the Communists after being subjected to a "people's trial" and experiencing the humiliation of imprisonment. Father Crotti personally knew Gertrude and published her testimony for the first time in Più forti della tormenta *[Stronger than torture], a little book that appeared in 1957. "While reading these pages," he writes, "the reader's heart will tremble many times with surprise, horror and emotion," as he himself did, "even though I was in the same prisons during the same period."*

Father Crotti says about the author: "I knew her personally, and even rather well, from 1947 on, when she began to help me in my work with the boys of our school. But as early as 1938, when she was scarcely thirteen years old and was baptized, she struck me by her timid and humble comportment. She was already burdened with family troubles (her mother was dead, her father was an opium smoker, and there were many younger siblings to raise) and was timid by nature; I had never seen her laugh or lift up her eyes. Her baptism gave her more serenity, but other than that she remained as she was, even when she turned twenty and distinguished herself by her abilities as a teacher, so as to merit the accolades of her colleagues."

From 1949 to 1951, during the stormiest period immediately before the overt persecution, Gertrude (who "managed to keep hold of the other three hundred non-Catholics") became "the unshakeable support of the fifty Catholic pupils who attended our elementary school". And Father Crotti adds: "On the day when she learned that the formation of the Red Handkerchiefs, a Communist association, could not be tolerated at our school, she did not hesitate to disband the squad made up of Catholics, with no fear of reprisals by the government."

Throughout the account there is an oft-recurring accusation of "imperialism" voiced by Gertrude's jailers and aimed at the foreign priests and, by implication, at their collaborators. Yet the affection that many Chinese people had (and have!) for the missionaries shows that charging them with that crime was just a pretext. Not to mention the abundant fruits of the evangelization activity conducted by the foreign missionaries in the form of social services: instruction, improving the status of women, aid to the poor and the like.

There is more. Anyone who has the patience to read the transcripts of the interrogations, as Gertrude presents them, will notice that the Catholics have never sought (and do not seek today) to confront the public authorities head-on. The point of friction—which in Crotti's and therefore Gertrude's case became a rupture—was the presumptuous claim of the Communist authority to control every aspect in the lives of individual persons, including religion. Illuminating in this regard is an excerpt from an interrogation, in the course of which Gertrude and Father Crotti were confronted by an official who intended to create misunderstandings.

> "What did Crotti tell you with regard to the government?"
>
> "To obey all its orders, except for those that are opposed to our faith."
>
> Minister Zhu turned to Father Crotti: "You know very well that the Christians are Chinese citizens before they are Christians. What, then, are we supposed to think about you if you order Christians to disobey the government?"
>
> "I told them to disobey only in the case where the government orders things contrary to the faith", Father Crotti defended himself.

Some expressions which crop up here and there in the narrative might give the impression of an outdated, anachronistic perspective tinged with propaganda. Actually it would be a mistake to consider Gertrude's autobiography as a highly rhetorical account. Gertrude is a genuine believer, but she is also a woman with her weaknesses. The author, in fact, does not deny them, and this is precisely what makes her testimony believable. "In the section of these pages in which Gertrude confesses an initial fall," Father Crotti notes, "there is so much sorrow and humility that we would be led to think ill of her, if it had not been duly presented. Therefore I advise the readers to wait until the end of the diary, when they will have admired this young woman's heroism, before judging her. Furthermore, allow me to speak well of her, not so as to make her a saint, since saints are made after they die, but rather to testify that she is certainly not the sinner that she thinks she is for having had one day of weakness in prison, overcome by the moral torture that she endured."

It is moving to read the dialogue between the author and that same Father Crotti, both of them perfectly aware of the disaster that was about to happen to them and to the entire Chinese Church. The missionary recalls: "Her apostolic zeal among the pupils, the help that she offered to her fellow teachers in the most difficult moments of the struggle and above all the courage that she showed in the final weeks of March 1950 enraged the government agents. On March 30, two days before my arrest, I saw her for the last time, in the evening, in the convent of the Sisters of Mary Consolatrix. She had made an appointment to meet me there so as not to be noticed; I found that she was very upset. 'Father,' she said, 'they have accused me of being a spy, a secret agent in your service.... What is to become of me?' I tried to console her. She calmed down and I saw in her a sign of resolve when she knelt down to receive my blessing.... She had agreed to drink the cup of suffering. The next day, April 1, I saw her again while she was defending her bishop at the tragic moment in which the chief of police tried to lay hands on our shepherd. Later on we saw each other again in prison, victims of the same antireligious hatred."

Proof of Gertrude's Christian maturity is the astonishing serenity with which the young woman endured her hardships and even the long-awaited end of the impressive series of interrogations, trials and detainments to which she was *subjected. You would expect a person who was proud, ready to show off her meritorious acts. But instead, she writes,*

> *When the meeting was over, no one else came to torment me. Then, after getting permission from the committee, I went back home in peace. The priest to whom I related the whole story commented: "Don't pride yourself on your victory. It was not your strength but the Lord who won it. As you see, for those who fight with courage and perseverance, the victory is always sure, because Jesus is fighting with them."*

Not exactly the happy end of a fine story—quite the contrary. Gertrude's human experience, unfortunately, had a bitter conclusion that deserves to be known. In a short appendix to Più forti della tormenta *("Latest news about Gertrude Li"), Father Crotti reports as follows:*

> *The tremendous mental torture of the indoctrination to which Gertrude was subjected, after her four months of imprisonment, had been prompted by a diabolical plan of the government: to make a heroine of the faith surrender. . . . But the plan foundered on the strength of that timid schoolteacher. . . . When she returned home, the terrible experience that she had gone through prompted her to flee. . . . She succeeded. After two months she was discovered and brought back to Kaifeng to live under house arrest, where several times a week she had to face appearances of the usual policemen and listen to the usual talks. But her strength was undiminished.*

Crotti then reports the testimony of Father Giovanni Carbone:

> *Gertrude is still herself: delicate, fine, quick-witted, decisive and strong. Her father landed in the gutter, life at home is a struggle and the government tries to win her over with lots of promises of assistance and prospects for employment. She told me about*

*the intrigues of the policemen in a very amusing way and con-
cluded by saying, "Better to die."*

Years later, the Communists succeeded in making Gertrude
surrender with one of their most treacherous and perverse techniques: forced marriage. Crotti writes:

> In 1991 I had the chance to travel to Kaifeng and to see many
> of my Christians. I did not see Li Minwen among them and I
> asked about her. They replied that certain individuals in the
> government had tried, successfully, to have her meet a young
> man from the reformed [Patriotic] Church and to make her
> marry him. When I went to Kaifeng, she did not have the
> courage to see me; she felt guilty. But in God's sight I think
> that the battles that she had to wage for her faith were what
> counted.

Attack on the Bishop

April 1, 1951, was the fourth anniversary of the episcopal consecration of Gaetano Pollio, Archbishop of
Kaifeng (Henan). The same day also marked the twenty-
fifth anniversary of the priestly ordination of Father
Dionigi Busnelli. In church, during the Solemn Mass
sung by Father Busnelli and concelebrated by the bishop,
Father Giovanni Battista Boracco, rector of the regional
seminary, gave a talk on the subject of "The priest,
mediator between God and men", in which he declared,
among other things: "The priest is the representative
of Jesus; his person is sacred and all Christians should
respect him."

On that day my recollection was often disturbed by
an unusual uproar coming from outside the church.

When Mass was over, I went out in haste and saw Father Amelio climbing the staircase to the bishop's palace, while the students from Hua Yang School shouted, "Down with the imperialist Crotti!" Father Crotti, smiling, withdrew. After taking off his sacred vestments, the bishop came outdoors, and the same students started shouting again: "Down with the imperialist Pollio!"

The Christians stood there watching and did not move. The bishop, smiling also, waved his hand in greeting and gestured for them to leave. But at that moment Father Edoardo Piccinini came out of church; in response to the outrageous yelling of the students, he started to shout, "Long live Monsignor Pollio! Long live the bishop!"

That shout was taken up and repeated by all the Christians. That started a heated quarrel between students and Christians. The students shouted, "Christians, you are all Chinese; stop calling 'Father' men who are robbers; stop being the hounds of the imperialists." And the Christians retorted: "What? You call us hounds because we are followers of the Christian religion?" And the yelling on either side got louder, causing more and more confusion.

The priests and the bishop had already withdrawn into the palace. Then I turned to Catherine: "It is impossible to resolve the situation in this way. Let us send some representatives, chosen from among us Christians, to inform those in charge of the school that it is not right for the students to shout that way in front of the bishop's residence."

Catherine agreed and eleven persons were chosen: the sisters Wang and Li, Li De, Yang Guiyong, He Guiying, Wu Xiuzhe, Zhao Zhe, her mother, another old woman, Catherine and I. But while we were choosing our representatives, the police arrived, called by the school, to find out what was happening. The soldiers immediately entered the episcopal residence. Fearing that their captain would lay the blame on the bishop, we followed them. Upon seeing them arrive, the bishop first addressed the police captain: "For two weeks now I have been putting up with those students who have been instigating similar disturbances everywhere to drive me out of China: I protest."

But Captain Liu looked very angry. Catherine intervened: "What happened concerns the students and the Christians; the bishop has nothing to do with this affair; he didn't say anything", she declared sadly.

The captain went outside to see what had been written in chalk on the walls, and then gestured for the Christians to disperse, threatening to book anyone who did not obey. We eleven did not go away, and he immediately had his men take down our names, professions and addresses. Moreover he wanted the bishop to follow him right away to the police station, but we and Brother Francesco offered to go instead. He did not permit it. After a short pause, he declared: "The incident is over; I warn you that such things must not happen in the future."

He went away but left some soldiers to guard the entrance, and we were forbidden to leave until five in the morning.

The Arrest

On the morning of April 2, Josephine Li De (the youngest schoolteacher in the group) and I were stopped by several armed guards as we were going into church for Mass. The bishop, Crotti, and Piccinini had already been taken away, while the brother (Francesco Quartieri) had joined them voluntarily. The guards forced us to go back home.

On the afternoon of that same day a large assembly was held to indict the Church and the priests; among the participants were representatives of all the schools and of all the public offices. Josephine and I heard Li Maode declare, besides the usual accusations: "The imperialists (that is, the bishop and the priests), in premeditated fashion, incited their lawless disciples to beat the students who love their country and to shout, 'Down with Mao Zedong! Down with Stalin!'"

Later, around ten in the evening, I was in the dormitory of Qing Yi College talking with the assistant principal, Agnes Zhao, when suddenly several police agents came in asking for me. They searched painstakingly through my things, took some of my books and ordered me to follow them. I obeyed and, outside the building, met up with Josephine and Sister Yu. All three of us were brought to the police station.

There my interrogations began. One official asked me, "Do you know why we have brought you here?"

"I think because of what happened yesterday", I answered.

"What happened yesterday?" he replied.

I recounted the whole incident.

"We did not call you for that little thing", he retorted contemptuously. "The government is not against religion and therefore cannot forbid you to perform your acts of worship. But tell me, didn't you offend someone yesterday?"

"I? No."

Then I was brought back to the front courtyard, where I heard the voice of Catherine He who, in the meantime, had been subjected to a similar questioning. I calmed down. After we had all been interrogated, they brought us back to the station and left us sitting there until dawn of the following day.

In Prison

At three in the morning of April 3 the police captain, as he stood up to leave, turned to us and said, "The charges against you don't amount to much; when I return I will interrogate you quickly so as to let you go as soon as possible, because I know that you all have much to do and I don't want you to lose any time."

Those words made me happy.

At four o'clock they led me to the rear courtyard, and suddenly I was brought into the captain's office. There a comrade gave me the lead article from the newspaper *Henan* to read, which described what had happened on April 1 near the Catholic church. The other women who had been arrested with me were there, too. After I read it, the comrade invited us to consider carefully our way of conducting ourselves and admonished us: "Stop harboring in your minds thoughts that are opposed to the teachings of the government and accept the education that the government offers you."

Then they separated us and questioned us one at a time.

Comrade Meng wanted me to repeat to him the story of April 1. At the end he commented, "Don't think that that happened by chance; this deals with one aspect in the warfare between imperialists and the people."

I responded that in reality it was nothing but a matter between Christians and non-Christians. In reply he advised me to reconsider, and he dismissed me.

At eight in the evening Comrade Wu came up to me and asked, "On that day did you also shout 'Long live the bishop'?"

"No," I answered.

"And why didn't you?"

"I thought that if we did we would get involved in a conflict, and I was anxious then and could not shout."

"This is a matter between imperialists and the Chinese people", he continued. "If you do not side with the Chinese people, it means that you want to remain with the imperialists. Whether you want to admit it or not, that is the reality."

Soon afterward I was taken to jail. Catherine He, Wu Xiuzhe and Josephine Li had arrived there before me. A female comrade took away my crucifix, rosary and [Miraculous] medal and locked me in prison.

The women's prison consisted of half a room (six square meters) and was divided from the men's prison by a partition wall half the height of the room. In one corner there was a wooden pail for the wants of nature, and on the floor some putrid straw. At the sight of it my heart sank, and I began to cry, but the other three immediately tried to console me. As it was, supported by their strength of character, I took courage and began to sit quietly.

A Sense of Bewilderment

On April 4, at two in the afternoon, they called me for another interrogation. The aim was to make me admit that the disturbances of April 1 had been organized by the bishop with a clearly determined plan and purpose.

"Whether the others were urged by the bishop to go against the students, I do not know; I, certainly, received no order", I declared.

"It may be", replied Captain Liu, "that before the fact you received no order. But tell me, during the conflict, didn't the bishop command something; didn't he make some sign to you? Because even that would have been enough to encourage you."

"No," I answered.

After that conversation I was taken back to the prison. We could communicate and admonish each other to pray only by our facial expressions and some hand signs, but I, in a few moments, managed to let the others know what I had said in the last interrogation and the composure that I had maintained. Then, being unable to speak further, we went back to praying.

I closed my eyes and began to think: "The principals of the two schools live in peace; only we four inexperienced young women have become involved in this situation ... and perhaps having created the present state of affairs by our behavior is not exactly advantageous for the Church. Maybe, because we are lacking in virtue, God will not grant us the grace of martyrdom; not only that, but a long stay in prison might be for us an occasion of sin as well. And if that happened, wouldn't it be our fault? The government is simply asking us to admit that the bishop is an imperialist. Does it do any good to put up resistance? And if the bishop pardoned Headmaster Chen, can't he pardon us, too? When the government tries to convince me to join the 'Triple Autonomy Movement', then I will resist!"

That evening the police captain called for me once again and told me: "This is the end now for the imperialists in China. The Chinese people can no longer let them carry on their disintegrating work. The less guilty ones will be expelled from China, while those who are considered more criminal will be sentenced to prison and even to death. Why do you still want to follow them, thus placing yourselves on a par with them? If for that reason the government had to sentence you to prison or kill you, think what a dishonor it would be for you and your families! Do you imagine perhaps that the government will not sentence you because you are young women? I tell you again that we will treat you just like enemies, and we do not have too much compassion with enemies: one dead is one less remaining. Well then," he continued, "the government thinks that you, blinded by the imperialists, are indeed in error, but that it is easy for you to realize your mistake. All you need is to liberate your mind from every imperialist idea and to acknowledge your offenses, siding with the government and revealing the crimes of the imperialists. The government will be ready to forgive you. Otherwise you will be sentenced by the same standard as the imperialists; this is the government's policy of leniency and oppression."

The result of this conversation was that my will was shaken even more. I thought that, although they could not kill me, nevertheless a one- or two-year prison sentence would be too difficult for me. In my heart, therefore, I prepared to give in a little and to persuade the others to yield, too, convinced that I was doing something beneficial for us all.

The Fall

That same night Captain Liu summoned me once again.

"We do not want to take the side of the imperialists," I explained to him, "but neither can we admit that our bishop is an imperialist. It is true that ever since the headmaster of the Hua Yang School declared that the bishop is an imperialist, many have repeated it. But what was the basis for the headmaster's accusation? And is the government really convinced that that assertion is true?"

"You are making a huge mistake, thinking that way," the captain then said, "but you deserve an answer. Know, therefore, that the government maintains that Pollio and Crotti are imperialists, not because they were recognized as such during the public accusations, but because there is evidence that confirms it. When we arrested the bishop, we found in his room documents proving that he was subsidized by America, and we also found subversive material. Maybe soon we will also find the radio transmitter that he was using. All this proves that he is an imperialist. If you don't believe it, the government can show you the evidence."

While the captain was speaking, I thought to myself, "If the government has evidence from two days ago, why did it insist long ago in saying that they were imperialists, when there was no evidence?" But I did not dare to ask that question. I only said: "At first I thought that the words spoken by Headmaster Chen during the public accusations were worthless and that the Catholic Church could neither receive subsidies from imperialist powers nor be in the service of a government; but now, if the government has proof, I must believe it. Based on that evidence, I admit that the bishop and the priests are imperialists."

"Good. What will you do now to demonstrate that your admission is sincere?"

"I will break off all relations with them."

"As for that, you would have to break off relations even if you did not want to", Comrade Wu shouted. "The government itself will see to that. It has already imprisoned the imperialists; how could you still have relations with them? What you have promised is worthless.

"You should declare instead that you will help the government, revealing their crimes", suggested Captain Liu. "And you will help the Christians to understand better the true face of the Church, by promoting from within it the Triple Autonomy Movement."

"All right", I accepted. "First I will make sure that the Christian women who are with me in prison come to know the things that I have learned today. Then, under the guidance of the Chinese priests [of the Patriotic Church], I will also try to promote the Triple Autonomy Movement."

"Will you do this work tomorrow among your fellow prisoners?" Captain Liu insisted.

"Yes, I will do it", I replied.

"Good. Change Li's room", he ordered the guards. "This is how the government deals with those who amend their ways."

Confess, and Confess Again

That same evening they moved me to a cell in the front courtyard, where Yu Wenxiu and another detainee had set up a cot for me.

April 5. In the morning, as soon as I got up, I looked around the room more attentively and saw that over my bed there was a little window. A piece of paper covered it; I lifted it and saw that on the other side of the glass another piece of paper had been glued. I heard coughing and realized that the bishop and Father

Piccinini were being detained in that cell. That was a great consolation to me.

At ten o'clock I was called by the captain, who asked me what I intended to do to start my work of persuasion. "I will tell my comrades", I answered, "what I said yesterday evening to you."

And so the other women were called and questioned in my presence. They all agreed in saying that they thought as I did. But Catherine and Josephine wanted us to clarify some things. "Gertrude says that she will obey the Chinese priests," Catherine specified, "but the foreign priests are our superiors, too; we must obey them, too."

I accepted the observation, but it greatly annoyed the captain. With an irate expression he suddenly ordered us to put in writing both the part that we had played in the events of April 1, and the crimes of the missionaries whom we knew. I thought that, without compromising myself, I could easily get out of it by writing something. Nevertheless the captain, after reading the draft that I had written, objected: "You have made progress, but you have said too little about the Europeans. You must be more courageous and say it all. Like Yu Wenxiu, who fearlessly revealed everything, going so far as to speak about Pollio's scandalous relations."

Those last words grieved me. When I returned to the cell, I asked Yu Wenxiu what she had said. And she replied: "I didn't say anything. At the captain's request, I just admitted that Father Piccinini knew Sister Candida well and that the bishop knew Mother

Superior Song well. Maybe he was referring to those remarks of mine."

Meanwhile Agnes Zhao and the little girl Xiaomei had been imprisoned also. That evening they brought them into our cell and moved the other detainee to Josephine and Catherine's cell. "I have been accused of shouting reactionary slogans", Agnes told us. "Afraid that they might lay the blame on Father Piccinini, I ended up admitting that I had shouted them. For that they put me in prison."

That evening I wrote a second draft of my confessions. This time, again, the captain was not satisfied and ordered me to rewrite everything. Only then did I realize my initial mistake, but it was too late: I had to continue down that wrong path and wrote a third time. I wrote about my work against the Triple Autonomy Movement, against the "pioneers", against the "New Democratic Youth". And then I wrote that I had also spoken ill of Russia, recalling the religious persecution by the government. I hoped in that way to be able to satisfy the captain.

Temptations

At three in the afternoon of the sixth day, Catherine's brother Joseph, by order of the labor union, came to visit us so as to exhort us to change our minds and to accuse the bishop and the priests. First Catherine, with a severe expression, curtly scolded her brother, saying, "The priests are the representatives of Jesus. If they had committed errors, one might discuss them. But they are innocent; what else is there to say?"

Facing me, she added, "We said that the priests are imperialists only because we are relying on the evidence that the government may have: besides that we know nothing."

Joseph, Catherine's brother, remained silent. The police captain could not conceal his great disappointment, but nonetheless spoke calmly to urge us to reconsider, and not to allow Joseph's fair observations to go unheeded. But Catherine's brother did not dare to speak further; shortly afterward he said good-bye and went away.

That evening there was another meeting. The captain informed us: "Zhao Lijie Agnes has admitted her mistake. For that reason the government is acting generously in her regard and this very evening she can return home.... Learn from her!"

Agnes, too, spoke some words of admonishment to us and then left. The detainee who had been transferred to the cell with Catherine and Josephine was brought back to our cell.

The Captain's Rage against Catherine

In the afternoon of the seventh day the captain sent for me. He informed me that he had read the third draft of my confessions, which he considered a little more satisfactory than the preceding one, but he ordered me to write them over. I was overcome with despair.

Late in the evening all of us were called together again. This time the captain's frown was more stern than usual. He accused us of conspiring so as not to let ourselves be influenced and to deceive the government.

"During these five or six days," he added, "the government, manifesting its great good will, has used the most persuasive words to convince you to accept Marxist education.... If you still do not want to submit, that means that it will punish you mercilessly."

Then, turning to Catherine, he again asked her for explanations about the events of April 1. But after a few words, he suddenly took out Catherine's diary and read a few lines: "Today the priest, during the Legion of Mary meeting, spoke about the future of the Church. He said, 'Almost all the words of the Church—schools, hospitals, Holy Childhood—will be confiscated. The priests will be imprisoned, the buildings occupied and the whole Church persecuted.'"

While reading these few lines the captain trembled and his face became increasingly livid. He yelled at Catherine to stand up and cursed her in these words: "*Hunzhang*[1] that you are! I sentence you to half a year in chains so that you will not be forced to walk on four paws. Handcuff her. Make sure her wrists are tightly bound."

Catherine fearlessly extended her hands, and they were quickly put into shackles. The captain continued: "Who is the fellow named Duan who often appears in your diary?"

[1] *Hunzhang* is an insult meaning "contemptible".

Catherine stared at the captain's face, without batting an eyelid and without speaking. The captain, still inflamed, pressed on with his questions, without giving Catherine time to think of an answer. Finally, pointing to a small pile of papers on the table, he became furious. "Look at how much material we have collected against you. We have investigated your whole life, from childhood to this day.... It is useless to lie, to try to confuse me with your falsehoods. We know everything about you. Tell me, what sort of relationship did this Duan have with you?"

"He is a friend."

"What sort of friend?"

"We were supposed to get married soon."

"Where did he work?"

"In the army printing office."

"And where is he now?"

"In Taiwan."

"Has he ever written to you?"

"Only once since the liberation."

"How many letters did you exchange?"

"Ten."

"Tell me the contents of those ten letters."

"I don't remember."

"Tell me what you remember."

Catherine spoke about the content of five letters and then declared that she did not remember anything else. The captain directed other curses at her, then turned to Josephine. "Your attitude toward the government is too harsh", he threatened. "Remember not to be so proud and uncompromising."

Wu Xiuzhe intervened, advising us not to imitate those who resist the government. Then, turning to me, he asked, "And you, what will you do?"

"I will say what I know."

So that terrible day came to an end.

Testifying about the "Imperialists"

In the afternoon of the ninth day, Comrade Wu questioned me again about the facts on April 1. I related that Father Piccinini had been the first to shout, "Long live the bishop!", and that that had started the scuffle between Christians and students. Then the comrade asked me, "Would you be willing to testify against the Europeans?"

"Yes," I answered, since I was unable to refuse.

"Prepare yourself well," the comrade continued, "so as not to be embarrassed when you confront them."

Father Piccinini was brought to the back courtyard and, after a while, Yu Wenxiu and Wu Xiuzhe were summoned also. Finally the comrade came to me and said, "The time has arrived to put the imperialists on trial. Pay attention to what I tell you, because in court all deference between father and children must disappear; in speaking you cannot let yourself be guided by affection. Remember then that the imperialists are very cunning."

When I had arrived in the back courtyard, the captain had me sit down and ordered me to speak. Trembling, I declared, "On April 1 Father Piccinini was the first to shout. After a few seconds all the Christians began to shout. Father Piccinini must take responsibility for having started the demonstration of the Christians."

Then the captain asked Father Piccinini what he thought. And he answered, "Before, I did not know what my share of the responsibility consisted of; now, if that is true, I accept my responsibility." And he signed the statements.

At five in the evening the captain called for me again. "Piccinini told me that he has nothing to do with the Christians," he informed me, "and therefore cannot take responsibility for the Christians' actions. Crotti is responsible for them. See how the imperialists behave: they accuse each other. Why don't you do the same? Why not blame others for everything? This evening you will testify against Crotti; put all the blame on him."

I understood that the captain's words were false and I was very upset, but I could not refuse.

At eight I arrived in the back courtyard and saw Father Crotti sitting calmly in front of the captain. I did not dare to look up at him. Agnes Zhao and Wang Weiyu had arrived before me. The captain ordered me to speak. "Father Crotti is our pastor", I began. "When the Christians became agitated, he did not come out to tell them to stop; his attitude can be interpreted as approval for what they were doing. For this Father Crotti must be held responsible."

Xiaomei's mother added a few words. Then Father Crotti spoke up. "What the two Christian women said is correct: I am the pastor and I did not prevent the Christians from shouting. I acknowledge that I am responsible for that."

"Do you take full responsibility for the incident?" the captain asked.

"No," Father Crotti replied. "I declare myself responsible, as Li Minwen says, for not having prevented the insurrection of the Christians; I am responsible only for that."

"Well, then, if you won't take responsibility for the incident, your Christians will."

Father Crotti remained silent. Then Agnes Zhao implored him: "Father, take this responsibility! If you don't do it, how will we be able to do it? At home I have an elderly mother and a little daughter.... What will become of them if the government puts the blame on me? I have always obeyed you, even at the cost of great sacrifices; now that the government has already pardoned me and has set me free again, would you want me to be arrested again?"

The captain insisted. Then Father Crotti, in a low voice, said, "All right." And he signed. I was terribly sorry.

At three in the afternoon of the tenth day Captain Liu ordered me to prepare myself because I would have to testify against the bishop. At four o'clock I was brought again to the back courtyard, where the bishop sat, serene and smiling. I repeated with regard to the bishop what I had said about Father Crotti. The bishop explained, "That is what the Christian women think. I am the bishop and must declare myself responsible for not having prevented the Christians from rebelling against the students and for not having called the police immediately; my responsibility cannot go any further."

"Well, then," the captain shouted, "the full responsibility will rest again with the Christians."

"No," the bishop replied, "the Christians are not at fault. The one who is really to blame is the director of Hua Yang School. He is the one who ought to have prevented the students from coming to cause an uproar on our churchyard."

The captain tried to argue with him, but the bishop did not back down from his position. I was very much consoled by that.

The Trial for Activity against the "Pioneers"

At four o'clock on the eleventh day the captain ordered me to get ready to accuse Father Crotti. I was terrified, but I was forced to obey. At eight in the evening the trial began and at nine I was called to make a deposition. In the back courtyard I saw a dozen armed men, some students and teachers from Hua Yang School and eight or nine judges. Wang Weiyu was there also.

The captain ordered me to relate the incident of the disbanding of the "Pioneers". "The organization", I began, "was formed at my elementary school on June 24, 1950. In mid-July Father Crotti informed me that the Pioneers were under the direction of the New Democratic Youth, which opposes religion of any sort, and that the Catholic students in the school therefore could not participate in the Pioneers. So then I assembled the Catholic students and repeated to them what the priest had said. Consequently those who were not yet in the organization did not join and those who had already joined withdrew."

"What did Crotti tell you with regard to the government?"

"To obey all its orders, except for those that are opposed to our faith."

Minister Zhu turned to Father Crotti. "You know very well that the Christians are Chinese citizens before they are Christians. What, then, are we supposed to think about you if you order Christians to disobey the government?"

"I told them to disobey only in the case where the government orders things contrary to the faith", Father Crotti defended himself.

Someone else who was present intervened: "Is it true that Crotti forbade you to enroll in the New Democratic Youth?"

Father Crotti immediately replied, "The rule book of the New Democratic Youth is clearly against religion of any sort; naturally anyone who does not want to lose his own faith should not enroll in that organization."

"Take the rule book and find that article for us", the captain of the New Democratic Youth shouted.

Father Crotti tried to remember the article without looking in the rule book. Finally he found it and read: "Communist youth must patiently convince everybody of the poison and falsehood contained in religions and superstitions."

Someone else in attendance stood up to say: "In the rule book it says that the youth must carry out this work patiently; therefore it does not go against your activity."

"The fact remains", the priest replied, "that the young people enrolled in this organization have to treat religion as something poisonous and false."

"Call Li Maode to testify", the captain ordered.

"The testimony of one", the priest replied, "is not valid. Besides, Li Minwen is present; ask her about this matter; if she accuses me of this, I am ready to surrender."

The captain was silent for a moment; then he ordered me to return to my cell.

Did Sabotage Occur?

At eleven that same night (April 10) I was again brought to the interrogation room.

"Crotti maintains that by disbanding the Pioneer organization he did not commit an act of sabotage. What do you say about it?" Captain Liu asked insistently.

"I was the one in charge of the organization. If a pagan Pioneers group didn't start up at the school, it was because of my inability. As for advising the twenty or so Christians not to join the association, I don't think that that is sabotaging the government's work."

"Who is talking about you?" the captain shouted. "I am speaking about Crotti."

"Crotti only advised me to dissuade the Catholic pupils from joining the organization."

The captain pounded his fist on the table and, enraged, continued. "What, Li Minwen? You are regressing? Say once again how Crotti ordered you to disband the Pioneers, and then you yourself tell me what sort of crime that is."

I repeated the story, but I did not draw the conclusions that the captain wanted.

"Isn't that sabotage?" he insisted.

"I don't know; let the government say that."

"You must say it."

I kept silence.

"Why don't you speak?"

"I don't know what to say; I don't know how to determine properly whether that action can be called sabotage or whether it is a simple defense of the principles of the faith."

"What, you don't understand? This question about the Pioneers is similar to the one about the New Democratic Youth. If it is sabotage to warn young people against the New Democratic Youth, then it will also be sabotage to advise Christian children not to belong to the Pioneers."

At that point Father Crotti lifted his head and intervened: "All right. You are only forcing Li Minwen to say that what I did was sabotage. Know, however, that even if she says that, I will never admit it."

I immediately understood what those words meant. I drew courage from them and remained steadfast in not seconding the captain. The judges no longer tormented me on that subject. It was already past midnight.

"Until tomorrow", the captain said to me. And he had me brought back to my cell.

After only a quarter of an hour I was brought again to the interrogation room. The captain resumed the questioning: "Li Minwen, what happened? At the sight of your priest, did your mind take a step backward? I do not understand the way you conducted yourself. Either you were overcome with fear that the blame you were supposed to lay on the European would fall back on you, or else the past was recalled to your mind in the presence of the priest."

"The trial was too serious", I replied. "I was afraid and did not dare to speak rashly."

"Today you have been pulling my leg", the captain added. "I praised you before the others because you had made real progress, and just look: now I have to take it back. What can I say to those who question me again on your account?"

Comrade Wu answered instead of me. "The blame is mine, too, because I did not prepare you well. I thought that since I had already predisposed you many other times, there was no need to repeat that work. If I had assured you in time that the responsibility would not be shifted to you, you would certainly have acted differently. Enough for this evening: think well about this and try to remain steadfast in Marxist principles. Tomorrow you will be called once more to testify against Crotti. And I advise you not to be so stubborn."

The Efficacy of Prayer

On April 11, at around two in the afternoon, Captain Liu summoned me again. "This evening the trial against Crotti will continue", he informed me. "Prepare yourself; just shift all the responsibility to him and be assured that nothing will happen to you. How bad you made me look yesterday! I have always treated you well because I was sure of your persevering progress and, instead, yesterday evening, you showed that you are faltering. I had to confess in front of the others that I have not yet helped you enough. You took five steps forward and three backward; but that is a little progress, and I hope that finally, with the help of the government, you will continue to progress to the point of deciding to reveal the crimes of the imperialists."

I bowed my head as a sign of submission, but my heart was in turmoil. I feared a repetition of what had happened the previous evening and that I would not have the strength to resist the pressures from the government. I feared above all that I would be forced treacherously to testify against Father Crotti. Then I fervently prayed to the Lord to free me from that anguish and I waited. The hours passed slowly. Midnight arrived, but no one summoned me. Great was my joy then; I thanked the Lord and went to sleep.

The Tables Turn

In the early morning of the twelfth day the captain called for me and informed me: "Yesterday the trial against Crotti was conducted. Confronted with the testimony of Wang Weiyu, Crotti had to admit everything. For that reason there was no need of you. Wang is much better than you; she told everything, so that Crotti was completely contradicted. Today it will be Pollio's turn: don't you want to accuse him?"

"I don't know him well; I am not on close terms with him."

"Well, then," the captain continued, "if you know Crotti better, get ready to accuse him."

At eight in the evening Comrade Wu notified me: "Today we will hold Pollio's trial. The representatives of all the government offices will be present. For you this is the last chance to rehabilitate yourself. If you do not conduct yourself as you ought, the government will settle all its accounts with you."

I did not dare to object.

"Pollio is arrogant and astute", he continued. "He says that the students of Hua Yang School are at fault, since they went in front of the church to disturb the ceremonies. We must counter that accusation by reasoning with the mind of the people. What do you say about this?"

"I, too, think that the students should not have gone into the churchyard to cause a disturbance."

"Careful, careful: this is not reasoning with the mind of the people! You must say that the Chinese people do well to demonstrate against the imperialists on any square centimeter whatsoever of Chinese land. Am I right or not?"

"Yes."

"Think it over well, then, so as not to be like Yu Wenxiu, who in my presence admitted Piccinini's offenses and then, while confronting him, recanted what she had said."

"I will say what I already said the other times. As for the incident with the students, it is up to them to defend themselves; if you want me to speak, it might happen that I, too, will do as Yu Wenxiu did."

"The students will do their part; but you, too, must prepare yourself."

I was struck by pangs of remorse, but I did not dare to reply. After me Wu Xiuzhe was summoned. When she returned, she said to me, "We two are just like Judas. Josephine and Catherine have not been summoned again, because they proved to be strong, while we are summoned continually. Today they are forcing us again to speak against our conscience."

These words increased my remorse. After a while Comrade Wu urged us once more to prepare ourselves, but noticing our agitation he added, "I see that your minds are shaken today."

We did not respond. But from the moment when the bishop was taken away to be brought to the courtroom, we began to pray. The bishop returned and we were not called to testify. I considered that a special grace from the Lord.

The thirteenth day passed without anything special happening. The next day Catherine and the other detainee were transferred to the first police department. Maybe that detainee, to curry favor with the government, had reported to the captain what we said about Catherine during the days when she was staying in our cell. Thus Catherine was perhaps incarcerated long-term through our fault.

On the fifteenth day the captain said to me, "See how much material has accumulated on my table? These are letters accusing the imperialists, which are arriving from all quarters. Hence we do not need your accusations. They will help me, however, to know what you are thinking and to set you free. Write quickly everything that you know about the imperialists."

But I had already decided not to give in and I wrote nothing.

After two days had passed, the captain, seeing that I did not want to write, threatened me, "I intended not to punish you, but I see that you are allied with the imperialists. We must wait for orders from Peking [Beijing] to determine their punishment. Therefore when the sentence arrives for them, it will go for you as well. As comfortable as you are here, it is better than He Yufen."

Spiritual Asceticism

For several days nothing new happened, and therefore we planned to establish communication with the bishop. While Wu Xiuzhe and Yu Wenxiu kept watch, I explained to the bishop what had happened to us in those dozen days and asked him whether it would be a sin to admit that he was an imperialist. "You could say that", was the Bishop's response. "I forgive you." Despite those words, which were spoken to reassure me, I was tormented by remorse.

Father Carbone was able to see to it that while in prison we had the Holy Eucharist along with our bread. In the presence of the Most Blessed Sacrament I felt even more the weight of our sins and sorrow for having committed them. We asked the bishop to grant us absolution. After Holy Communion, I promised the Lord never again to say a compromising word. If the government didn't release me again, I would accept prison as a penance that the Lord sent me to atone for my sins. And finally a great peace came over my soul.

On April 24, at ten o'clock, we were brought to the People's Theater to participate in the great assembly of indictments that the Catholics had to attend in preparation for the celebration of May 1. They told us that they were taking us there so that we, hearing the indictments of the Catholics, would finally decide to change our minds. Onstage Captain Liu sat behind us and spoke to us now and then in a very familiar manner. Below, in the audience, almost everyone knew us and their eyes were fixed on us. In some you could read compassion, in others—derision. I saw again all my regular students right in front of me, motionless. I felt great sorrow at the thought that, being unable to teach my lessons, I was failing in my duty toward them.

Many Christians came up onto the stage to make their accusations. These accusations differed, of course, depending on who was speaking. The headmasters, the priests, the seminarians and the students followed one after the other on the stage: there were some apostates in the last-mentioned group, too. But what all those people said had no effect but to urge me to be more steadfast in the faith, proud of my status as a prisoner.

At four in the afternoon we were brought back to the prison; by five I had already informed the bishop about what had been said during the assembly.

Reawakening of Conscience

It was now a month that I had spent in prison and, still unable to tolerate the situation, I was not able to pray well. But little by little, thinking over what I had done and said during that month, I realized that I had committed serious mistakes. Comparing myself then to Catherine and Josephine, I was assailed by even greater remorse, because they had truly shown strength and perseverance in prison, while I had done nothing but sin. I understood then that staying in prison was for me a great grace, a good opportunity to do penance and conform myself to the Lord's will. I thanked God for his goodness and found consolation.

The Lord then let me understand that other more serious trials awaited me and that I would therefore have to dedicate myself more completely to prayer in order to obtain the necessary graces. I fervently promised this also. And suddenly the Lord gave me a sign of his goodness. On May 1 the bishop was able to begin celebrating Mass in prison with us: I was able to attend it through the usual little closed window. It became easier for me to make progress in prayer and meditation.

On May 10 Captain Liu summoned me again so that I could make a deposition against the bishop and the priests; we women had all agreed that we would not say a word. In the afternoon of that same day the captain opened the door of our cell and told us: "Today someone else will be added to you: Zhao Lijie. She was unwilling to gather material against the imperialists to expiate her crimes. For that reason she is going back to prison." Having said that, he exhorted us once more to reveal the crimes of the imperialists, but his words did not influence us in the least.

Agnes Zhao

At four in the afternoon Agnes Zhao, with her little daughter Xiaomei in her arms, came into our cell. The little girl was crying, the mother was sobbing, and we, too, were unable to hold back our tears. At that sorrowful scene, suddenly the events of the previous month and a half passed before the eyes of my mind as though on a cinema screen. I reflected in particular on the incidents concerning Agnes. I saw again the evening of April 6 when, before leaving prison, she praised the clemency of the government and exhorted us not to be too obstinate; I saw her again as she appeared on April 24, when she uttered words of apostasy on the stage, accused the bishop and the priests and said that she was willing to carry on propaganda for the reformed Church. And now here she was again in prison because she had refused to provide documents against the bishop.

Faced with that picture, I rejoiced in my heart. Although I had made mistakes, the Lord in His mercy offered me a vivid example of what would have happened to me if His grace had not assisted me. Therefore I decided to abandon myself completely to Divine Providence.

When Xiaomei stopped crying, Agnes told us that, after April 24, Father Giovanni had reproached her and she had repented of her sins, resolving never again to comply with anything proposed by the government. She wanted to make her confession to the priest at Pentecost, not imagining that she would be sent back to prison so soon. She also told us that because of her sin she had made the priest weep and that now, as soon as he learned about her return to prison, he would be saddened even more.

This account made me even more determined: in the future, nothing would ever make me fall again.

On May 14 we received a note from Father Giovanni which said, "You are the glory of the Church, the pillars of faith in the midst of the Christians; you have become an example for all." This note, too, served to make us more steadfast. On Pentecost the bishop exhorted us to meditate on the seven gifts of the Holy Spirit. After this meditation we were all strengthened; we decided then to find an occasion to demonstrate our faith publicly and promised that, when we left prison, we would hear two Masses each day and receive Holy Communion daily.

An Unforgettable Day

On the first day of the fifth moon, Father Crotti was brought into the interrogation room; on the third day the bishop was brought there; on the fourth, first Father Crotti and then the bishop. When he returned, the bishop told us that in the course of two weeks everything would be over.

This news consoled us at first. We immediately asked the bishop how he had learned that, and he replied, "These last two times the interrogations have been conducted much more amicably; they no longer insisted on the question of American subsidies. They only asked me whether I have ever preached against Communist teaching, whether I have prevented Christians from participating in Communist organizations and whether I have sabotaged the Triple Autonomy Movement. I replied that I have preached openly against Communism, that I have prevented and sabotaged everything, and I repeatedly said that I will continue to do so until I die. Captain Liu declared that within two weeks everything will be over and that the government will let us go home."

Thinking that only a few days were left now before our separation, we were moved to tears. Wu Xiuzhe asked the bishop whether he had anything to say to all the Christians before leaving us. Monsignor Pollio noted, "Although the captain said that they would let us go, it is not certain. Maybe there will be a sentence. If they sentence me to two or three years in prison, I certainly will not be able to tolerate the heat and the cold in prison. If I must die, remember that I sacrificed myself willingly for my diocese; tell the Christians that they must remain steadfast in the faith at the cost of any sacrifice whatsoever. If, on the other hand, they do send me away, then I will always remain Bishop of Kaifeng and will never forget you even for an instant."

These words, spoken with affection and compassion, moved us to tears. Agnes sobbed. We noticed that the bishop's voice, too, was muffled by weeping, and we felt even greater sorrow.

Deceit and Firmness

Two weeks later the bishop was again brought to the interrogation room. He returned after only fifteen minutes. "Today I signed the final statement", he informed us. "My errors are having sabotaged the reform of the Church, having prevented young people from joining the New Democratic Youth, having spoken against Communism and having circulated books that oppose Communism. Then there are lesser sins, such as having announced that the Third World War is near. But in general the offenses that I am charged with concern the faith; I am very glad about that. In two or three days everything will be over."

We, too, were glad; we took turns making our confessions and were very much consoled by it. The story, however, didn't end that soon. Little by little the heat became unbearable and we all began to feel the effects. My cell-mates commissioned me to act as spokeswoman with the captain, which I was quite willing to do.

On June 1, I asked for and obtained permission to be brought to see the captain. "What we have to say to you we have already said", I began. "The heat is suffocating now, and they need us at home; we ask the government to decide the question as soon as possible."

"You are impatient, aren't you?" the captain sneered. "But who reduced you to these conditions? It wasn't the government that urged you to side with the imperialists and to offend the students of Hua Yang School. Now you want everything to be finished quickly. If you, by revealing the misdeeds of the imperialists, had come to the aid of the government, everything would already be over; but you persist in remaining silent about it, and so the government is forced to lose time inquiring elsewhere about the crimes of these imperialists. As for you, not only must you keep waiting in prison, but, once your lack of sincerity is proved, you will be punished severely. But since you have come to me spontaneously, I set one condition: if you reveal the crimes of the imperialists, I promise you that within a week you will be free. Otherwise there will be no limit to your arrest or you will be transferred to the prisons of the court. You are my spokeswoman: go back and try to convince the others."

These words provoked me sorely and made me regret that I had gone to speak with the captain. At the same time, I thanked the Lord that once again, by means of that disappointment, He was warning me to be strong to the end and that between suffering to preserve my faith and apostasy there was no middle way. I was beginning to understand better that the Lord had arranged this sorrowful path for my good, and I resolved to walk it steadfastly so as to avoid the danger of sin.

When I returned to the cell, I repeated what the captain had said, but at the same time I added what I was thinking also. My companions shared my view and resolved to conform themselves completely to the divine will. The heat had become oppressive; we, however, exhorted each other to endure it by meditating on the sufferings in purgatory.

Incentives and Consolations in the Darkness of Prison

During the first few days of July all the priests were assembled at the police station. While they were waiting in the first courtyard, they had an opportunity to inform the bishop about what was happening in China. "The facts prove that today in China there is a real persecution against the Catholic Church", the bishop concluded. "Monsignor Riberi, the papal internuncio in China, has been imprisoned and so have many, many of the priests and bishops, both Chinese and foreign, in each case because of the reform that the Communists want to impose on the Catholic Church. You are suffering now, but you should be proud, because your sufferings are for the Church. The Pope has come to know about our tribulations and has blessed us in a special way. But pray for the many Christians who unfortunately, through fear or for some other reason, have fallen into apostasy or have suffered to the point of becoming sick."

The bishop's words were very consoling to me; I understood that I was extraordinarily fortunate to be suffering together with him, that it was a real honor, both because I thereby came to receive the special blessing of the Holy Father, and also because in prison I was not subjected to all the persecutions that the

Christians outside underwent, and therefore I was less in danger of losing the faith. After the bishop spoke I felt that I was filled with a great strength that would help me to endure better the sufferings in prison.

Desire for Martyrdom

One day, as the heat was becoming more and more oppressive, Yu Wenxiu was transferred along with Josephine Li. When the bishop learned this, he told her to tell Josephine that every morning, during Mass, he offered to God the sorrows of those who were imprisoned for the faith for the conversion of everyone.

Another time, convinced that sooner or later I would be sentenced to long years in prison, I had the opportunity to send a few lines to Agnes Mary Zhao and Teresa Shen (two professors at the girls' high school). Agnes Mary was able to reply, saying, "Follow the bishop courageously, and fight along with him to the finish, even if it costs you your life; the fear of torments must never make us submit." Together with the letter from Agnes Mary I received also a note from Father Giovanni, which included news about everything that was happening outside.

That evening I informed the bishop about the contents of the two letters and, the next day, I spoke to him as follows: "What struck me the most in the two notes that arrived yesterday evening were the words of Agnes Mary: they moved me to tears. I am happy to hear that she is so strong but grieved by all that she has to go through. Every day I pray for every one of our

Christians, especially for those who suffer the most. Their sufferings cause me so much pain, yet I am ready to forgive those who have turned their backs on me, and I pray that the Lord will convert them as soon as possible, so that they will not be doomed to die in sin."

This letter and the words of the bishop gave me fresh fervor. I thanked the Lord for having chosen me as an instrument of His glory and I prayed for Him to accomplish in me His holy will.

In those days the bishop's exhortation was always the same: offer our sufferings to God. On the feast of Saint Mary Magdalen he exhorted us to think about the love of Mary for Jesus and about Jesus' love for that saint. "The government is treating you unjustly", he added. "I cannot refuse to let you go. If you allow it, I will speak on your behalf in no uncertain terms. I have already told the captain once that I wanted to sacrifice myself for the Church and to die a martyr in their hands, and these words have worked great wonders in him."

From that day on, the bishop's desire became mine as well. I, too, desired to be as strong as he and hoped that the day of martyrdom would come for me. That thought was constantly in my mind, so that often, during the night, in prison, I dreamed that the bishop was being led away to be martyred, but I wasn't in the least bit afraid.

The End of Our Imprisonment

On July 28 I was able to see Father Crotti from my window and get his attention; with a hand gesture,

I asked for his blessing and he promptly made the Sign of the Cross. That same day the captain asked me, "Was the government right or not to put you in prison?"

"It was."

"And why?"

"To reeducate us."

"Good, you have answered very well. Tomorrow you five will be set free, while He Yufen and Li De will be sentenced."

What the captain said did not cheer me up. I spoke for the last time with the bishop.

"I am not happy that you are going away," he confided to us, "because once you are outside, you will be victims of a more ruthless persecution during the course of the indoctrination that you will certainly have to undergo. There it will not be easy for you to defend yourselves as it is now. I bless you: tell the priests and the Christians that I am always praying for them. Be strong in the faith."

At eight o'clock Secretary Meng notified us that, as soon as we left, an initial course of indoctrination awaited us; immediately afterward there would be a big public meeting during which we would have to go up onstage to accuse the Church.

Our predictions and those of the bishop were not mistaken. Chao Agnes Mary quickly reassured the bishop that we would not waver; I tried to let Josephine know what awaited us outside so as to console her while she remained in prison.

At nine in the morning I was already home.

Exhortations by the Spiritual Director

On July 30, in the morning, I went to the convent of the Sisters of Divine Providence to make my confession and to speak with Father Giovanni. "The true friends of Jesus", he told me, "are those who know how to suffer and sacrifice themselves for Him even unto death. Unfortunately Jesus finds few of these faithful servants, and no wonder. Just go to the course of indoctrination, but remember always to be strong; don't yield even one step, and put all your trust in the Lord. Be prepared for all sorts of sufferings and sacrifices, and the Lord will grant you a superabundance of His grace; respond generously to the Lord, who is calling you to holiness."

I obeyed the spiritual director's orders and thanked him for his encouragement.

That same day I had to go to Qing Yi School (the girls' school that once belonged to the Church) for the announcement of the indoctrination program. The purpose, they told us, was threefold: to learn about the harm that imperialism did to China; to understand the need to love the fatherland and to counteract imperialism; to help the government unmask the imperialism of the Catholic Church of Kaifeng and the subversive goals of the Legion of Mary.

On August 2 one prefect of the course exhorted me to pronounce publicly a sample accusation against the Church. I energetically refused, saying, "In the government's view I was guilty of having obeyed the bishop and the pastor in disbanding the existing

Pioneer organization at my school. I, however, think that dissuading Catholic students from joining that organization is the right thing to do, so as to protect their faith. Besides, that order comes from the pope, not from the bishop or the pastor."

At seven in the evening Chen Tianruo, the director of the course, came to urge me to sign a statement declaring that the Legion of Mary was a reactionary organization. His manner and his brilliant eloquence disturbed me. He told me that if I signed that declaration, it would not go against my faith. I asked him to let me think about it until the following morning. Meanwhile I would have a chance to ask Father He and Father Carbone for their opinion. Both of them urged me not to sign that document and explained to me why not. Enlightened by their counsel, I promised that during the whole course I would never again give any answer to questions concerning the Church.

But as the course went on, the suggestions, the traps, the interrogations became more and more compelling. I tried to avoid all the questions but could not refuse to answer questions of a general nature, which often concealed snares. Then I decided to use a firm strategy with everyone: I denied absolutely that the bishop and the priests were imperialists, I denied that the Legion of Mary was a reactionary organization and I denied at all costs that I approved of the reform movement promoted by the Triple Autonomy Movement. Everyone was of the opinion that I was resolutely conservative-minded, and so the course directors and participants harassed me. The teachers treated me harshly and kindly in turn.

I remained immovable, although that complex of forces arrayed against me frightened me.

New Stratagem

On August 6 the central committee of the indoctrination course was inaugurated, made up of the director, several prefects, teachers and students: seventeen members in all. The purpose of the committee was to plan and present to the student body day by day the topics for study. I, too, was included. The committee had to meet every evening from eight until ten.

Chen Tianruo, the director of the course, was likewise president of the committee. The first evening he announced: "In our committee, unfortunately, there is still someone who dares to say that Pollio and Crotti are not imperialists. This is a worrisome question, and this evening we will spend the first twenty minutes discussing and clarifying it."

One of the participants urged me to present my objections immediately, to which those present would then reply. I was extremely agitated and did not want to speak. But one prefect began to get angry: I absolutely had to speak. Then, taking my courage in my two hands, I said, "Anyone who asserts that the bishop is an imperialist bases his statement on the fact that he boycotted the Triple Autonomy Movement. But how can anyone claim that it is possible to support that movement without falling into heresy? And if it is heresy, is it fair to declare that the bishop is an imperialist because he opposes heresy?"

Those present began to rail at me and to say that I had sold out to the imperialists, that I would accept the ideas of others only if the bishop gave me permission, and other accusations of that sort. They then asked me a thousand other things, which I refused to answer; and so at eight-thirty nothing had been accomplished.

Finally the president concluded: "Well, then, tomorrow evening at seven o'clock we will resume; be prepared to answer." That prospect terrified me. I feared that I would not be ready to answer their sophistries and would therefore fall into their traps. Before going to bed I turned very fervently to Our Lady and asked her to help me. At six the following morning I was at the convent to receive Holy Communion so as to gain the strength to do the Lord's will. I asked Father Giovanni what canon law prescribed with regard to admissions extorted under pressure. He replied that in any case I had to be strong. I went back toward the school, afflicted and sorely troubled.

Unbearable Torment

At school I met two teachers who began to speak to me and ask me why I was so stubborn. I replied that it was not because I wanted to protect guilty parties or was playing favorites, but because I was a Christian and wanted to remain faithful to my principles and to the precepts of the Church. They proved to be agreeable enough; it seemed that they understood me.

But the course continued inexorably; everyone said that they wanted to help me and free me from the old ideas. The teachers did not leave me alone for an instant. Little by little that torment became unbearable. Then I thought of the justice of God which was chastising me because I had fallen and had become an occasion of falling for others, whereas the Lord was granting peace in prison to Catherine and Josephine, who had managed to remain faithful.

Like Jesus before Pilate and the Crowd

Many times I had asked the Blessed Virgin for the grace to be able to make a general confession so as to prepare for the great trials that were yet to come and, finally, my prayer was heard on Sunday, August 13. That evening, to my great joy, it was possible for me to go see Father Giovanni and to have my desire granted. The priest urged me to trust entirely in the Divine Mercy, assuring me that my soul was now purified of every stain. Finally he recommended that I consecrate myself to Mary on the day of the Assumption, which was now near.

On the afternoon of August 15 the course committee forced Giovanni Liu and me to go up onstage to declare our attitude publicly. We obeyed. Those attending were free to interrupt with their objections. The prefect of the course leveled several accusations against me and asked me to reveal, without deceit, the reason for my last visit to Father Giovanni. I tried to excuse myself, saying that I was not prepared to answer questions like that. Those present began to rail against me and to curse me. Many times the committee tried to force me onto the stage, from which I had come down. Since I was resolved more than ever not to go back up, the girls from the school were mobilized against me and dragged me by force onto the stage. With rebellion in my heart and greatly agitated, in front of about a thousand people, I declared: "During these days of indoctrination Comrade President and all the rest have been very helpful to me. I acknowledge that their kindness has surpassed the limits of propriety and I am moved by it. But I must admit that, unfortunately, my mind has not made any progress, that I do not feel capable of obeying the order to join the reform and to denounce the Catholic Church, and I refuse to respond to what the president has just asked me."

"But why did you go visit the European?"

"Because I intended to make use of my freedom."

The directors were perplexed by my answer. They consulted among themselves before haranguing the crowd as follows: "Li Minwen admits that we have helped her, yet she refuses to submit to the law. The course committee suggests that we turn her over to the government again to be punished according to the law, but we take pity on her because she is still young. Therefore we have decided to turn her over to you. Continue to help her: if indeed there is nothing to be done about this, we will hand her over to the government."

The crowd approved by raising their fists. In the afternoon I forced myself to go to school.

Our Lady, who had granted me the first grace, obtained a second for me the following morning: I was able to go to church for Mass. Although it was the great feast of the Assumption, the church was almost deserted. I consecrated myself to the Blessed Virgin, saying to her, "If the Lord knows that I am about to fall by pronouncing words of apostasy, take my soul immediately."

Second Course of Indoctrination

On the day after the feast of the Assumption the second battle would begin for me: the second course of indoctrination started, this time on the Triple Autonomy Movement. A new central committee for the course was formed, made up of seventeen members, headed by the director Chen Tianruo, and the meeting began.

Many of the Christians enrolled in the new course did not want to hear about that movement. They all said that, if it were an orthodox movement, the example would have come from the Chinese priests, whom we would have agreed to follow.

One day Instructor Meng, returning from Hua Yang School for boys, announced to us: "I have good news to tell you: now we don't have to worry any more about accepting this movement, because the Chinese priests are ready to take it as their guide. Today the two priests who are at the seminary, Father Li and Father Ma, were here. I spoke with Father Li and he told me that at the seminary the Triple Autonomy Movement has already been organized. Father Giovanni Boracco (the rector) resigned; Father Ma is the new rector. As for the money, Father Boracco handed over to the two Chinese priests the eight ounces of gold that he had and all the real estate and furnishings of the seminary. Father Li authorized me to tell you all this, and he himself urged you to join the movement; the seminarians, seeing that he was a priest, accepted willingly, raising their fists. Father Li would have liked to come right away to our school as well, but he was prevented by other duties. Certainly we want to follow our Chinese priests; therefore now, in union with them, let us raise our fists as a sign of approval for the movement itself."

Most of those present, taken by surprise, raised their fists, but I did not trust Meng's words and refused to give my approval. As soon as I was free, I quickly ran to visit Father Ma to ask him what had happened.

The priest answered, "The change in the administration of the seminary took place because Father Boracco informed the Propaganda Fide about the situation in our seminary. Everything happened with the approval of Rome."

The following day they asked me: "The Chinese priests are now poised to lead the movement. Will you join or not?"

"Seminary reform is one thing, and reforming Christians is another. What happened at the seminary was a simple transfer of power, in keeping with instructions from Rome; on the other hand, an oath is being required of the lay people. If the oath required of us is approved by Rome, then I will join. Get in contact with Rome first."

"Rome will not listen to us," replied one of the committee members, "because this movement is against the imperialists and Rome is in the hands of the imperialists."

"If that is the case, then I will never be able to join you."

Confounding the Adversaries

During those days Father He had to participate in a congress convened by the provincial government. Two days after the congress, the newspapers published a declaration signed by Father He saying that Monsignor Pollio and Father Crotti were imperialists, that the Legion of Mary was a reactionary organization and that he belonged to the Triple Autonomy Movement.

Our prefect read that declaration in the presence of everyone and ordered the various teams in the course to discuss it. My team asked me, "You said that you would follow the example of the priests; now that Father He has admitted everything, what do you think?"

In my heart I did not quite believe that what they read from the newspaper really reflected the thinking of Father He, and so I replied, "I must find out what happened to Father He during the two days of the congress. Before giving you an answer, I must see him."

They forbade me to do that, but I was still determined not to answer before seeing the priest.

At midday I went to his office, but he was in the seminary. I returned at eight and asked him whether what we read about him in the newspapers was true. Father He, with a pained expression, confided in me: "I never said such things. It is true that a journalist approached me, but he added to my statements words that I have never uttered."

I would have liked to find out from him more precisely how all this had happened, but the members of the reform movement committee kept coming to bother him about other matters. Finally Instructor Meng told me, "We have the published declaration; that is enough for us. We will try to prepare the oath of membership in the movement, based on that declaration."

I would have liked to keep questioning Father He, but I was not allowed to. At nine o'clock I went back home, without knowing how to prepare my answer for the next day.

The following morning they assembled everyone participating in the course to confront me. The director asked me, "You said that you would follow the Chinese priests; now they have joined the movement. Why do you still persist in not joining?"

"It may be that the priests have said some things in conversation, but in practice what have they done? I have not yet succeeded in finding out from Father He exactly what he admitted and what he did not admit. For now I cannot join."

"You visited Father He yesterday: What did you talk about?"

"I went specifically to find out whether or not the newspaper had reported what the priest thinks. Unfortunately, just as he was about to tell me something, the members of the committee for the movement kept coming in and interrupting us. After an hour I was forced to go back home without learning much more about it."

"Why did you go to question him? Don't you believe the newspaper?"

"I believe it, but in matters concerning my faith I have to verify everything first. For example, Instructor Meng reported to us what Fathers Li and Ma, priests at the seminary, had said by way of urging us to join the reform, whereas it turns out that the two priests had agreed to a simple change of appointments, with the approval of Rome. It could be that the same thing happened with Father He. I cannot join the reform just because the newspaper reports his words; I need to know clearly what the priest thinks."

"You are stubborn!" a prefect shouted. "What is presented by the imperialists is good to you; what is presented to you by the people you reject out of hand. When we cited Father Ma to you as an example, you did not follow him, because we were the ones praising Father Ma. But when you learned that Father Ma had done everything according to the imperialists in Rome, then you approved his actions. When you were sure that the priests would always be subject to the imperialists in Rome, you said that you were ready to follow them; now that you know that Father He follows us, you say instead that you must first check everything.

From this we understand that you are obstinately siding with the imperialists."

Instead of frightening me, those words gave me courage. "In public", I continued, "you held up Father Ma as an example to imitate, and now you say that his reform is promoted by the imperialists. How do you explain your way of proceeding?"

"Yes," Instructor Pi admitted, "we knew very well that the reform of Ma Changshe had been promoted by the imperialists, but we cited it as an example so as to get you to make some progress."

"If we had imitated Father Ma, our effort would not have been a step forward in the reform movement."

Then Pi, infuriated, exclaimed, "Yes, it would not have been a step forward, but in that way it was hoped that we would begin to wake you up in earnest. Do you want to understand this or not? As for the reform that took place at the seminary, we understand better than you that this is a move of the imperialists against our movement. But we will be vigilant and will block every move they make."

I made no further answer. It was twelve o'clock, and the meeting was concluded. In the afternoon, worn out by the stress from that morning, I did not show up at the meeting.

Conclusion

The following day the conclusions were drawn. The judgment rendered in my case was: "Hostile to the course of indoctrination; very loyal dog of the imperialists;

defender of the imperialists' crimes (such as disbanding the Pioneer association)."

After the judgment was read they asked me, "Do you have any objection?"

"None."

"How can that be, after such a severe judgment?"

"That is the committee's judgment; it would do no good for me to object."

"Do you know", one prefect continued, "that everyone is amazed by your stubbornness? We know that you are very intelligent; we hope to be able to convert you so as to have you work for the people. That is why we have spared neither words nor encouragement to help you. Unfortunately we have not noticed any change in you, and we are all the more disappointed."

"No," someone else added, "she is not intelligent. She is a poor, stubborn imbecile. It is impossible to convert her."

Finally they asked me whether I wanted to see Father He again. "I don't want to see him", I replied. "I don't need to ask anything else concerning the reform of the Church, because I don't want to know about it. When it is possible to communicate with the pope, then we will know whether the reform that you promote is orthodox or not; only then will I agree to discuss it again."

"If all of China's problems", a prefect interjected drily, "had to be dealt with as you are doing, what matter would ever be resolved?"

"I am ready for anything; just don't let anyone talk about religious questions."

"Ah! Since you don't intend to come over to our side, it will be impossible from now on for us to help you."

That day the course ended. The director took the paper spelling out my judgment and held it up to my eyes, shouting, "Li Minwen, have you seen the judgment that has been handed down against you? And you dare to remain indifferent? Doesn't it matter to you? Can you imagine what might happen to you?"

I remained silent.

"Think about it", he continued. "If you want to convert there is still time for you." And he went away.

I gave the paper back to the group leader. When the meeting was over, no one else came to torment me. Then, after getting permission from the committee, I went back home in peace. The priest to whom I related the whole story commented: "Don't pride yourself on your victory. It was not your strength but the Lord who won it. As you see, for those who fight with courage and perseverance, the victory is always sure, because Jesus is fighting with them."

THE VIA CRUCIS OF THE TRAPPIST
MONKS OF YANGJIAPING

Introduction

Father Anthony, who served the monastery as cellarer (the monk in charge of business and provisions for the community), and two of the monks who assisted him, were arrested. They were stripped of their clothing and hung on trees in the bitter cold, their thumbs and big toes tied together behind their backs. Soldiers fired rifles past their heads in order to frighten them into revealing the existence and location of additional stores of arms. There were no more arms, though, and at last, satisfied that they had obtained all that Our Lady of Consolation had to offer, the troops left Yangjiaping. In departing, however, the communist authorities left behind political cadres to keep an eye on the monks. As Father Stanislaus Jen, the historian of the community, later wrote, "The monks were now like silent lambs driven to slaughter."

So James T. Myers narrates, in his book Enemies without Guns, *the beginning of the dramatic adventure of the Trappists from the monastery in Yangjiaping, a story which by its brutality and violence is undoubtedly unique in the vast scenario of anti-Catholic persecution. Of the experiences related in this book, that of the monks is the only one that ends in true martyrdom, strictly speaking: at the end of their Way of the Cross, thirty-three religious would pay for their fidelity with their lives.*

This is a story that is known in Italy to only a few specialists. However, because of both the cruelty of the executioners and also, more importantly, the extraordinary witness to the faith given by the monks who suffered those cruelties, it is radiantly emblematic of the many experiences of suffering that were written in blood in the following years. For this reason it is reprinted here: there is perhaps no more violent or stirring account of persecution and martyrdom with which to conclude The Red Book of Chinese Martyrs.

The experience of the Trappists of the Monastery of Our Lady of Consolation in Yangjiaping has been reconstructed with a wealth of particulars in the weighty tome, Monaci nella Tormenta, *a collection of many interesting firsthand accounts which was published by the General House of the Cistercians of the Strict Observance. As the editor, Father M. Paolino Beltrame Quattrocchi explains in the Introduction that the incidents being narrated have come down to us clear and intact, having miraculously survived the tumultuous series of events. All this was possible thanks to the rediscovery of contemporaneous documents that were providentially preserved in the archives of the Order; invaluable also was direct testimony by some of the protagonists of those events and by eyewitnesses who are still living, though scattered throughout the world, and who have been contacted patiently by the General Councilors, sometimes in almost unbelievable ways. All this material made it possible to describe in detail what has rightly been called the "Death March".*

The text that we are reprinting, excerpted from an article by Father Antonio Dall'Osto in Testimoni *(for further details see the bibliographical references at the end of this volume) is ultimately based on one of the reports published in* Monaci nella Tormenta. *It was composed by Father Charles J. McCarthy, a Jesuit, who at that time was stationed in Peking [Beijing] as a correspondent for Fides News Service and National Catholic News Service; when the first young monks released by the Communists arrived in the city, Father McCarthy met with them, offered them assistance and interviewed them in turn, with the help of a confrere who had a good command of Chinese.*

The Trappists' odyssey began in July of 1947, when the monastery, situated in the northeastern region of China, was overrun by the devastating fury of the revolutionary armies. As early as 1940 the Abbot had told thirty monks to flee and take refuge in the Monastery of Our Lady of Joy; subsequently relations between the Communist authorities and the religious had improved to the point where in 1941 the monks returned to Yangjiaping. In the following years, however, the Monastery of Our Lady of Consolation found itself on the line of demarcation between the belligerent Maoist forces and the Nationalist troops; in the summer of 1947 the line was swept away by the Maoist formations. The monastery was devastated by repeated pillaging and finally set on fire. The monks—for the most part old and infirm—were all arrested and subjected to repeated and tumultuous "popular trials", exhausting interrogations and inhumane physical and moral torture. They were then deported en masse, ruthlessly driven to make a "long march" without destination. For months on end they were forced to walk along the tortuous and steep paths in the northern mountains, exposed first to the baking heat of the summer, then under the torrential rains of the autumn and then in the bitter cold of winter, beyond the Great Wall, through the narrow passes of the Dalongmen wilderness. With their hands tied behind their backs with iron wires, their shoulders bent under the heavy baggage of the soldiers, subjected to countless cruelties and torments, half-naked, devoured by lice, their bodies stooped, the monks watched their companions die little by little along the way (and often they had to abandon them on the spot without burying the corpses). Another six were executed. All told, the "long march" imposed on the monks took the life of thirty-three of them, fourteen priests and nineteen lay brothers.

The monks' faith was challenged and sorely tried; like Christ on Golgotha they suffered piercing physical pain and the mockery of their captors.

> *The guards continued to ridicule them, saying, "We have seen that you pray while you are being beaten. You don't feel the first ten blows much, but when you have received a hundred you weep and ask God to help you. But does God help you not to feel the other blows? He is a God who does not care to help you or else cannot."*

For weeks on end the Trappists had to respond to weighty but patently false accusations, ranging from collaboration with the Japanese to the generic crime of being foreigners (actually the majority of the monks were Chinese). "One of these accusations", the testimonies relate, "reproached the priests for having built the monastery forty-six years previously, at the time of the disturbances caused by the Boxers, using taxes extorted from the Chinese government by the foreign powers." The accusation could not be more unfounded, given that the foundation of the monastery dates back to the end of the nineteenth century. Particularly painful for the Trappists must have been the "martyrdom of ingratitude", in other words, the about-face of the local farmers who had been longtime neighbors of the community.

Not only that: the monks had been close friends with the local, largely non-Christian population and had been very generous to them in times of need, as the same account testifies. For that reason the farmers had proved to be reluctant, at least initially, about the idea of seizing the monks' property by force so as to use it as their own, just as they had refused to cut down the trees that encircled the monastery. The Communists themselves, at first, had refrained from attacking the monastery violently, so as not to arouse the hostility of the people. The picture that emerges from the account is somewhat analogous to the situation that the Trappists at the Monastery of Our Lady of Atlas in Tibhirine, Algeria, happened to live in decades later: in that case too—we know from firsthand sources—there was a widening network of daily contacts between the monks and the people of that place, the great majority of whom were Muslim, leading to a mutual sympathy. As in China, so too in Algeria: it was not the local population but a group of violent extremists (Maoist in the one case, Islamist Shiites in the other) who put the foreign religious to death. In the case of Yangjiaping, the atmosphere of mutual respect deteriorated over time, with fatal results, because of the insistent Communist propaganda, aimed at depicting the monks as usurpers of the "people's property".

By destroying the monastery, the Maoists managed to strike a severe blow to the monastic presence in the country which, though numerically slight, was quite significant, if we recall that it was monks, incorrectly described as "Nestorians", who first brought the seed of the gospel to the "Middle Kingdom". The Maoists hoped furthermore to inflict a serious wound on *the very life of the Church in China. "The monks returned to the place of their imprisonment with hearts full of sorrow and reported to the others that Yangjiaping had been razed to its foundations. With satisfaction, the Communists said, 'For a long time there will be no more Catholic Church in our territory.' "The sinister prophecy proved true: for a long time the vitality of the Catholic Church in that area was stifled. Today, decades later, in that area, as in many others that had become scorched earth, Christian life is gradually flowering again.*

The secret of this unexpected fruitfulness is in the evangelical character of the witness that was given. Forgiveness offered to the persecutors, right in the midst of such painful and atrocious trials, indeed constitutes the seal of a faith that is "refined like gold in the fire". The monks' Via Crucis was an extremely eloquent example of fidelity to the cross; this is demonstrated by the fact that not once do we find words of hatred or revenge on the lips of the religious. Not even during the furious outbursts of the persecutors themselves: "Now it is no longer time for mercy. It is time for revenge!" Dall'Osto writes, quoting Father McCarthy:

> I asked Brother Joachim how he felt during those weeks. He answered that his heart was at peace and even joyful. "The reason", he said, "was that we were not guilty of anything." . . . When asked what he would do to the Communists if they were taken prisoners and handed over to him, he answered, "I would forgive them."

This is the odyssey of Yangjiaping. Few know, however, that before its tragic end, the monastery had an interesting history going back to the final years of the nineteenth century. In April of 1883, the former prior of the Trappist monastery in

Tamié in Savoy, Dom Ephrem Seignol, had boarded in Marseilles, together with a lay brother, a ship bound for China. His intention was to lay, in the vicinity of the Great Wall, in the former province of Chahar (the apostolic vicariate of Peking), the foundations of what would become the first Trappist monastery in the Far East, Our Lady of Consolation. The title "of Consolation" had been suggested to Dom Ephrem by none other than his friend Don Bosco, recalling the shrine of the Consolata *in Turin.*

Over the course of several decades the community came to number more than one hundred twenty members, almost all of them Chinese, so that in 1928, less than half a century after the original foundation, it was capable, in turn, of sending off a group of monks to the south of Peking, in Hebei, to found the new monastery of Our Lady of Joy, which in 1941 obtained full canonical autonomy.

The photographic documentation of the era shows two well-designed complexes that were not without a certain grandeur. And, indeed, both communities were flourishing with regard to their apostolates and vocations. Unfortunately, the political situation continued to heat up with the start of the Maoist revolution, putting an end to the development of the two monasteries.

The First Portents of the Disaster[1]

The first portents of what was about to happen occurred on July 1, when two monks were summoned before a

[1] The author of this testimony is Dehonian Father Antonio Dall'Osto, director of the biweekly *Testimoni* (see the bibliographic references).

"people's tribunal" in Xinzhuang, a little village about two kilometers north of the monastery. The community was accused of having oppressed and exploited the people, and so it was sentenced to hand over a certain number of cows and goats. But the worst was yet to come.

From July 2 to 8 two priests—Father Seraphim Shi, who was responsible for maintaining contacts with the outside world, and Father Chrysostom, the superior of the monastery—were forced to travel to Lijiawanzi, a village about three kilometers south of the monastery, to make arrangements at a people's tribunal to compensate for (supposed) past infractions. Both priests were Chinese: Father Seraphim was around thirty-eight years old, and Father Chrysostom was thirty. The leaders of the people had assembled the inhabitants of the villages and determined beforehand the accusations and responses that were then to be proclaimed publicly, without any opportunity for a defense. One leader, for example, was supposed to shout, "The monks are guilty of collaborating with the Japanese; do you agree?" The answer was supposed to be, "We agree!" Once again the leader was to proclaim, "For that reason the monks must hand over their equipment to the people. Do you agree with us or not?" The response was to be: "We agree with you."

Then other completely absurd accusations were leveled against the monks. One of them, for example, reproached the priests for having built the monastery forty-six years previously, at the time of the disturbances caused by the Boxers, using taxes extorted from the Chinese government by the foreign powers.[2] One farmer claimed compensation because his parents had been alarmed by the arrival of the foreign troops in China forty-six years before. The people's tribunal authorized him to take possession of a considerable number of goods belonging to the monastery. Fathers Seraphim and Chrysostom pointed out that when the monastery of Yangjiaping was founded, they were not there; indeed, they had not yet been born. "Nevertheless," they continued, "if there is no other alternative and we must pay, we will do everything possible to comply with your requests." No opportunity was given to them, however, to tell about all the good that the monastery had done for the poor people of the region.

The Sack of the Monastery

On July 8, Father Seraphim and Father Chrysostom returned to the monastery, followed by a group of people from Lijiawanzi. The latter came to take possession of the property that was supposed to be handed over to the farmers according to the verdict of the people's tribunal.

The most coveted booty consisted of around fifty quilts and blankets. In a flash the news that the people of Lijiawanzi were seizing the goods of the monastery spread through the mountain villages. Rumor had it

---

[2] Actually the monastery had been built in 1883: see the introduction to this chapter.

that the monastery would thereafter be closed. Throughout the night of July 8, people from around thirty villages rushed to Yangjiaping, eager to take part in the pillaging. Toward midnight the unexpected arrivals forced open the outer gates, beat the porter who had tried to speak with them and burst into the inner courtyard.

The priests, who enjoyed a certain authority, tried to calm them, but in vain. They did not want to hear about explanations or formalities; everyone was trying to grab as much as possible before someone else did. The people, lighting the way for themselves with torches, entered the monks' dormitory, took all the blankets and whatever other pieces of fabric that they found. At two in the morning of July 9 the pillaging was over, and little by little the people went away.

Nevertheless, even on that tumultuous night, at two o'clock, the monastic community assembled in chapel as usual to chant the Divine Office. The monks felt a great weight on their hearts, however. Around four o'clock, when the community gathered for Mass, another wave of farmers arrived to sack the monastery. At Yangjiaping there were seventy-five Trappists: eighteen were priests, five of them foreigners and the rest Chinese. That morning of July 9 saw the celebration of the last Holy Mass in the long, fervent history of that monastery.

The farmers roamed through the dormitory. One of the brothers was sick; they made off with his mattress and the cushions beneath it, regardless. Above all, the people were looking for fabric, which in that region was very scarce and was even easier to carry than mattresses and cushions. They tore down the curtains that separated the monks' cells from each other. After Mass there was a moment of respite.

The pillaging began again toward seven o'clock, and this time the storehouses, the workshops and every corner of the monastery were targeted. Fortunately the hosts in the tabernacle had all been consumed during the last Mass so as to avoid profanation of the Eucharist. Indeed, the crowd even reached the chapel. They tied up the sacristan and, after taking the keys away from him, stole the chalices, some other sacred vessels and some vestments and altar cloths.

During the pillaging the sacristan met a group of Christians and said to them: "Tie me up and pretend to mistreat me." So he led them into the sacristy where, with the doors closed, the pillaging began under his direction. The Christians took all the ordinary chalices, the pyxes, a monstrance, the cruets containing the holy oils, the crozier, the processional cross and many ornaments. "Later on," the priest reported, "they faithfully brought all those objects back to me. I always considered that as a sign of the continuity of the monastery." [3]

At breakfast time the brothers were gathered in the scriptorium. Some of them were desolate because the prospect of dispersal meant the end of their hopes and their peace of mind. The older priests tried to console them. But one brother said, "You have the priesthood, which cannot be taken away from you. But when

---

[3] This episode is mentioned in the account by Father Jean-Marie Struyven.

we no longer have Yangjiaping, how will we be able to approach the altar? How will we be able to live our life as Trappists?" They felt overcome by a profound sense of bewilderment. Father Michael, the prior, then wrote a letter for each one commending him to the charity of whatever bishop they might meet once they were dispersed. That simple document, written in pencil on crumpled paper, was a great comfort to the students. Several of them managed to keep those little pieces of paper hidden under their clothing even during the subsequent three months of tribulations.

The Great Popular Trial

Everything that had happened in those few dramatic hours was only the beginning of the sufferings that were about to befall the community. Immediately after the pillaging, all the monks were shut up in the chapel. Meanwhile, some bandits had been sent around to announce "the great assembly for the common trial on behalf of all the villages against Yangjiaping". The trial was to be held in the open air, before a crowd of more than a thousand persons gathered from around thirty villages.

The first one to be put on trial was Father Seraphim. The old accusations were repeated against him: that the monastery was responsible for the repression of the Boxer Rebellion by the foreign powers; that the monastery had received firearms from the French government to be used against the people of the region ...

The priests were also charged with owning a radio transmitter and with having provided information to the enemies of the Communists—an absolutely false accusation—and furthermore, with having illegally kept a certain number of Mexican silver dollars, money that was in circulation twenty years before, and other accusations of that sort. The trial of Father Seraphim lasted about two hours, but since he had not declared himself guilty, he was repeatedly struck with rods in the hope of being able to break down his resistance and courage.

Then it was Father Chrysostom's turn: the same accusations and the same acts of violence. They told him, "We have found Father Seraphim guilty of these crimes against the people; if you do not accept our verdict and do not confess, you are as good as dead. Do you accept or not?"

Next up was old Father Augustine. He, too, refused to confess to having committed any hostile act whatsoever against the people. "However," he added, "if we have done wrong, take everything that we have. But to give you what you are asking and demanding, ten Yangjiapings would not be enough."

The three priests were taken away, escorted by guards.

Immediately afterward the other seventy-two Trappists were told to take off their cowls, and those who wore glasses were told to remove them as a sign of their unworthiness and submission to the court. At the end of the trial the Trappists were brought back to the monastery chapel and held prisoners for six days, until Sunday, July 20. Then they were placed under surveillance in the dormitory.

A New Public Trial

Meanwhile, preparations were being made for another public trial. The monks were brought back to the chapel where they prayed and received the Eucharist daily, and there, of all places, they were once again put under indictment.

Eyeglasses were confiscated from those who still had them, this time for good. The old charges were trumped up again. During his interrogation Brother Rocque, a convert, was savagely beaten with rods by three or four guards at the same time. To the preceding accusations another was now added: sometimes it happened that in the mountain villages a sick Christian needed the sacraments; in that case one or another of the monks who were priests left the monastery to go bring them that religious comfort, given the scarcity of priests in that area. The Communists, informed about these excursions, immediately accused the priests of having gone to the mountain villages or to the isolated cottages to gather intelligence for the Japanese during the war. Father Seraphim denied all the charges and was brutally beaten. Exhausted by the blows, he begged for mercy. To his pleas one of the judges responded, "Now it is no longer time for mercy. It is time for revenge. The time for mercy is over!"

A woman from one of the villages had also been summoned before the judges in order to confirm the accusation against the monks of collaborating with the Japanese.

That woman, whom we know to be Mary Zhang, was around forty years old, a Christian, and for many years she had been a catechist. The judges asked her to confirm the accusations against Father Seraphim. She replied, "It was not Father Seraphim who came to our village, but Father Maurus. He did not come to spy or to gather intelligence for the Japanese; he came to bring the sacraments to the sick and the dying."

These statements infuriated the judges. The woman was savagely beaten on the head and back until she collapsed on the ground, senseless and inert. The monks thought that she was dead, but later, with her body covered with wounds, she was thrown in prison.

During the whole trial, that woman seems to have been the only person to have the courage to defend the victims of Communism publicly. Father McCarthy, the author of the account, comments, "This is just one of the many details of the trial that reminds us of Christ's passion, in the passage where it says, 'Standing by the cross of Jesus were his mother, and his mother's sister, Mary the wife of Cleopas, and Mary Magdalen.' I remarked to Brother Joachim", the priest continues, "that Our Lord, too, had seen the same people, for whom He had worked miracles and to whom He had shown every possible consideration, remain silent about it and finally become hostile toward Him during His Passion." Brother Joachim replied, "The same thing occurred to us. Many priests and brothers have spoken about it. We just cannot understand this mystery of ingratitude, but, ultimately, we are enduring it together with Jesus."

Sentenced to Death

The long, drawn-out people's trial lasted until July 23. The delegates from the villages declared that the whole community of Yangjiaping deserved death.

The Trappists did not know to what extent the sentence was to be taken seriously. Some thought that it had been issued only to frighten them. The officials of the Red government, to whom belonged the power of life and death, approached the table to "receive the people's judgment". The spokesman for the village delegates said, "They must die. Hand them over to us, if you want. We will take up stones and kill them." The official in charge replied, "The Communist government is the government of the people; we can only make the people's decision our own." Then he asked, "Do you want all the Trappists to be punished or only those who are most guilty?" The delegates answered that all had to be punished without distinction.

One by one the monks were brought to the corner where the vigil lamp of the Most Blessed Sacrament was hanging, and there they were bound hand and foot with chains.

The cinctures, scapulars, rosaries and medals were snatched away from the others. Then they were all brought to the refectory of the monastery. From that moment began an imprisonment in the strict sense.

Farewell to the Monastery

For two more weeks, from July 26 to August 12, a whole series of trials and individual interrogations took place. One brother was interrogated thirteen times, others even more often. On the night of Tuesday, August 12, the Trappists were compelled to leave Yangjiaping. The older ones were taken away first, while the younger ones left later. Before moving them from there, an official named Li said that their minds had been blinded by their monastic superiors and clouded by the enclosed life of the monastery. He urged them to look at how things had changed outside under the Communist regime.

The monks left the monastery during the night. The Communist soldiers had placed on the shoulders of each one a heavy load, mostly food supplies. Like beasts of burden, they climbed by narrow paths the whole night and the following morning. They were given nothing to eat until midday. Finally they reached the village of Zhangjiazhuang, and for three days they camped in what had originally been the house of a landowner. The Communists had confiscated it for the people.

They spent the feast of Our Lady's Assumption in that place. Brother Joachim remembered it well, because on that day he had gone to confession and received absolution from one of the priests in a room crowded with prisoners.

There in Zhangjiazhuang, Brother Bruno Fu, an eighty-two-year-old Chinese religious, died. "If I understood correctly," Father McCarthy writes, "Brother Bruno died right on the fiftieth anniversary of his religious profession." He was buried without a Mass and without any ceremony.

On August 18 the prisoners returned to Yangjiaping. They traveled mostly at night, bent under the heavy
loads on their shoulders; at the village they were kept
under strict surveillance and packed into overcrowded
rooms. After they returned to the monastery, several
other prisoners, besides the eight in chains, were put
in bonds for varying periods of time. If there were no
chains, they used iron wire which, tightened around
the wrists, amounted to real torture.

In those days two other lay brothers died: Brother
Clement Gao, who was around seventy-five years old,
and Brother Philip Liu. During his research, Father
McCarthy asked the witnesses, "Did they die from
beatings?" The answer was "No!" Was it "from hunger or malnutrition?" "No." "Then what did they die
from?"

Of a broken heart.

The Death March Resumes

The march resumed on the night of August 24 and
was prolonged for between forty and fifty kilometers.
The group of prisoners never stopped long in one place.

Very soon the strength of the monks, especially the
older ones, began to fail. Some had to be transported
on improvised litters by four younger monks. The guards
gave them nothing to eat but dry foods (cereals without broth, vegetables or meat). In the village of Taip-
ingcun most of them were held in a pigpen, while for
the others a somewhat more "tolerable" environment
was found. The march continued in this way through

various sorts of weather with no destination and amidst cruel sufferings.

Once they reached the village of Dengjiayu, in the middle of the mountains, the prisoners remained there for twenty-five days. In that place, Father McCarthy writes, the treatment became even more brutal than it had been until then. Beatings were more frequent and more severe. Many monks had their hands tied together with an iron wire. The flesh around the wrists of those who were bound in that way was swollen and inflamed; in some cases it had caused extremely painful lacerations.

Those who had their hands tied in front could still manage somehow at mealtimes. But those who had their hands tied behind were forced to eat their bowl of rice like animals. Generally the guards absolutely forbade speaking: the monks were even forbidden to make use of the sign language (*bihua*) with which Trappists can exchange necessary information during the regular hours of silence. The Communists seemed to fear also the slightest hint of moving lips. Indeed, almost all the monks instinctively spent their hours in prayer and often, while reciting prayers that were familiar to them, they involuntarily moved their lips. Every time that movement was noticed, the punishment started.

The captains said, "You can believe in your God if you like, but we have no God. You say that God made you. But if a man and a woman are strong, they make children: if they are not, they don't. And God cannot do anything about it."

From the testimonies that have been gathered it appears that no monk was asked to apostatize. The accusations, as we have seen, were of another sort. In their effort to wring confessions from them, the Communists threatened them with death. They said, "We know that you have no fear of death, but we will beat and torture you without respite until you are half-dead. And in that state we will induce you to agree with us."

Meanwhile, during the first week spent in Dengjiayu, three priests died, among them Father Alphonse L'Heureux, a Canadian. He, before becoming a Trappist, had been with the Jesuits. He had taken the monastic habit in Yangjiaping. He had an extraordinary ability for work in the fields. Every time that he returned from work, he used to go to the chapel and stay a few minutes in prayer before the altar of Our Lady and then the altar of the Sacred Heart. He was very fastidious and had an extraordinarily tender conscience, as is witnessed by the fact that he used to go to confession every day.

During the last week of his life he was afflicted by a painful case of dysentery. He had been separated from the other monks, without blankets or any medical treatment. On Friday the twelfth, the guards told the monks that one of them should give the sick man something to eat. A priest went and gave Father Alphonse absolution and the blessing of the dying: the sick man said that he would like to die the following day and that in heaven he would pray for the others. He did in fact pass away on Saturday. A few days later Father Emilio Ying, a Chinese man who was around sixty-five years old, died also.

During the next three weeks another five brothers died, all of them Chinese. Every time that someone expired, a group of prisoners was brought to the mountain slope outside the village to dig a grave for him. The guards were often impatient and said that any shallow hole was enough. It was the rainy season and the ground was drenched. Thus the corpses were prey to the wolves and wandering dogs. Finally, despite the opinion of the guards, the people of that place decided to bury them properly.[4]

Joy Even amidst Sufferings

Meanwhile the public and private "trials" continued. During every interrogation Father Seraphim was beaten with rods. Upon returning to the other monks, he said nothing and did not complain, but for hours his poor body trembled with pain.

Father Chrysostom, on the other hand, had been imprisoned separately, in a pigsty. The monks came to learn about the treatment that he had received during the public trials. He had asked for a sheet or a blanket so as to be able to sleep at least a little, and also so as not to have to lie down on the ground without some protection from the pigs.

One of the judges told him, "You are not thinking correctly, or else, if you are, you are not saying what

---

[4] Father Maur Bougon, author of a detailed account of the *Calvary of Our Lady of Consolation*, has edited also a precise necrology of the monks who died during the ordeal from August 15, 1947, to April of 1948: there were thirty-three of them, of whom fourteen were priests.

you think. It is quite right that you should speak with the pigs." In that way his request was refused.

Among the monks bound with their hands behind their backs were Fathers Michael, Theodore and Nivard and Brothers Alex and Damian. The latter had suffered from frostbite in his feet some years before, and walking was very painful for him. At the beginning of the imprisonment at Dengjiayu he fell at every third or fourth step. Later he was put into solitary confinement. It is difficult to understand how he was able to move with his hands tied behind his back.

Father McCarthy again writes,

> I asked Brother Joachim how he felt during those weeks. He answered that his heart was at peace and even joyful. "The reason", he said, "was that we were not guilty of anything." He added that the monks offered their sufferings to God. When asked what he would do to the Communists if they were taken prisoners and handed over to him, he answered, "I would forgive them."

Two or three days after the Trappists had left Yangjiaping, the guards let them know that their monastery had been destroyed by fire. The monks did not believe it. The soldiers took a perverse pleasure in repeating the news. To prove it, seeing that they were not convinced, they took three of the younger monks and brought them back to the spot. In fact the monastery had been reduced to a pile of ruins. One little building was all that remained standing, but the fires set by the Communists had destroyed everything else.

The monks returned to the place of their imprisonment with hearts full of sorrow and reported to the others that Yangjiaping had been razed to its foundations. With satisfaction, the Communists said, "For a long time there will be no more Catholic Church in our territory."

Toward Liberation

Toward the end of September this tragedy advanced to its conclusion. It was becoming increasingly apparent that the trials were nothing but a theatrical production. The people were tired of it, and it seemed that the Communist officials themselves wanted to get rid of the monks and were looking for a way to do it.

On September 29, an initial group of four brothers was released with instructions to go back home.

On Monday, October 13, Brother Joachim and six other monks were set free. Before their release the text of their "confessions" was read also. The chief crime of Brother Joachim was that he had prayed to God to free China from the Communists and had helped the army of Chiang Kai-shek.

Each of the prisoners who were released was asked to sign a document prepared by a civil servant: it was an admission of guilt. It declared that the party in question acknowledged the crimes of Yangjiaping, repented of them and hoped that the priests responsible would also see the errors of their ways.

The civil servant then turned to the young monks who stood in front of them, and said, "You are young, and like boys you have been misled; therefore you deserve fewer reprimands. But you are members of the Trappist community and in a certain sense share the blame with them. We will take you all immediately to northern China. Now we have your photographs and fingerprints. If we come to some city and find out that you have relapsed and entered a seminary again, we will no longer be so gentle as this time. We will kill you."

The documents were signed and then read to the prisoners who had not yet been released, and perhaps again later to the people. Signing the documents was another occasion of humiliation for the prisoners: it was a sort of safe-conduct for the guards themselves, who wanted to protect themselves in case the monks were subsequently found innocent.

The group of seven who were released, along with an escort, set out in a northerly direction from the vicinity of the monastery of Yangjiaping, then turned east, through the mountains and the Great Wall, toward the plain lying to the west of Peking. The journey lasted five days. On the fifth afternoon of the march, the company was approaching the line of demarcation between the Communist troops and the Nationalist armies. The soldiers who had accompanied them stopped and told them to continue by themselves into the no-man's-land.

The monks had scarcely gone past an abandoned village when suddenly a tommy-gun fired. An armed soldier came forward, and the monks told him their story. The soldier carefully examined what sort of passport the Communists had issued to them; then they were allowed to cross the line. When they arrived at the camp another interrogation took place. Nearby, however, there was a Catholic official who listened to them, and suddenly the attitude of suspicion and mistrust turned into gestures of courtesy. They were loaded into a truck that was bound for Peking. Toward midnight of October 18, the vigil of World Mission Sunday, they arrived in Xizhimen, near Peking, and soon after they were knocking at the door of the Marist Fathers' school in Zhala, a suburb of the capital.

A Brief Resumption and a New Catastrophe

Once they had regained their physical and moral strength, the monks who had been set free did not delay in reestablishing a regular community, settling in quarters placed at their disposal by the Apostolic Nuncio nearby the East Gate of the city. The prior of the community of Our Lady of Joy, Dom Paolino Li, came to their aid, together with another monk, the Belgian Father Jean-Marie Struyven, leaving the latter as their superior.

Little by little the monks resumed their monastic observance. In a short time there was a new influx of vocations, new professions of young monks and new priestly ordinations. By February of 1953 the community was made up of forty-three monks, including thirteen priests.

But in the early months of 1954, with the new course of Mao Zedong's revolution, the steamroller passed again

over the flourishing, promising community of Peking,
followed this time definitively by total silence. The arrest
in April 1954 of the young superior, Father Benedict
Wang—who succeeded Dom J. M. Struyven after the
latter was expelled from China—is the last certain date.[5]

From the little information that was still able to fil-
ter through in the following months it was learned
that in October of that year the community was completely dispersed. After that a curtain of silence fell.[6]

---

[5] According to what J. T. Meyers has written, the very few survivors from
the abbey managed to arrive in Peking, which at that moment was not yet
under the control of the Communist forces, and there they opened a cheese
factory. With the help of several brothers from the community of Our Lady
of Joy and other new monks, they tried to lead the rest of their lives in
accordance with the Cistercian and Trappist tradition. The cheese factory
was somewhat successful (it is said that Mao Zedong himself had tasted the
milk that was processed there), but in 1954 it was confiscated by the Communist government.

[6] The monastery of Our Lady of Joy, too, was the object of persecution and
had its martyrs: Fathers Emmanuel Robiat, Vincent Shi and Albert Wei. A particularly touching report has come down to us of the martyrdom of Vincent,
which took place in 1951. Among the various testimonies there is also one of a
nonbeliever, a fellow prisoner. "I never heard a complaint from his lips. When
the Communists pressured him to deny God, he just answered, 'I cannot.' How
moving it was to see him kneeling in prayer! Indeed, he was a saint."

With the coming of Mao Zedong and the intensification of anti-
Christian hostility, the monks of Our Lady of Joy fled and were welcomed in
Hong Kong, where they established a little community on the island of Lantau. At the time when it was founded, the island was almost totally deserted
(although the large international airport was built nearby); for a long time
the monks dedicated themselves to agriculture and livestock breeding.

The Trappist community on Lantau—a priory until it was made into an
abbey in 1999—houses twelve monks; it also welcomes young men and priests
for spiritual retreats. As of January 22, 2005, the abbey of Lantau received a
new abbot: Dom Anastasius Li, who took the place of Clement Kong, who
resigned in 2003 because of health problems. At the time of his election,
Dom Anastasius expressed the desire that the Trappists would become witnesses to the contemplative life in hectic Hong Kong.

Appendix 1

CHRONOLOGY OF THE CATHOLIC CHURCH IN CHINA

(1921–2006)

1921. In July the Chinese Communist Party is founded in Shanghai; Chen Duxiu is elected secretary.

1935. In January Mao Zedong consolidates his leadership within the Chinese Communist Party and takes control of the Red Army; this event takes place in Zunyi (Guizhou), inside a Catholic church. In 1938 the book *Red Star over China* by Bernard Snow will catapult the figure of Mao onto the international scene, a decisive factor in the creation of the myth.

1937–1945. Japan invades northern and south-central China; in 1938 it conquers Canton. Between 1941 and 1945 the Pacific War is waged; the Chinese anti-Japanese resistance becomes part of the world-wide conflict. The occupation by Japan ends in August 1945 following its defeat at the end of World War II.

1946–1949. Civil war rages between the Nationalists of Kuomintang and the Red Army, which gradually occupies all of China. After their defeat, the

Nationalists of Chiang Kai-shek flee to the island of Taiwan, from which base the government of the Republic of China continues to operate.

1949. On October 1 the People's Republic of China is proclaimed in Peking. At that time there were around three and a half million Catholics in China: 190 thousand of them catechumens; 5,788 priests (2,698 Chinese and 3,090 foreigners); 7,463 nuns (5,112 Chinese and 2,351 foreigners) and 840 religious brothers (442 Chinese and 398 foreigners); there were more than 300 seminarians, counting both diocesan and religious. The ordinary ecclesiastical hierarchy had been established in China in 1946. In 1949 there were twenty archdioceses, eighty-five dioceses and thirty-four apostolic prefectures in China. There were twenty Chinese bishops; around thirty would be appointed by the Holy See in the following years, until 1955, when it became impossible to maintain contact with the Church inside the country. The Church also conducted many social service apostolates: 216 hospitals and nursing homes, six leprosaria, 781 medical dispensaries, 254 orphanages, 3 universities, 189 high schools, 2,011 elementary schools, 2,243 schools for catechesis, 32 publishing houses and around fifty newspapers and magazines.

1949–1950. After seizing power, the Communist Party engages in intense propaganda for atheism. In July 1950 the repression of "counterrevolutionary activities" (including religious activities) begins. The population becomes involved in a frantic "system of mobilization" through repeated mass campaigns with various political objectives. The "agrarian reform", conducted with drastic methods, instigates the physical elimination of around two million landowners and the confiscation of lands, including church property. Church buildings in rural areas are closed. In autumn of 1950 the three Catholic universities and various high schools come under state control. On September 24, 1950, the government disseminates the *Manifesto* of the Triple Autonomy Movement, drawn up by the Protestants with the help of Pastor Wu Yaozong. The three autonomies concern: the propagation of the faith, i.e., forbidding the presence of foreign missionaries; administration, i.e., the churches must be guided by local personnel; and finances, i.e., no economic aid from abroad. In December 1950, Peking imposes compliance with these same measures on the Catholic Church as well. Practically all Catholics refuse to accept regulations that imply separation from the pope; from then on many bishops, priests and lay faithful are arrested.

1951. This is a crucial year in the persecution against the Catholic Church: the Proclamation of Guangyuan (Sichuan) is published, proposing "the independence of the Catholic Church". The persecution extends to all religions: in February the government institutes the Office of Religious Affairs with the task of superintending the implementation of the policy of controlling religions; on February 20, the decree for the "suppression of counterrevolutionaries" is promulgated. Attacks in the press against Catholics increase; there are more arrests and closures of seminaries, convents and Catholic schools.

Foreign missionaries leave China or are imprisoned and expelled. On September 5, after two months of house arrest, the apostolic nuncio, Monsignor Antonio Riberi is expelled. In October there are mass arrests among the Chinese and foreign clergy in Peking, with torture, libel, trials and death sentences. By the end of 1951 twenty-two bishops are imprisoned and fourteen bishops are expelled, together with 1,136 foreign missionaries.

1952. On January 18, Pius XII publishes the Apostolic Letter *Cupimus imprimis*, to express solidarity with the Chinese people and Chinese Christians and to reaffirm the need for union with the See of Peter. At the end of 1952 there are only 537 foreign priests left in China, and around 300 of the Chinese priests are in prison.

1954. In September a new Constitution of the People's Republic is promulgated, which lays the foundations for Chinese Communist Party control of the State and of any organized activity whatsoever, especially in the educational field. On October 17, Pius XII publishes the Encyclical *Ad sinarum gentes*, in which he denounces the Triple Autonomy Movement as contrary to the Catholic faith and condemns the establishment of a national Church. In response, the government carries out a new wave of arrests of Catholics. There are 121 foreign missionaries, including five bishops, still present in China, of whom twenty-three are in prison.

1955. September 8 is the most tragic date for the flourishing Catholic Church of Shanghai: the bishop, Ignatius Gong [Kung] Pinmei, is arrested with several hundred priests, religious and lay faithful. They are brought to the dog-racing stadium, where Bishop Gong is summoned to confess his crimes. To the dismay of his captors, the courageous bishop shouts: "Long live Christ the King; long live the Pope", thus giving a clear signal to his faithful that they should resist. Over the course of the year there are reports of the arrest of around seventy Chinese priests and three thousand Catholics, considered "unsuited for collaboration with the Party" (among them, Father Li Chang). At the end of the year only sixteen foreign priests (two of them bishops) and eleven foreign nuns remain in China; thirteen priests and a bishop are in prison, while the nuns are confined to the school for the children of foreign diplomats in Peking. In the mid-fifties seminaries and convents are closed. The Church in China is almost completely confined to the prisons and the labor camps.

1956. In spring Mao promotes a brief campaign of liberalization, the so-called "Hundred Flowers Campaign", launched under the slogan, "Let a hundred flowers bloom and a hundred schools of thought contend with each other." The people are invited to express their own opinions and to criticize the regime. But after a few months harsh repression of the "rightist elements" follows, with the arrest of those who have voiced criticism, in particular the intellectuals and also priests and Catholic laymen.

1957. On August 2, the Patriotic Association of Chinese Catholics is established, the instrument of the Communist Party which—according to the logic of the United Front—is to exercise control of the Catholic Church.

1958. The Patriotic Association is imposed in many dioceses. The Catholics must choose whether to belong to this association or to remain faithful to the Holy See and to end up in a labor camp. Quite a few bishops, priests and lay faithful are arrested. The first two autonomous episcopal consecrations, which are illicit, take place on April 13 in Wuhan, and twenty-two others follow in the same year. On June 28, Pius XII publishes another Encyclical on China, *Ad apostolorum principis*, denouncing the persecution and declaring the consecration of bishops without the approval of the Holy See to be gravely illicit. Nevertheless the bishops and priests involved are not personally excommunicated, inasmuch as it is maintained that they did not act freely.

1958–1962. These are the years of the tragic "Great Leap Forward", with which Mao aims to achieve a radical economic transformation and to increase industrial production massively, in particular the production of steel. The traditional Chinese social fabric, based on family and village life, is revolutionized with the establishment of the "people's communes", whereby the Communist regime attempts to collectivize every aspect of the farmers' lives. Officially instituted in August 1958, they would not be suppressed until the beginning of the 1980s. The disastrous consequences of this campaign are felt especially in agriculture. The overturning of traditional methods causes a drastic decrease in agricultural production and in control of tillable land, resulting in the death of at least forty million Chinese. (It is said that an internal Party document exists which speaks of about eighty million deaths by "non-natural causes".)

1960–1961. In 1960 trials are conducted against Bishop Gong Pinmei of Shanghai, who is sentenced to life imprisonment, and against the American Bishop James Walsh, a Maryknoll Missionary, who is sentenced to twenty years in prison.

1962. The second Congress of the Patriotic Association is held in Peking, emphasizing the primacy of the Party, even in ecclesiastical questions, and affirming the reactionary character of the Holy See, which is thought to be collaborating with American imperialism to destroy the new China. On January 21 seven more bishops are illicitly ordained, among them the Bishop of Taiwan (later executed at the beginning of the Cultural Revolution). In autumn during the first session of the Second Vatican Council, the sixty bishops of China who are in exile (among them forty-nine foreigners) convey to John XXIII a document on the situation of the Church in China, which states that those who have joined the Patriotic Association should not be condemned but rather understood, because of their lack of freedom. The Church of China is represented at the Council by the bishops in exile and by the bishops of Hong Kong, Macao and Taiwan.

1965. On December 31, Paul VI sends greetings in a message to Mao Zedong, which remains unanswered.

1966. The "Circular of May 16" marks the beginning of the proletarian Cultural Revolution, a radical movement based on Mao's thought which proposes to eliminate the remnants of the ancient Chinese cultural tradition by trying to impose an abrupt and complete ideological change. With it, Mao aims to reaffirm his control of the Party, which was called into question after the disastrous Great Leap Forward. The most acute phase of the Cultural Revolution, carried out with the destructive fury of the Red Guard, lasts until autumn of 1967. The last eight European nuns who were running a school for the children of foreign diplomats are expelled from Peking. Between 1966 and 1969 the very few churches still open will be closed; many churches will be vandalized and destroyed by the Red Guard. Priests and bishops will continue to be arrested, put on trial, and imprisoned, including those belonging to the Patriotic Association. China will present itself to the world as a completely atheistic country, with the radical elimination of all religion and the prohibition of any manifestation of faith whatsoever. The Cultural Revolution, declared officially concluded after the death of Mao in 1976, is condemned by today's Chinese leaders as the most serious disaster since the foundation of the People's Republic.

1970. In July, Bishop Walsh is released from prison, in view of American President Richard Nixon's visit to Peking. In December, Paul VI broadcasts a message to China from Hong Kong, which he visits during his travels in Asia.

1971–1972. On November 20 an Italian delegation visits China. For that occasion, at the request of the Honorable Vittorino Colombo, who heads the group, a Mass is celebrated in the Catholic Cathedral of Beijing ("Nantang"). From then on the church will remain open especially for the foreign diplomats in the capital; it will remain the one authorized place of worship in all of China until 1978. In 1971 the apostolic internuncio to Taiwan, Monsignor Edward Cassidy, is placed on leave. From then on the nunciature with the Republic of China (on Taiwan) is entrusted to a *chargé d'affaires*.

On the international scene, the People's Republic of China is received into the United Nations (October 1971); this is followed by the famous journey of Nixon to China (February 1972), a prelude to the opening up of China to the West, accompanied by a progressive closure of China to the U.S.S.R.

1974. The first tourists and Chinese living abroad can visit China. The first news leaks out about the Christian communities that have preserved the faith despite the persecution. On the occasion of the 25th anniversary of the foundation of the People's Republic of China, some bishops, priests, nuns and lay faithful are released from prison and from the forced labor camps.

1976. On September 9, Mao Zedong dies; after a few weeks the Gang of Four is routed. These four leaders dominated the Chinese political scene during the Cultural Revolution: Jiang Qing (Mao's wife, who would commit suicide in prison on May 16, 1991),

Zhang Chunqiao, Yao Wenyuan and Wang Hongwen. The new leaders begin to allow limited religious freedom, and gradually many Christians detained in the prisons and labor camps are released. The victory of the reformists opens the way to the Four Modernizations (agriculture, industry, technology, armed forces), which require the support of the West and of Japan.

1978. On February 16, representatives of the "religious circles", among them some Protestants and two Catholic bishops, are invited to the Fifth Consultative Political Conference in Peking. For the first time since 1962–1963, the Chinese regime admits the existence of believers in the People's Republic. There are signs of a return to the policy of "religious freedom" formulated in the 1950s. The release of detained Christians continues; many churches are reopened to the public. The press begins to report some news about religious events abroad, including the death of Paul VI and the election of John Paul I and John Paul II. To overcome the difficult ecclesiastical situation, the Congregation for the Evangelization of Peoples prepares a special document, "Faculties and privileges belonging to the Chinese Catholic clergy and laymen living in continental China". In December, the third plenary session of the Eleventh Central Committee of the Communist Party recognizes Deng Xiaoping as absolute leader; reforms in the economic field are initiated.

1979. On June 30, in the course of his first consistory, John Paul II creates fourteen cardinals, one of them *in pectore*, the Bishop of Shanghai, Ignatius Gong

Pinmei, whose name would not be made known until the consistory of June 28, 1991. In China lay Catholic initiatives are multiplied, but only members of the Patriotic Association are officially recognized; the others, even though they are released from the labor camps and prisons, do not have permission to open worship centers and, if they are priests, to carry on their ministry publicly. Many churches are reopened for worship and entrusted to bishops and priests controlled by the Patriotic Association. On December 21, Michael Fu Tieshan is consecrated Bishop of Peking: it is the first "official" episcopal consecration after those from the years 1958–1963. On Christmas churches in various cities are reopened for the liturgical celebration.

1980. The third "Conference/Congress of Chinese Catholic Representatives" is held in Peking. The College of Chinese Bishops is established, made up of the "official bishops" only. That same year the central government issues a series of instructions aimed at managing the return of confiscated properties to the Catholic Church. The policy of "religious freedom" causes division, which from then on roils the Catholic Church. The official communities are subject to the control of the Patriotic Association (the Party) and of the Office of Religious Affairs (the government). The non-registered (so-called "clandestine") communities, which refuse to recognize State interference and explicitly profess their communion with the pope, are considered subversive of the regime and hence are persecuted. The latter comprise the majority of Catholic laity.

1981. In Manila, during his pastoral visit to the Far East, John Paul II addresses a message to the people and the Christians of China (February 18), in which he expresses his esteem for the country and its culture, emphasizing that Chinese Catholics contribute "fully to the building-up of China, since a true and faithful Christian is also a good, honest citizen", a concept that John Paul II will often stress.

1982. On the Solemnity of the Epiphany, John Paul II writes the letter *Caritas Christi* to the bishops throughout the world, expressing his lively concern for the situation of the Chinese Church and inviting Catholics to pray. It even includes a precise reference to the persecution: "In these painful sufferings they [the Chinese Catholics] have given proof of their fidelity to Christ and to his Church; such courageous testimonies can very well be compared with those of the Christians of the first centuries of the Church." On March 31 the Central Committee of the Communist Party issues "Document #19", effective immediately: it is the "Magna Carta" of the religious policy of Deng Xiaoping's regime. Direct hostilities against religions are abandoned. The disappearance of religions is foreseen, however, in the long term, and they are tolerated insofar as they support the leadership of the Communist Party and the modernization of the country. The freedom to believe is not understood as an inalienable and original right of the human person, but rather as a concession of the State to the individual. "Citizens have the freedom of religious belief. . . . No one may use religion to damage the social order, to harm the welfare of the citizens, or to obstruct the educational system of the State. Religious associations and affairs are not to be manipulated by foreign influences." On April 17, Article 36 of the new Constitution sanctions the principle of "freedom of religious faith" and subjects the exercise thereof "to the requirements of the stability of the State". Catholics are still constantly the object of strict control and the "clandestine" Catholics are openly persecuted. The repression is especially strong in some areas of the country, where the clandestine communities are the most solidly established: Hebei (particularly the Diocese of Baoding), Shaanxi, Fujian and Inner Mongolia. In the same year the seminary of Shanghai is reopened.

1985. Zhao Fushan, assistant director of the Chinese Academy of Social Sciences, in a talk presented to the Consultative Political Conference of the Chinese People, declares that "it is an error to say that religion is the opiate of the peoples." Starting in the mid-1990s, records show the presence of a certain number of foreigners at Chinese universities, in the capacity of instructors. Some of them are religious, but their identity is concealed: indeed, they are allowed to carry on academic activities exclusively, under pain of expulsion.

1988. In May, John Paul II for the first time raises a Bishop of Hong Kong to the rank of cardinal: Monsignor John Baptist Wu Cheng-chung, originally from the province of Guangdong. In September, the Congregation for the Evangelization of Peoples sends to all the bishops in the world a confidential document entitled

"Directives of the Holy See concerning some problems of the Church in continental China", in response to the so-called "13-point Document" drawn up by the clandestine Catholics of Baoding. Subdivided into eight articles, the Vatican document reaffirms the Catholic position concerning papal primacy and authority and touches on the three questions raised by the existence of "official" communities that are independent of Rome: the excommunication (*latae sententiae*) of the bishops ordained without pontifical mandate; the validity of the sacraments administered by the "official" priests; the legitimacy of the seminaries that have been opened, even though they are subject to the control of the Patriotic Association. Meanwhile the government, with "Document #3" issued on December 24, 1988, reaffirms that the Church must submit to the leadership of the Communist Party.

1989. On November 21, the Chinese Bishops Conference is founded, made up of clandestine bishops loyal to the pope. (The organization, however, has never been officially recognized by the Holy See.) Within a short time all who participated in the foundational meeting are arrested. In the same year a representative of the Pope, a member of the nunciature in Manila, begins to reside permanently in Hong Kong, formally engaged in a "study mission". His presence and activity, carried out discreetly but not secretly, is ongoing and will become a matter of common knowledge in 1999.

1992. The Fifth National Conference of Catholic Representatives is held from September 14 to 19. It approves the bylaws of the College of Bishops which agree to "act in accordance with the principles of independence and self-government".

1993. On May 17, the Standing Committee of the College of Chinese Bishops meets in Jinan (Shandong) and draws up norms regarding the election and consecration of bishops. On June 19, John Paul II expresses esteem and love for "the illustrious Chinese nation" and admiration for "that beloved Catholic community which, despite the many and grave difficulties, continues to give a luminous example of fidelity to Christ and to the Church". The Pope adds that it is his "fervent desire to be able to meet those Christians personally".

1994. In order to control the "clandestine Catholics", the Chinese government introduces obligatory registration for places of worship and ordained ministries with its "Decree #145" dated May 1. In the second half of the 1990s this policy of inflexible control will weaken the "non-official or clandestine" communities yet will not be able to subdue them.

1997. In October the government published a *White Book on Religious Liberty in China*, reaffirming the regime's control over religious activities and its negative judgment on the work of foreign missionaries.

1998. John Paul II invites Matthias Duan Yinming, Bishop of Wanxian (Sichuan), and his coadjutor, Joseph Xu Zhixuan, to participate in the Synod for Asia in Rome, but the government forbids them to travel.

Throughout the proceedings two seats symbolically remain empty. Monsignor Duan sends a moving message to the Synod.

1999. At the conclusion of the Synod for Asia (held the previous year) a journey of the Pope to Hong Kong is envisaged as the occasion for delivering the Post-Synodal Apostolic Exhortation, *Ecclesia in Asia*. Previously during his long pontificate, John Paul II avoided visiting Hong Kong and Taiwan so as not to provoke the authorities of the People's Republic of China. On July 4, the spokesman of the Chinese Foreign Ministry declares that Beijing is opposed to a papal journey to Hong Kong.

During the summer, news spreads of an imminent restoration of diplomatic relations between Beijing and the Holy See. During that same period a secret "Document #26" comes to light, entitled "On reinforcing the work with regard to the Catholic Church in the new circumstances" and issued (presumably) on August 17 of that year. The document proposes, prior to the establishment of diplomatic relations with the Holy See, eliminating the "clandestine Catholics" and definitively extending government control over the official communities and over the appointment of bishops.

The following months see stricter control over the official communities and a series of arrests of bishops and priests of the clandestine communities. On December 8, on the eve of the Opening of the Holy Year, John Paul II sends a message to the Chinese Church and grants a special jubilee indulgence to the Chinese faithful who find it impossible to make pilgrimages to Rome.

2000. January 6 is a "black day" for the Catholic Church in China. In the church of Nantang, the cathedral of Beijing, five bishops are consecrated illicitly with major media coverage. There were supposed to have been twelve, mirroring the consecration in Rome of twelve bishops by the Pope on the Solemnity of the Epiphany. Seven candidates, however, withdrew from the ordination enjoined by the Patriotic Association and by the Office for Religious Affairs. This constitutes a serious act of rupture with Rome, after much talk in the preceding months about signs of détente and even about possible diplomatic relations between China and the Holy See. Prestigious bishops, such as Bishops Aloysius Jin Luxian of Shanghai and Anthony Li Duan of Xi'an, by means of various stratagems, manage to excuse themselves from participating in that ritual, which is clearly a challenge to the Pope. The 120 seminarians of the national seminary in Beijing, once informed that the ceremony was plainly contrary to directives from the Holy See, also refuse to participate. In the following months the courageous seminarians undergo wearisome political propaganda sessions, forced self-criticism and other harassment from government officials and the police. Those responsible for the rebellion, both seminarians and instructors, are expelled from the seminary. Some observers interpret the noisy gesture as an attempt on the part of the leaders of the

Patriotic Association to nip in the bud the diplomatic negotiations between the Holy See and China.

In September Cardinal Roger Etchegaray celebrates the first public Mass by a Cardinal in China in Sheshan, the principal Chinese Marian shrine near Shanghai. But his visit to Beijing is marred by the furious opposition of the regime to the imminent canonization of the martyrs of China.

On October 1, the Feast of Saint Thérèse of the Child Jesus, John Paul II canonizes 120 martyrs of China. According to Beijing the date (the anniversary of the institution of the People's Republic) is a polemical act against China. Moreover the government accuses some of the missionaries being raised to the honors of the altar of colonialism and crimes against the people. All the Chinese media participate in a gigantic campaign to defame the saints and the Holy See. The Catholic communities celebrate in secret the canonization of the 120 martyrs, while Hong Kong is the only place in Chinese territory where they are honored publicly. The reaction of the Chinese authorities to the canonization is the high point of tension between Rome and Beijing since the inauguration of the new religious policy (1979).

2001. On the occasion of the 400th anniversary of the arrival in Peking of the Jesuit Father Matteo Ricci, October 24, John Paul II sends a written message in which he once again expresses his affection and his great esteem for the Chinese people, their culture and their traditions and, at the same time, asks pardon for the errors committed by the "sons of the Church" in China.

2002. On September 23 Cardinal John Baptist Wu Cheng-chung dies in Hong Kong and is succeeded by Bishop Joseph Zen Ze-Kiun, his coadjutor since 1996. Monsignor Zen, described as "the conscience of Hong Kong", has distinguished himself as a major figure in the local Church, in China and in the worldwide movement that fights for human rights and freedom. In past years he waged important battles for democracy, for human rights, against the national security law, in favor of the "right of residence" and in defense of Catholic schools.

In December, the Central Committee of the Chinese Communist Party convenes, by way of exception, a National Conference for Party and government personnel responsible for implementing the "policy of religious freedom". Their determination to maintain strict control over all public religious manifestations is confirmed. The initiative fits in with the campaign to suppress spiritual movements along the lines of the Buddhist Falun Gong which, after experiencing a tumultuous success in the 1990s, was declared illegal in the summer of 1999.

2003. In March, three new documents are made public which formalize procedures for directing the Catholic Church in China. They define the role of the Patriotic Association of Chinese Catholics and of the Episcopal College of the Chinese Church. The three documents are entitled "Management Procedures for the Catholic Dioceses in China", "Working Procedures for the Joint Conference of the Directors of the Patriotic Association and the Directors of the College of Bishops" and "Bylaws for the Work of the Patriotic Association". Several observers point out that these norms are a serious departure from the tradition and the canon law of the Catholic Church and are aimed at consolidating political control over it.

On March 15, the Bishop of Beijing, Michael Fu Tieshan, is appointed one of the vice presidents of the National People's Assembly. It is the first time that such a position was granted to a churchman. The appointment can be explained in light of the request by Jiang Zemin to make the regime more "representative" of the more vital forces of society, including religious elements. Bishop Fu, President of the Patriotic Association of Chinese Catholics and thus a leader of the official community, is highly compromised with the regime but enjoys no support among the Catholic population.

From September 1 through 4 in Louvain, Belgium, during a "Colloquium of European Catholics for China", participants receive copies of an "Open Letter to My Friends" by Monsignor Han Zhihai, Bishop of Lanzhou [Gansu], who is not recognized by the government; the letter invites all the Chinese bishops to strive to overcome the divisions between the two communities and to set out on the path to reconciliation. "I am convinced", Monsignor Han writes, "that we can no longer ignore the prayer of Jesus, our Lord: 'That all may be one'. As bishop and pastor of the flock of the Diocese of Lanzhou I feel obliged to say to all my brother bishops: 'Free the Chinese Catholics from this ambiguous situation of division.' "

On October 5, John Paul II canonizes Joseph Freinademetz, a Tyrolean missionary who died in Shandong in 1908. In contrast to what happened in 2000, there are no polemics on the part of the Chinese.

2005. In March, the *Asia News* agency of PIME [Pontifical Institute for Foreign Missionaries] and the Holy Spirit Study Center of Hong Kong publish a list of nineteen bishops and eighteen priests who have been arrested and prevented from exercising their ministry or whose whereabouts are unknown. In the international campaign for their release, petitions arrive from the European Parliament and from the United States Conference of Catholic Bishops.

On the occasion of the death of John Paul II (April 2), the spokesman for the Chinese Foreign Ministry expresses his condolences but stresses the two well-known "preconditions" for an agreement with the Holy See: non-interference in Chinese internal affairs (that is, the appointment of bishops), and breaking off relations with Taiwan. The People's Republic of China sends no official representative to the funeral, which is celebrated in Saint Peter's Square on April 8.

On June 14 the Bishop of Hong Kong, Joseph Zen, declares that the Holy See is "anxious" to establish diplomatic ties with China, adding that "it is wrong to think that diplomatic relations can be initiated first and that religious freedom can be discussed only in a second step." On June 22 Monsignor Giovanni Lajolo, the Holy See's Secretary for Relations with States, explains that "there are no insurmountable difficulties for the establishment of diplomatic relations between the Holy See and China."

In the succeeding months two important episcopal consecrations take place, both with the approval of the Holy See and the tacit consent of the political authorities. On June 28, Monsignor Joseph Xing Wenzhi is ordained Auxiliary Bishop of Shanghai and announces publicly that his appointment had the approval of the Holy See; on July 26, Monsignor Anthony Dang Mingyan is ordained Auxiliary Bishop of the Archdiocese of Xi'an, which is governed by Monsignor Anthony Li Duan, a bishop who is greatly esteemed at the Holy See. In August, for the first time, a group of young Chinese Catholics from the underground community participates in World Youth Day. Among them are Catholics who are already studying abroad and young people coming directly from the People's Republic: priests, nuns and laity from various dioceses (Beijing, Tianjin, Hebei, Fujian, Inner Mongolia).

On September 9, the press office of the Holy See announces the appointment of four bishops for the People's Republic of China to members of the Synod on the Eucharist (held in Rome from October 2–23, 2005). The clerics in question are Monsignor Anthony Li Duan, Archbishop of Xi'an; Monsignor Aloysius Jin Luxian, Bishop of Shanghai; Monsignor Luke Li Jingfeng, Bishop of Fengxiang [Shaanxi], all of whom are recognized by the government; the fourth, Monsignor

Joseph Wei Jingyi, Bishop of Qiqihar, is not recognized by the Chinese authorities, however. After the names are made public, Liu Bainian, vice president and general secretary of the Patriotic Association of Chinese Catholics, reacts by accusing the Vatican of discourtesy because the request to the bishops was made without going through the official channels that manage the Church's affairs. Permission to go to Rome is not granted to the bishops. Monsignor Luke Li Jingfeng sends a letter of thanks to the Pope, which is read during the Synod proceedings; Benedict XVI writes a personal reply. On October 22, the Synod Fathers send a message to the four Chinese bishops who were invited to participate in the Synod: "Your absence from the work of the Synod caused deep regret in our mind."

On November 18, six priests of the unofficial community of Zhengding are arrested. On November 23, sixteen nuns of the Congregation of the Missionary Franciscan Sisters of the Sacred Heart in Xi'an are beaten by a group of "thugs" and two of the nuns are seriously injured. The sisters were organizing to prevent the demolition of a school, originally their property, which the city government handed over to a commercial business. On November 30, the Vatican, with an official note from the press office, strongly condemns the violence against the nuns and expresses concern about the fate of the priests.

2006. On February 22, it is announced that Monsignor Joseph Zen will be created a cardinal in the consistory on March 24. The bishop concerned explains the appointment as follows: "The Pope wants much good for all of China." Beijing, however, reacts with polemics: in an interview Liu Bainian, vice president of the Patriotic Association, criticizes the Pontiff's choice, describing it as a hostile act against China. On the day when he receives the cardinalatial biretta, Zen celebrates a Mass of thanksgiving in Chinese broadcast by Vatican Radio. In his homily, the newly-created cardinal sends a message to Chinese Catholics, urging them to bear patiently with the lack of religious freedom, adding that the red color of his vestments recalls "the tears and the blood of the many unnamed heroes of the Church in China".

On March 25, the *South China Morning Post* in Hong Kong publishes an interview with Monsignor Giovanni Lajolo, Vatican Secretary for Relations with States, who explains that Zen's elevation to the College of Cardinals is a recognition by Benedict XVI "of the lofty values of culture and wisdom of the great Chinese tradition, and of the role of modern China in contemporary society". Lajolo also states that "the time is ripe" for overcoming differences and initiating direct negotiations and full diplomatic relations. In another interview televised from Hong Kong, he adds that he trusts in "the open-mindedness of the supreme authorities of the People's Republic of China, who cannot ignore the expectations of their people, as well as the signs of the times", declaring finally that Benedict XVI wishes to visit China soon, perhaps before the 2008 Olympics.

On April 30 and May 3, more than six years after Epiphany of 2000, two new illicit episcopal ordinations take place. The bishops in question are Joseph Ma Yinglin of Kunming (province of Yunnan) and Joseph Liu Xinhong of Wuhu (province of Anhui). On May 4 the Holy See issues a note expressing the Holy Father's sorrow and declaring that those appointments represent "a serious violation of religious freedom" and an obstacle to the dialogue between the two parties. The Holy See, moreover, notes that as of June 2000 episcopal ordinations in China had always taken place with the Pope's approval.

On May 7 in the cathedral of Shenyang (Liaoning, in northeastern China), Father Paul Pei Junmin is consecrated Coadjutor Bishop of Shenyang by his Ordinary, Monsignor Jin Peixian, this time with the approval of the Holy See.

On May 25, the most beloved and respected leader of the Catholic Church in China, Archbishop Anthony Li Duan, dies in Xi'an; he was recognized by the Chinese authorities, with whom he sought to dialogue, but with whom he did not make compromises. Monsignor Li Duan spent more than twenty years in prison and was esteemed for his courage, kindliness and optimism. Thousands of grief-stricken Catholics attend his funeral, and his tomb is already the destination of pilgrimages. In an interview granted to *Mondo e Missione* in 2004, Monsignor Li Duan expressed clearly and courageously his mind with regard to the situation of the Church in China: complete loyalty to the pope; the right of bishops to govern the Church without government interference; the openness of many Chinese people to evangelization. The Holy See placed great trust in him, so much so that many commentators have suggested that he was the cardinal appointed *in pectore* by John Paul II in 2003.

Appendix 2

THE STRUCTURES THAT CONTROL
CHINESE RELIGIOUS POLICY

Whether in the civil or the ecclesiastical sphere, the People's Republic of China (PRC) manifests a series of organizations quite different from what we are accustomed to in Italy [and the rest of the Western world].

— Political power is in the hands of the *Chinese Communist Party* (CCP), with its operating structures. The government is an executive sphere, not a political decision-making entity.

— In the religious field, the PRC recognizes four religions: Buddhism, Islam, Taoism and Christianity (Catholicism and Protestantism). Each of these has within it, as a controlling instrument, an association that takes orders directly from the Party and the civil authority.

— The Party organization in charge of "following" religions is the *Department for the United Front* (DUF). In the organizational chart of the CCP, the DUF has the task of "uniting all the forces" of the country under the direction of the Party itself. The idea of a "united front" goes back to the 1920s; it subsequently developed

337

into a theory that was articulated for the strategic purposes of winning and maintaining power. The DUF was suppressed during the Cultural Revolution (1966–1976) and reactivated with the Dengist reform in the late 1970s. Section 2 of the DUF is concerned with religions.

— The *State Administration for Religious Affairs* ("SARA" is the common acronym; until a few years ago the structure was called the *Office for Religious Affairs*, "ORA"), under orders from the Council of State, is the executive arm of the DUF and of the government in religious matters. Section 2 is concerned with the Catholic Church. SARA (formerly ORA) was created in January 1950; for long periods of time it was dominated by the public security forces (a sort of secret police).

— The mouthpiece of SARA within the Catholic Church is the *Patriotic Association of Chinese Catholics* (PACC). Founded in 1957, it is clearly an extra-ecclesial organization implanted inside the Church by the regime. It constitutes an element of interference and control and is the organization largely responsible for the conflicts that are still evident. On many occasions the PACC has informed the authorities against Catholics who are reluctant to acknowledge its role. In many dioceses the PACC has unlimited power, in others its function is more limited.

— The *National Conference of Chinese Catholic Representatives* (NCCCR) is, according to its own bylaws, the supreme organ of the Chinese Church. It meets at intervals of five or six years (although eighteen years elapsed between the second and the third assemblies), and it is dominated by the invisible presence of civil servants from SARA and DUF. It, too, is an essentially extra-ecclesial, "democratic" organization, which nonetheless makes (obviously unacceptable) claims to exercise authority within and over the Church.

— The *College of Chinese Bishops* (CCB) was created in 1980 by the third NCCCR. It is composed exclusively of those bishops which the regime recognizes as such and who at least ostensibly accept the CCP's "guidance" of the Church. The NCCCR is an organization superior to the CCB and has the power to dissolve it. Many of these "official" Catholic bishops are privately in communion with the pope and with the universal Church, and hence Catholic in the full sense. The College, however, is by statutory definition "independent" and "autonomous".

— The *Chinese Episcopal Conference* (CEC) was founded clandestinely on November 21, 1989, in Zhangerce, in the province of Shaanxi by the "unofficial" bishops who are not recognized by the regime. Its "clandestine" nature prevents it from being fully operative and from acting in the open. It has no headquarters, and those in charge of it are not publicly known. It is made of up those bishops who have no relations with the regime or with the PACC. Its members are in full communion with the Holy See: some of them are known, usually because of the harassment that they suffer from the regime.

BIBLIOGRAPHY

The Diary of Father Francis Tan Tiande

The diary of Father Tan Tiande was written in Canton in 1990, seven years after his final release from the forced labor camp, and it was originally published in the biweekly Catholic newspaper of Hong Kong, *Kung Kao Po* [*Sunday Examiner*].

In Italy the text appeared in *Cina Oggi*, a supplementary report of the PIME agency *Asia News* (at that time for print media only), dated November 15, 1990 (no. 10, pp. 189–207). The Italian translation was revised by Father Mario Marazzi, a PIME Missionary, who also provided the notes. Extensive excerpts from this testimony were subsequently published in an article ("Ho piantato il seme delle mie 'disgrazie'") in the PIME monthly magazine, *Mondo e Missione* (August–September 1992, pp. 462–69). Accompanied by watercolors depicting scenes of detention and persecution in China, the article is part of a dossier entitled "Cina in croce" ["China on the cross"] edited by the same Father Marazzi.

The Diary of Father John Huang Yongmu

The diary of Father John Huang Yongmu was published for the first time in Italy on the pages of *Cina*

Oggi (July 1990, no. 8, pp. 142–61), a supplement to no. 73 of *Asia News*.

Father Mario Marazzi had before him the English translation of the manuscript, which specified that the text was not to be published: indeed, Father Huang feared reprisals against persons in China. Only later did he agree to its publication, with some of the names changed. Hence the diary, which contains the memoirs of almost twenty-five years in prison and forced labor camps endured by the author (who died in Hong Kong in Autumn of 2005), appeared then anonymously.

The Life of Father Joseph Li Chang

The life of Father Li Chang, the first and only work by Li Daoming, appeared posthumously in Hong Kong in 1990, through the initiative of the Holy Spirit Study Centre (HSSC), which published the text in Chinese and English (the original Chinese version was edited by Teresa Yeung). In Italy, by the kind offices of the HSSC, the book was published by CEAM (*Cultura e Attività Missionaria*) in 1996 under the title *Pioggia di primavera: Una testimonianza attraverso trent'anni di storia cinese* [*Spring rain: a testimony spanning thirty years of Chinese history*; for English edition, see Analytic Bibliography]. The title recalls the verse by Du Fu (one of the greatest Chinese poets, who lived in the eighth century A.D.): "The good rain comes in the season when spring returns; / the clouds thicken, and it creeps in gently, / like a nocturnal sigh, / and falls lightly on the ground." [From an Italian translation by Gabriella Novati.]

The revision of the text and the notes are by Father Mario Marazzi, a PIME Missionary; the project was supervised by Father Massimo Casaro (also of PIME).

The Prison Diary of Gertrude Li Minwen

Translated from Chinese and edited by PIME Missionary Father Amelio Crotti (who also wrote the introduction), the testimony of Gertrude Li appeared for the first time in *Più forti della tormenta: Documenti sulla Persecuzione Religiosa in Cina* [Stronger than torture: Documents on Religious Persecution in China], published by the Pontifical Institute for Foreign Missions (Milan: PIME, 1957, in the series Oltremare under the direction of Father Piero Gheddo). In the Preface, this little book reprints a letter from Monsignor Giovanni Battista Montini, later Paul VI, who was then Deputy Secretary of State. It was then republished in A. Crotti, *Con i Communisti in Cina nei Primi Anni del Nuovo Governo: Raccolta di Articoli Pubblicati negli Anni Sessanta* [With the Communists in China in the First Years of the New Government: Collection of Articles Published in the 1960s] (Lecco: PIME, 2000), pp. 62–97. In this edition *pro manuscripto*, which also includes a photo of Gertrude, the text is accompanied by a brief concluding note on the most recent experiences of the young Chinese woman.

The *Via Crucis* of the Trappist Monks of Yangjiaping

The report by Father Charles J. McCarthy (which was the basis for the article in the magazine *Testimoni* that appeared in no. 7, dated April 15, 1992, written by Dehonian Father Antonio Dall'Osto and published here in excerpt form with the permission of the editors) was published in the January/February 1948 issue of the *Catholic Review* of Shanghai under the title "Trappist Tragedy". This source was consulted by many in the mass media; even the Trappist monk Thomas Merton used the same source in *The Waters of Siloe*, which appeared in 1949, two years after Merton made his solemn vows.

This written account was anthologized, together with many others, in the aforementioned *Monaci nella Tormenta*, a groundbreaking work edited by Father Beltrame Quattrocchi and published by the General House of the Cistercian Order of the Strict Observance (Cîteaux, 1991), which contains other very important firsthand documents. Among them: the testimony of Father Jean-Marie Struyven, a monk of the other Chinese Trappist, the Abbey of Our Lady of Joy, and that of Father Maur Bougon, who from 1930 on experienced intensely the whole history of Yangjiaping. Even though he was not present at the moment of the outbreak of the catastrophe, he was able to reestablish contact with the monks while they were still in chains and was a firsthand witness of their sufferings besides being a victim of torture himself.

Another interesting document is that of Father Louis Scanlan, formerly a monk at Yangjiaping; after being interned by the Japanese in Weixian together with his European confreres, he left China shortly before the catastrophe befell the monastery. He worked tirelessly to reconstruct the story of his confreres, managing also to correspond with one of the surviving monks, Father Sebastian Pian.

The plight of the Trappists of Yangjiaping was concisely but powerfully recounted also in Chapter I ("Portents", pp. 1–19) of the book *Enemies without Guns* (New York: Paragon House, 1991), written by Dr. James T. Myers and one of the most complete and rigorous studies of the history of the Chinese Church in the last century.

Father Paolino Beltrame Quattrocchi's account, *Monaci nella Tormenta: La Passio dei Trappisti di Yan-Kia-Ping e di Liesse* (published by the General House of the Cistercian Order of the Strict Observance in *Cîteaux, Textes et documents*, vol. III, Cîteaux, 1991), also relates the experiences of another Chinese Trappist monastery, that of Our Lady of Joy in Hong Kong, on the island of Lantau, again in the province of Hebei.

Analytic Bibliography

Testimonies and documents

Adeney, David. *China: Christian Students Face the Revolution.* Downers Grove, Ill.: InterVarsity Press, 1973.

Camps, Arnulf, and Pat McCloskey. *The Friars Minor in China, 1294–1955: Especially the Years 1925–1955.* Rome: General Curia of Friars Minor, 1995.

Cervellera, B., G. Criveller, G. Fazzini, A. Lazzarotto, and S. Ticozzi. "La Nuova Cina Cerca Dio." *Mondo e Missione* (special issue), January 2003, 41–56.

Crotti, A. *In Cina Ieri e Oggi Testimoni di Speranza: Breve Storia della Missione di Kaifeng (Henan) negli Anni 1941–1991*. Milan: PIME, 1992.

Dufay, Francis, and Douglas Hyde. *Red Star versus the Cross: The Pattern of Persecution*. Carlisle, UK: Paternoster Publications, 1954.

Fazzini, G., ed. "Una Chiesa, Molte Sorprese". *Mondo e Missione* (special issue), August–September 2006, 33–64.

Gheddo, Piero., ed. *Lettere di cristiani dalla Cina*. Bologna: EMI, 1981.

———. *Lawrence Bianchi of Hong Kong*. Strathfield, Australia: Catholic Truth Society, 1992.

Grasselli, F., and M. Marazzi, eds. *Io Prigioniero del Signore Francesco Saverio Zhu Shude, Sacerdote e Martire Cinese*. Bologna: EMI, 1991.

Li, Daoming. *Spring Rain*. Edited by Yeung Cho Woo. Translated by Woo Lo Ming. Hong Kong: Holy Spirit Study Centre, 1990.

Liao Shouji, G. *La Mia Vita nel Gulag: Diario di un Cattolico Cinese*. Bologna: EMI, 1992.

Marazzi, M. ed. "Cina in Croce". *Mondo e Missione* (special issue), August–September 1992, 461–476.

Monsterleet, Jean. *Martyrs in China*. Translated by Antonia Pakenham. Chicago: H. Regnery Co., 1956.

Politi, G. "Cattolici in Cina: La Primavera della Fede". *Mondo e Missione* (special issue), December 1995, 29–44.

———. *Martiri in Cina: Noi Non Possiamo Tacere*. Bologna: EMI, 1998.

Strizoli, G. ed. *Criminali . . . o Vittime? Testimonianze di Vescovi e Missionari del PIME, Espulsi dalla Cina di Mao*. Milan: PIME, 1954.

Suigo, Carlo. *In the Land of Mao-Tse-Tung*. Edited by Clifford Witting. Translated by Muriel Currey. Wellington, New Zealand: George Allen and Unwin, Ltd., 1953.

_____. *K'ou min: Povero Popolo! . . . Diario di un Prigioniero*. Milan: PIME, 1948.

Tang, Dominic. *How Inscrutable His Ways! Memoirs 1951–1981*. Hong Kong: Aidan Publicities and Printing, 1987.

Taylor, James Hudson. *To China with Love*. Bloomington, Minn.: Bethany House, 1972.

Valente, G., and M. Quattrucci. *Il Tesoro Che Fiorisce: Storie di Cristiani in Cina*. Rome: Associazione amici di *30 Giorni*, 2002.

Xiaoling, Wang. *L'allodola e il Drago: Sopravvissuta nei Gulag della Cina*. Casale Monferrato (Al): Piemme, 1993.

_____. *Many Waters: Experiences of a Chinese Woman Prisoner of Conscience*. Hong Kong: Caritas Printing Training, 1988.

Socio-political Analyses

Bays, Daniel, ed. *Christianity in China, from the 18th Century to the Present*. Stanford, Calif.: Stanford University Press, 1996.

Becker, Jasper. *Hungry Ghosts: Mao's Secret Famine*. New York: Holt Paperbacks, 1998.

Bush, Richard. *Religion in Communist China*. New York: Abingdon Press, 1970.

Cervellera, B. *Missione Cina: Viaggio nell'Impero tra Mercato e Repressione*. 2nd ed. Milan: Ancora, 2005.

Charbonnier, Jean-Pierre. *Christians in China: A.D. 600 to 2000*. San Francisco: Ignatius Press, 2007.

Etchegaray, R. *Verso i Cristiani in Cina, Visti da una Rana dal Fondo di un Pozzo*. Milan: Mondadori, 2005.

Fogel, Joshua. *Chinese Women in a Century of Revolution 1850–1950*. Stanford, Calif.: Stanford University Press, 1989.

Hayward, Victor. *Christians in China*. Dublin: Cahill, 1974.

Lam, Anthony. *The Catholic Church in Present Day China: Through Darkness and Light*. Hong Kong: Holy Spirit Study Centre, English ed. 1997.

Lazzarotto, Angelo. *The Catholic Church in Post-Mao China*. Hong Kong: Holy Spirit Centre, 1982.

———. *Politica Religiosa in Cina: Contradditoria Ricerca di Una "Società Armoniosa"*. Seregno [MI]: Edizioni OCD, 2006.

Leung, Beaqtrice. *Sino-Vatican Relations: Problems of Conflicting Authority (1976–1986)*. Cambridge, Mass.: Cambridge University Press, 1992.

Madsen, Richard. *China's Catholics: Tragedy and Hope in an Emerging Civil Society*. Berkeley and Los Angeles: University of California Press, 1998.

Minamiki, George. *The Chinese Rites Controversy, from Its Beginning to Modern Times*. Chicago: Loyola University Press, 1985.

Myers, James. *Enemies without Guns: The Catholic Church in China*. New York: Paragon House, 1991.

Politi, G. "Cina, l'Illusione della Libertà". *Mondo e Missione* (special issue), April 1999, 31–46.

Salisbury, Harrison. *The New Emperors: China in the Era of Mao and Deng*. New York, 1992.

Tang, Edmund, and J. P. Wiest, eds. *The Catholic Church in Modern China*. Maryknoll, N.Y.: Orbis Books, 1993.

Whyte, Bob. *Unfinished Encounter, China and Christianity*. London: Fount Paperbacks, 1988.

Wu, Harry. *Laogai: I Gulag di Mao Zedong*. Naples-Rome: L'ancora del Mediterraneo, 2006.

_____, and Carolyn Wakeman. *Bitter Winds: A Memoir of My Years in China's Gulag*. New York: John Wiley and Sons, 1995.

For updates on the current situation of the Church in China, it is helpful to consult on the internet the agency *Asia News* (www.asianews.it), directed by Father Bernardo Cervellera, PIME Missionary.

INDEX